Also Available From the American Academy of Pediatrics

Other Books by Dr Kenneth Ginsburg

Raising Kids to Thrive: Balancing Love With Expectations and Protection With Trust *(coming soon)*

For Youth-Serving Professionals

Reaching Teens: Strength-Based Communication Strategies to Build Resilience and Support Healthy Adolescent Development

Common Conditions

Allergies and Asthma: What Every Parent Needs to Know

The Big Book of Symptoms: A–Z Guide to Your Child's Health

Mama Doc Medicine: Finding Calm and Confidence in Parenting, Child Health, and Work-Life Balance

My Child Is Sick! Expert Advice for Managing Common Illnesses and Injuries

Sleep: What Every Parent Needs to Know

Waking Up Dry: A Guide to Help Children Overcome Bedwetting

Developmental, Behavioral, and Psychosocial Information

ADHD: What Every Parent Needs to Know

Autism Spectrum Disorders: What Every Parent Needs to Know

CyberSafe: Protecting and Empowering Kids in the Digital World of Texting, Gaming, and Social Media

Mental Health, Naturally: The Family Guide to Holistic Care for a Healthy Mind and Body

Newborns, Infants, and Toddlers

Caring for Your Baby and Young Child: Birth to Age 5*

Dad to Dad: Parenting Like a Pro

Guide to Toilet Training*

Heading Home With Your Newborn: From Birth to Reality

Mommy Calls: Dr. Tanya Answers Parents' Top 101 Questions About Babies and Toddlers

New Mother's Guide to Breastfeeding*

Newborn Intensive Care: What Every Parent Needs to Know

Raising Twins: Parenting Multiples From Pregnancy Through the School Years

Retro Baby: Cut Back on All the Gear and Boost Your Baby's Development With More Than 100 Time-tested Activities

Your Baby's First Year*

Nutrition and Fitness

Food Fights: Winning the Nutritional Challenges of Parenthood Armed With Insight, Humor, and a Bottle of Ketchup

Nutrition: What Every Parent Needs to Know

A Parent's Guide to Childhood Obesity: A Road Map to Health

Sports Success R_x! Your Child's Prescription for the Best Experience

School-aged Children and Adolescents

Caring for Your School-Age Child: Ages 5 to 12

Caring for Your Teenager

For additional parenting resources, visit the HealthyChildren bookstore at shop.aap.org/for-parents/.

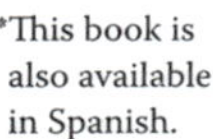
*This book is also available in Spanish.

Building Resilience in Children and Teens

Giving Kids Roots and Wings

3RD EDITION

Kenneth R. Ginsburg, MD, MS Ed, FAAP

With Martha M. Jablow

Published by the American Academy of Pediatrics
141 Northwest Point Blvd, Elk Grove Village, IL 60007-1019
847/434-4000
Fax: 847/434-8000
www.aap.org

Building Resilience in Children and Teens: Giving Kids Roots and Wings was created by Kenneth R. Ginsburg, MD, MS Ed, FAAP, and Martha M. Jablow.

Cover design by Daniel Rembert
Book design by Peg Mulcahy
Back cover photo courtesy of Robin Miller, www.robinmillerphotography.com.
Illustration on page 194 by Talia Ginsburg, age 10.

Third Edition—2015
Second Edition—2011
First Edition—© 2006 as *A Parent's Guide to Building Resilience in Children and Teens: Giving Your Child Roots and Wings*

Library of Congress Control Number: 2014932928
ISBN: 978-1-58110-866-8
eBook: 978-1-58110-870-5
EPUB: 978-1-58110-874-3
Kindle: 978-1-58110-875-0

CB0080
9-354

1 2 3 4 5 6 7 8 9 10

Critical Acclaim for *Building Resilience in Children and Teens*

Awards

Book of the Year—Gold Award, *ForeWord Reviews*
Parenting/Family—Silver Award, Nautilus Book Award
Parenting/Child Care/Family—Silver Award, eLit Awards

What People Are Saying

Building Resilience in Children and Teens provides a rich and valuable resource for anyone who cares about overcoming the increasing pressures of student achievement. Dr Ginsburg has created a great way for adolescents to manage stress and offers effective strategies to prepare this often-overlooked age group to thrive. It was a super pick for our school and community books clubs — a must-read for any adult involved in middle schools!

David Schrag
Principal, Stanley Middle School, Lafayette, CA

This book is about recognizing your child's strengths and parenting from a place of what you *can* influence. By helping parents understand what is normal developmentally, [Dr Ken Ginsburg] helps us refocus our impression of teens as difficult, and in the process helps us enhance our child's feelings of competence, setting the groundwork for raising children who can cope on their own in today's complex world. As a parent of 9- and 19-year-olds, and as someone who has brought Dr Ginsburg to speak to parents and teens in our community, I can tell you his genuine concern for children comes through on the pages of this book. Not only is he a parent himself, but he is on the front lines with teens in his office every day. There's no magic answer, but this book gives parents well-thought-out advice on raising children so they have the tools they need for authentic success in life. This book is one you will keep on your shelf to refer back to and share with friends.

Sharon B. Greenstein
Parent Education Chairperson, Los Altos-Mountain View PTA Council

Dr Ginsburg has focused on one of the most critical traits necessary for students on their path to self-actualization. This book provides a commonsense approach and time-tested exercises for stress reduction for students. *Building Resilience* can be the "spark" to assist students in their social-emotional growth.

Ray Piagentini
Professional school counselor and Past President,
Illinois School Counselor Association

Dr Ginsburg masterfully integrates cutting-edge theory and research with his rich, insightful, and compelling vision for enhancing the lives of youth. No book better serves parents, practitioners, policy makers, and educators in its respective effort to promote the health and positive development of children and adolescents.

Richard M. Lerner, PhD
Bergstrom Chair in Applied Developmental Science and
Director, Institute for Applied Research in Youth Development,
Tufts University, and author or editor of more than 70 books,
including *The Good Teen: Rescuing Adolescence from the Myths of the Storm and Stress Years*

Dr Ken Ginsburg's work on resilience forms the basis of our entire adolescent medicine practice. Teaching young people to use their strengths to prevent and manage problems helps them to be in control of their own futures; teaching parents to recognize and build resilience in their children fosters productive family-based partnerships that last a lifetime and save lives. Whether 3 years old or 30, whether struggling with "normal" developmental issues or major medical or psychological stresses, Dr Ginsburg empowers parents to raise children who love, accept, and protect themselves. Isn't that what we all want for our kids?

Susan Sugerman, MD, MPH, FAAP
President and Cofounder, Girls to Women Health and Wellness

[Dr Ken Ginsburg's] book...has become a vital part of our training and support resources for parents, professionals, and community volunteers. Over the years we have found...that Ken Ginsburg's research-based and evidence-informed training and practical scholarship is an incredible asset in helping us support parents and expand the convoy of other supporting adults that understand the challenges of mobility and transition faced by America's military-connected children and youth.

Mary M. Keller, EdD
President and CEO, Military Child Education Coalition

With love to my wife Celia,
who has taught me so much about good parenting,
and to Ilana and Talia,
who as young adults are the generous, compassionate,
and creative people I dreamed they would become.
I pray that
they will continue to find joy
in the simple pleasures
of life while remaining
strong enough to bounce back
from life's challenges.

Contents

Acknowledgments

It would not be possible to thank all the people who supported me in writing this book or inspired me to feel that it should be written. My colleagues at the Council on Communications and Media of the American Academy of Pediatrics (AAP), formerly chaired by Donald Shifrin, MD, FAAP, deserve special mention because they had the wisdom to know it is insufficient just to suggest what we *don't* want children to do. They knew that we must make clear all the wonderful expectations we have of youth. I thank the AAP for trusting me to take on this important project. In particular, I thank Mark Grimes and Carolyn Kolbaba for the vision to make this happen, and Eileen Glasstetter for making it happen by shepherding every step of the process with grace and skill.

I thank Martha Jablow for her wisdom, patience, and clarity of thought. This book never could have become a reality without her skills and perseverance. And I never would have had such joy in writing it without her kindness and good humor. I also must thank Elyse Salek, MEd, my project manager, for her deep understanding of resilience and constant presence as a supportive colleague.

I am so appreciative of the experts who contributed to portions of this work. Mary Keller, EdD; Patty Shinseki; Donna Earle; and Avlyn Bolton of the Military Child Education Coalition offered critical appraisal and guidance that helped me to write Chapter 22. I am deeply grateful to Jed Michael, MOM (Master of Oriental Medicine), for contributing heavily to Chapter 29. We worked together at Covenant House Pennsylvania to facilitate the healing of youth. He is one of the most gifted practitioners I have ever witnessed. I am also grateful to Princess Skyers for the wisdom and perspective she shared in the section about avoiding prejudice in Chapter 24.

I offer my heartfelt thanks and respect to the leaders of the positive youth development and resilience movements who have inspired me. In particular, Rick Little and his team at the International Youth Foundation first elucidated the importance of the primary ingredients needed for healthy youth development—confidence, competence, character, connection, and contribution. Although I have modified these a bit to include coping and control, they originated and solidified the core ideas. I have been honored to know Richard Lerner, PhD, of Tufts University, who was part of that team and is one of the great developmental psychologists of our time. Dr Lerner has spent decades demonstrating that positive youth development efforts indeed work and that caring is another core trait we must actively nurture through our own demonstrations of caring. In my own field of adolescent medicine, Robert Blum, MD, FAAP, and Michael Resnick, PhD, have led the way and motivated me to shift from a risk-based to a strength-based approach to youth, and Karen Hein, MD, FAAP, has made us understand we need to support youth so they can reach their full potential. I was always deeply impressed by how Peter Benson of the Search Institute helped communities and parents understand that we need to develop core assets in children and not just bemoan their deficits. The Communities That Care process developed by David Hawkins, PhD, and Richard Catalano, PhD, has advanced the field substantially by helping communities mobilize to promote the positive development of and prevent problem behaviors in youth. Karen Pittman of the Forum for Youth Investment has called for our nation to understand quite simply that "problem free is not fully prepared."

I thank my professional mentors, Gail B. Slap, MD, and Donald Schwarz, MD, FAAP, who have had the experience to guide me, the knowledge to enlighten me, and the passion and love of youth to transmit to me. Above all, they have repeatedly demonstrated they cared not just about my academic career but about me. I also thank the best teacher I ever had, Judith Lowenthal, PhD, who inspired me (when I was an adolescent) to grasp the potential in every young person. I also need to thank my colleagues at the Craig-Dalsimer Division of Adolescent Medicine at The Children's Hospital of Philadelphia for teaching me so much and being uniformly supportive of these efforts. In particular, one could only dream of having a division chief like Carol Ford, MD, who cares so deeply about work that supports youth and families.

I have been blessed to work in regional, national, and international settings to promote resilience. I must highlight, however, the opportunity I have had to work with an inspirational group of strength-based youth development organizations in Philadelphia, PA. I am learning from colleagues in each of these organizations how best to engage youth and families in strategies that will help them to *thrive.* We hope to take all that we are learning to help programs throughout the nation understand the power of respectful, loving adult relationships in the lives of youth. Joanna Berwind, Catherine Murphy, and Trean Bock are my partners in this journey. None of it would be possible without Joanna's vision to explore the power of connections that are rooted in unconditional love.

My first mentors and first teachers, of course, were my parents, Arnold and Marilyn Ginsburg. I learned much of what I have come to see as good parenting in their home. I was also blessed to learn about the strength of family from my grandmother, Belle Moore, who demonstrated unconditional love better than anyone I have known, except for her daughter Marilyn. They were two of a kind. I hope that I have passed along in some small measure what I learned from them to my own daughters.

Above all, I thank the young people and their families who have let me into their lives. I am awed by the love I see every day by parents who bring their children to me at The Children's Hospital of Philadelphia, and I hope that I have served them well. I am moved by the resilience of many of my patients, but in particular the youth of Covenant House Pennsylvania, who serve as a constant reminder of the tenacity and strength of the human spirit.

Preface

We limit our goals, and young people's potential, when we see children only in the moment. We rarely view a cute 5-year-old or a texting preteen as the 35-, 40-, and 50-year-olds they will become. If we are to prepare children to become the healthy, productive, contributing adults that will repair our world and lead us into the future, we must set our vision for the long term. For them to thrive over their lifetime, we need to consider their happiness and achievement today, as well as the skills they'll need to navigate an increasingly complex world tomorrow. We want them to be able to overcome adversity and view challenges as opportunities for growth and innovation. We need them to be *resilient.*

Why Another Edition?

A Parent's Guide to Building Resilience in Children and Teens: Giving Your Child Roots and Wings (2006) hoped to translate the best of what was known about positive youth development and resilience into strategies that parents could apply in their homes. We were gratified to learn that many people who care for children, in addition to parents, used the strategies to develop young peoples' strengths. Because children thrive best when they have many layers of support, we were eager to prepare a second edition that would serve parents well but would also better inform other caring adults who are so critical to building a child's resilience. Therefore, *Building Resilience in Children and Teens: Giving Kids Roots and Wings* (2011) offered new research findings and approaches that would be useful to all the adults committed to the well-being of children.

When I speak to parents and young people throughout the nation, I am always enriched by their feedback. I learn about the additional information they desire and gain from their pearls of wisdom. It is important that this work evolves to meet their needs and that it shares their wisdom and experience. In addition, research continues to advance our understanding of how best to prepare children to thrive. Parents and communities deserve to know the latest in thinking, and this third edition keeps them abreast of some of the latest strategies. But this new *multimedia* edition does so much more than update information; it expands the reach of how that information can be delivered. Now, videos reinforce and solidify the strategies offered in the book.

Building Resilience has been used in book clubs in hundreds of schools throughout the nation. Now, parenting organizations can begin their debriefs or meetings with videos to initiate or serve as focal points of discussion. Further, this vitally important message of building youth resilience can now reach people whose learning style is better suited for watching or listening than reading. It also allows ideas to be offered in "snackable" portions to spouses and teens who may not be able to invest the time and energy in reading a work as comprehensive as *Building Resilience.* Now, many of these ideas can be shared in just a few minutes. Teens may benefit particularly from the sections on stress and coping (Chapter 2 and Part 4) and on avoiding perfectionism while becoming a high achiever (Chapter 8).

Finally, *Building Resilience* can serve as a companion to the comprehensive body of work prepared for professionals, *Reaching Teens: Strength-Based Communication Strategies to Build Resilience and Support Healthy Adolescent Development.* This multimedia work helps professionals apply the best of what is known from the positive youth development, resilience, and trauma-informed movements. It has 69 chapters and more than 400 videos and offers up to 65 hours of continuing education credits. Schools, health practices, and youth programs throughout the nation are using it. *Building Resilience* allows parents and other caring adults to easily get on the same page as professionals to create the kind of partnerships that best serve youth.

If we all work together as parents, schools, communities, and policy makers to nurture our children today, they will become the strong, compassionate, creative adults we need tomorrow.

Please Read This Book With 2 Lenses

Resilience is a wonderfully positive concept, but it should never be confused with invulnerability. Just as children can reach their limits of resilience, so too can the adults who love and care for them. As you read this, for your own sake and for that of the young people in your lives, please read this with an eye to building your own resilience as well.

PART 1

Resilience and Stress

Why Resilience?

Every parent's dream is to raise children who lead charmed, happy lives free of physical pain, worries, and emotional hurt. They'd never break a bone, lose a ball game, or receive a grade lower than an A. Never smoke a cigarette, use a drug, or wreck a car. Never have sex until they're married...

We would love to live in a world so idyllic that children wouldn't have to be concerned about peer pressure, bullying, parents fighting or divorcing, lurking strangers, disease or death, poverty, crime, terrorism, and war. We fantasize that we could safeguard them from every possible loss, heartache, and danger. We'd like to wrap our children in a downy quilt and insulate them from every misfortune. But even if we could, would it really benefit them?

If we could immunize children from all disappointments and stress, would they ever have the chance to experience the satisfaction of facing a challenge, recovering, and discovering that they are able to cope with tough situations? Would they be able to revel in success or experience joy and pleasure if they never faced some struggle, failure, or rejection? Would they appreciate good fortune if they never knew its opposite? If we could wave a magic wand to isolate children from the pain around them, wouldn't we produce cold individuals incapable of empathy and unable to feel and express love, compassion, or a desire to help others? Would they be prepared to make the world a better place?

No parent wishes any adversity to befall a child, but realistically we have to expect problems. We cannot raise totally invulnerable kids. Our goal must be to raise children who can handle the bumps and bruises that the world has in store. We need to prepare them to cope with difficult challenges and bounce back. We must help them find happiness even when things aren't going their way. We want them to develop deep, strong roots now so that their wings will carry them successfully and independently into the future.

If we want our children to experience the world as fully as possible—unfortunately with all its pain, and thankfully with all its joy—our goal will have to be *resilience.* Resilience is the capacity to rise above difficult circumstances, the trait that allows us to exist in this less-than-perfect world while moving forward with optimism and confidence.

Resilience is commonly defined as an ability to recover from setbacks, the quality of bouncing back. Resilience is similar to buoyancy. When pushed under water, our bodies instinctively rise back up to the surface. That's a useful image to keep in mind as we consider resilience throughout this book. It's what we want our children to be able to do: when pushed under, rise to the top again.

Resilience is a mind-set. Resilient people see challenges as opportunities. They do not seek problems, but they understand that they will ultimately be strengthened from them. Rather than engaging in self-doubt, catastrophic thinking, or victimization *(Why me?),* they seek solutions.

Resilience is uneven. A person might be highly resilient in one aspect of life and need much higher levels of support in another. Resilience is not invulnerability, not perfection, not isolation from all risk. Resilience is the trait that parents hope to develop in children so they will be equipped to navigate a stressful, complicated world while relishing its abundant pleasures. Resilience is not a trait of "perfect" people. Perfectionists fear making any mistakes. They perform well but don't take chances to perform at their very best. Resilient people are more successful because they push their limits and learn from their mistakes. Resilience may be a core factor in determining not only who will adapt, but who will thrive.

Stress and Resilience

All children are born with a natural resilience. If you watch a group swimming lesson, it's apparent that kids have different degrees of natural buoyancy. Some float more easily than others, but all children can learn to float. In terms of resilience, some children seem naturally graced with an ability to recover from obstacles, while others need extra support. But all children can become *more* resilient.

We all recognize how real stress can be. Families are endlessly rushed. Kids are heavily scheduled with academic and extracurricular activities. Friends dare them to take bigger risks. Parents and teachers push them to get higher grades. Coaches demand better performance. The media bombard youth with messages that they aren't thin enough, cool enough, sexy enough, or attractive enough.

In this high-pressure atmosphere, children need to tap into their strengths, acquire specific skills to cope, recover from adversity, and be prepared for future challenges. They cannot do it completely on their own. Parents take the lead in building resilience, but children's ability to thrive is also deeply affected by the community of adults that surround them.

On These Pages

I hope to reinforce the best approaches you already use and help you support children in developing skills that will make them happier and more resilient. We will discuss building resilience in children as young as 2 years and as old as 18 years. I will suggest ways to help them learn to reduce stress and cope with challenges as well as deal with peers and self-doubt.

While resilience is the theme of this book, please understand from the outset that much of this is commonsense parenting. Don't expect each page to address dangers or risks. It's about building on children's existing strengths. Many of the situations addressed may not seem obviously related to resilience development. For example, discipline strategies will be discussed, as they are in every parenting book. The difference is that I intend to show you how to approach some of these issues in ways that tie into an overall strategy to enhance resilience.

Chapter 42 is a special chapter to share with children and teenagers. This stress-management plan can be individualized for every child.

The Resilience Movement

The resilience movement began as an effort to determine why children from the same challenging environment achieve different levels of success. It looked at what protective forces in children's lives buffered them from all that was wrong. This approach remains a stark contrast to the more commonly used approach—learning what went wrong. The leaders of the resilience movement come from a wide variety of disciplines and perspectives. Sociologists look at the social fabric and how it supports or harms communities. Psychologists examine individuals' thoughts and experiences and how they influence their ability to bounce back from difficulties. Anthropologists study human survival and how culture and communities influence resilience. Most books about resilience favor the discipline or interest of the author. I want to offer you the best from all disciplines because kids are whole human beings whose behavior never can be fully explained by any textbook or single theory. So while we have to understand how kids think, we also have to consider the social and community forces that affect them.

There is no way to do justice to every good idea out there about building resilience. If there is an approach that you feel is important to explore further for your child's individual needs, I want you to know where to turn. The Resources section on this book's Web site (www.healthychildren.org/BuildingResilience) can guide you to explore further areas of interest or special concern.

My goal is to present many different ideas about building resilience. I will introduce the 7 Cs model of resilience in Chapter 3. Those Cs are competence, confidence, connection, character, contribution, coping, and control. Every C is a different layer or individual piece of a total approach to blanket your child with protection, while reinforcing his own strengths.

Several essential themes weave through the book. Here is a preview.

- To be strong, children need unconditional love, absolute security, and a deep connection to at least one adult.
- Sometimes the best thing we can do to help children learn is to get out of their way.
- Children live up or down to adults' expectations of them.
- Listening to children attentively is more important than any words we can say. This applies to routine situations as well as times of crisis.
- Nothing we say is as important as what children see us doing on a daily basis.
- Children can only take positive steps when they have the confidence to do so. They gain that confidence when they have solid reasons to believe they are competent.
- If children are to develop the strength to overcome challenges, they need to know that they can control what happens to them.
- Children with a wide range of positive coping strategies will be prepared to overcome stressors and will be far less likely to try many of the risk behaviors we fear.

This is not an instruction manual. I won't give you a list of steps and say, "Proceed from step 1 to 2 to 3." It's more like putting together a recipe, making sure first that you know all of the right ingredients. I want to give you a wealth of material that stimulates thought and debate. Discuss these ideas with your partner or other significant adults in your child's life. I believe you will recognize that you already know most of this information on an instinctual level. This book will reinforce the best of what you know. Never trust an "expert" more than your own instincts about what is right for your family. From working with families for more than 28 years, I know that I could learn a great deal about parenting from each of you. In fact, much of what I will share has been taught to me by my patients and their families.

Using This Book

I hope you will think about the ideas on these pages, try them on for size, and see how they fit your individual children, depending on each one's character, temperament, likes and dislikes, and strengths and weaknesses. Because I hope you will return to this book as your children grow, examples apply to different stages of development.

Most of these techniques require practice and reinforcement. You'll probably need to go back from time to time to review skills and adapt guidelines as your child backslides or moves to a new developmental milestone. You may think you've taught your child a particular lesson or helped him acquire a certain coping skill, but he may not retain and use it. Kids need ongoing support—not nagging, lecturing, or criticism, but gentle reinforcement and practice. Like developing a good jump shot or mastering a musical instrument, skill-building takes time, practice, and patience.

You'll also discover (although you probably already know it) that children mature in fits and starts. Whenever an important, new situation is about to occur, such as entering a new school, moving to a different community, or starting summer camp, your child will probably regress a bit. You may notice this pattern with some children in even less momentous circumstances, such as going to a sleepover for the first time.

Most children take a few developmental steps forward and, just as parents are taking pride in their progress, something challenging appears on the horizon that's beyond their capabilities. Then they regress a step or two, behave as they did last year, or lash out at their parents. This is normal!

Think about how you'd leap across a chasm. You wouldn't stand on the edge and just jump across. You'd take several steps backward to get a running start before you leap, and then cover your eyes as you soar across. Visualize every major developmental stage or challenge as a chasm that children worry about crossing. Don't be surprised when they take 2 or 3 steps backward before their next attempt to move forward. And don't be shocked if they sometimes leap with blinders on.

Please don't feel defeated if you do your best to help your children across that chasm and your efforts seem to fall short. Children are listening, even when they roll their eyes or ask, "Are you done yet?" Keep plugging. Keep caring. You can make a big difference even when it feels like you've slipped backward.

The standard line I was taught over the years was, "Consistency is the most important ingredient in parenting." If that means consistency of love, I agree. But I can't be completely consistent with my own children. Each of my daughters has her individual temperament. On any given day, they may live the same experience, but each requires a different response from me.

I don't mean we have to just go with the flow. We certainly need to have clear, unwavering values, and our love for our kids has to be the most consistent, stable, and obviously expressed force in our homes. Children benefit from knowing that there are reliable routines in their lives. But life is always changing, so we need to give our children and ourselves a break by being flexible. To be resilient, we must adapt as circumstances require, for our own sake as well as to model this valuable quality for our children.

We want to make crossing that chasm a bit easier when we can. We know our children need to get across on their own, but we'd like to help them build a bridge. This book is about giving kids the tools they need to construct that bridge while maintaining the kind of relationships that will make them more likely to welcome our presence alongside them.

Why Me?

My life's work is about guiding youth toward a socially, emotionally, and physically healthy life. I am a pediatrician who has degrees in child and human development and who has specialized in adolescent medicine for more than 28 years at The Children's Hospital of Philadelphia and the University of Pennsylvania Perelman School of Medicine. Early on, most of my guidance tended toward telling kids what not to do. I learned pretty quickly that this problem-focused approach sometimes instilled shame and rarely worked. On the other hand, when youth are noticed for their strengths and expected to rise to their potential, they become self-motivated to overcome their challenges. While my service could spark their motivation, it was really their parents' support that made the long-lasting difference. In short, there is nothing I can do that carries even a fraction of meaning compared with what parents do at home and what communities do to support children and youth.

Outside of medicine, my purest joys have included teaching in nursery school, where I learned more than I ever taught. Much of what I believe about resilience was absorbed on a Lakota Native American reservation in South Dakota. There I learned about the strength of community to help individuals overcome great hardship.

I am a qualitative researcher—that is, I learn about children and teens from kids themselves. I developed a method with one of my mentors, Gail B. Slap, MD, that helps adults essentially get out of the way so that we can learn from the wisdom of youth. This research allows young people to teach us how they determine whether adults are trustworthy and what they think makes a difference in whether they will thrive.

The majority of my knowledge has been acquired from working directly with young patients and their parents. I have a medical practice that is widely varied—I treat suburban and urban youth, children of college professors and children in poverty, some who have thrived despite social inequities and some who have not.

From homeless families, children, and youth, I have learned great lessons about individual strength and the extremes from which people can recover. As the health services director of Covenant House Pennsylvania, I work with homeless youth who have survived lives that would have destroyed me. I am showered with their wisdom about what it takes to move beyond pain and what ingredients could have been in place that would have enabled them to thrive. From them, I know that children and teens have the capability to overcome almost anything. Because many have absorbed a great deal of condemnation and low expectation, some begin to see themselves as problems. I sometimes help them identify and build on their strengths. While I may serve as a guide, they do the heavy lifting. They possess a different kind of credential, one that is earned through survival. I am consistently amazed by how many of them want to devote their lives to guiding children to overcome difficulty. With the right kind of investment in them, we will find many of the healers of tomorrow. From my colleagues who work at Covenant House, I have learned that a loving, strength-building environment that offers structure permits young people to flourish and move beyond a troubled past.

I have been blessed with the opportunity to translate what is known from research and best practices into *applied* efforts to optimize resilience in youth and their families. It is a privilege to work with the Boys & Girls Clubs of America to further build resilience strategies in their programs. The mission of the Boys & Girls Clubs of America is "To enable all young people, especially those who need us most, to reach their full potential as productive, caring, responsible citizens." It has also been an honor to work on building resilience among the children, adolescents, and families of those who serve our nation in the military. I have travelled extensively over the last decade to support military communities but have always left genuinely inspired by the strengths I witness in these families. In particular, it has been a pleasure to work with the Military Child Education Coalition in helping to design resilience-based strategies to support the emotional health and well-being of military-affiliated children. Especially because so much of what I know to be true about resilience I learned from the Lakota people, I am humbled to be to working with the National Congress of American Indians to further develop national resilience strategies for our indigenous youth.

Just as parents fantasize a safe, idealized world for their children, I wish all the kids I care for would be protected and headed toward a positive future. In truth, most of the kids I see, from all backgrounds, are using their built-in resilience and are ready to tackle whatever lies ahead. But nearly every day I see some young people in trouble—drug-abusing, depressed, and suicidal kids; pregnant 14-year-olds; homeless youth who ricochet from the streets to shelters and back; kids with sexually transmitted infections; victims of gunshots on street corners; and those who wield the weapons. It would be incorrect to assume that only the homeless youth I serve or those who live in urban areas of concentrated poverty have problems. I care for young patients from upper-income suburbs who binge drink; are anxious, depressed, and suicidal; use drugs; get pregnant; have sexually transmitted infections; and have eating disorders. Most of them attend "good" schools, but they are so overstressed that they deal with pressure in destructive ways.

These similar yet diverse groups suffer the consequences of poverty and the different but very real pressures of affluence. In between these extremes, many other young people struggle to make their way through childhood and adolescence. Although all will take some bumps and bruises, most will use them to become stronger, more adaptable people. You can make a difference in making sure children will become healthy, emotionally intelligent adults; that's why you are taking the time to read this book. You are already proving your commitment, and that bodes well for your children.

While children have many natural abilities and strengths, they can always develop greater resilience, but it's difficult to do on their own. All children need caring adults to guide and support them. It will take a coordinated effort on many levels if we are to raise future generations of resilient young people. The best starting point is at home as early as possible in a child's life. Parents are the pivotal force in children's lives. The actions they take years before adolescence, starting even in infancy, can make a difference in the health of teenagers and their success and well-being as adults. Regardless of a child's age, keep in mind that it is never too late to begin new approaches to building resilience. The fruit of your efforts will grow throughout childhood, culminate in adolescence, and serve your child well through adult life. Parents' efforts, in turn, must be supported by professionals, communities, and society.

This brings me to my utmost joy, my greatest challenge, and my most important job—I am the parent of wonderful teenaged daughters, Ilana and Talia. I certainly learned more about children, and infinitely more about parenting, after I was privileged to become their daddy. I know, just like you, what it means to have your heart on the outside of your body, love like you never imagined possible, and have worries and fears that didn't exist until you knew you had something so very precious to protect. You can be sure that I come very humbled to these pages. I know there is no magic plan for raising children, only love and the very best of intentions.

To learn about the full offering of* Building Resilience *videos, please turn to page 327.

Stress and Its Effects

In 21st-century America, stress seems to permeate everyone's lives 24/7. Families are strained by financial and work tensions. Separation and divorce are common. Children are stressed at home and school ("Hurry up, finish this, do your homework, try out for the team, audition for the school play, do your best, stay out of trouble, make more friends, don't drink or do drugs..."). Their peers continually pressure them ("Be cool, try this, show us you aren't a loser, don't hang out with those dorks..."). Many children put even more stress on themselves ("I need to lose weight, wear the right clothes and shoes, get a tattoo, show my parents I'm not a baby and can do what my friends do...").

Contemporary society and the media add to family stress every time we turn on the television, click on a news Web page, or open a newspaper—terrorism, school violence, hurricanes, tsunamis, nuclear threats, economic instability, globalization that threatens to take your job overseas...

Adults deal with ongoing stress in various ways—exercise, meditation, long walks, turning down overtime or weekend work, painkillers, smoking, or another glass of wine. How do children deal with stress? Depending on their ages and temperaments, some kids choose healthy, positive strategies like play, exercise, or talking, but others withdraw, sulk, or zone out. Still others act aggressively, talk back, and toss tantrums. Older children may turn to the coping mechanisms that they see peers using—smoking, drugs, fighting, sexual activity, eating disorders, self-mutilation, and delinquency. Adults usually see these activities as "behavior problems." In actuality, these negative behaviors are often attempts to counter stress, push it under, chill out, and make it all go away.

When kids are stressed, their first impulse is to relieve the discomfort. They don't rationally think about the best way to do it. They find relief by acting impulsively or by following the paths most readily available to them, the ones they see other kids taking. Many young people simply don't know more healthy and effective alternatives. Unless we guide them toward positive ways to relieve and reduce stress, they choose the negative behaviors of peers or the culture they absorb from the media. They become caught up in a cycle of negative coping methods and risky behaviors. We need to help them avoid that cycle.

Before a child or adult can change a behavior, it's critical to understand its function as a coping mechanism—how it works, why we do it, and what need it fills. Simple examples: When pressures build at work, an adult may relieve the tension for a while by stepping outside for a cigarette or venting about the idiot boss to a coworker. When a child is hassled on the school bus, she may withdraw and act unaffected or slug the child who's bothering her. When friends are drinking at a party, a teenager feels pressure to be accepted by the crowd, so she guzzles beer to keep up with them. She does this partly as a response to peer pressure, but other factors also come into play. The dilemma of whether to drink increases her stress. She has seen how alcohol relaxes her parents after a difficult day at work, so she decides to drink to relieve her own stress.

Most of these behaviors are actually effective—in the short term—at relieving stress. The child who's hassled on the school bus lets off steam by punching the kid who's bothering her. A teen who feels that she has little control over her life may seize control of whatever she can. Although she may have no control over how her parents treat her or what school she must attend, she decides that she can control her body size and shape. By denying herself food, she takes some control, which temporarily decreases her stress, but the long-range result can become disordered eating. A young person who feels little connection with family may turn to a gang for a sense of belonging, loyalty, and protection. Although the gang may fill a void, the choice to join it is deeply destructive. A teen who is anxious about living up to expectations of parents or teachers may turn to drugs for relief. Her feelings of inadequacy or fear of failure are diminished in that haze of marijuana. The feelings resurface after the high wears off, so she may use drugs more frequently to keep her stress at bay.

Negative strategies are quick fixes that do relieve stress, but they have consequences that are harmful to individual children, families, and society. Our job is to convince young people that although stress is part of life, healthy ways of coping with it can ultimately be protective, productive, and satisfying.

Can Stress Be a Good Thing?

It is too simplistic to see stress only in a negative light. In fact, stress is designed to be a lifesaver. In times of danger, stress gets our adrenaline going so we can move quickly to dodge a harmful threat.

An appropriate level of stress may be a driving influence that leads us to positive achievements. A little stress pumps us up to perform well for a presentation at work. A little stress energizes a child to play an instrument at a recital or train for a race. Without occasional, well-timed stress, we might become too passive, decreasing our ability to reach new heights. Problems arise, however, when stress becomes chronic or we don't manage it well enough to perform the tasks and responsibilities before us. Then stress can become a destructive force that harms our bodies, paralyzes our efforts, or drives us toward dangerous behaviors.

Stress as a Lifesaver

The human body can transform quickly to meet multiple needs. Intricate connections between nerves, hormones, and cells allow for rapid changes to occur based on the emotions, thoughts, pleasures, and fears that our brain experiences. Our bodies are finely tuned machines whose functions differ depending on our surroundings and states of relaxation, vigilance, arousal, or fear.

But our bodies were not designed to survive 21st-century lifestyles. If they were, our bodies would grow stronger when fed fast food. Our skin would welcome that extra ultraviolet light that the hole in the ozone layer offers us. We would become temporarily deaf when our boss threatens to fire us.

Our bodies were designed to survive in the jungle when, at any moment, a tiger might leap out of the brush. Imagine that moment. Our great, great ancestor is feasting on berries and basking in the sun. Suddenly he sees a tiger. His brain registers terror before he can bring the danger to consciousness. His nervous system immediately begins firing; hormones surge throughout his body. Some hormones, such as adrenaline, give him the needed initial burst of energy to run, while others spark a cascade to mobilize his body's immediate needs (increased blood pressure and a release of sugar for energy) and prepare for some of its longer-term requirements (replenishing water and sugar).

The first feeling our ancestor—let's call him Sam—has is one we're familiar with: butterflies in the stomach. Sam has that sensation partially because blood circulating in his gut to digest food now swiftly shifts to his legs so he can run. In times of rest, muscles use only about 20% of the blood that the heart pumps, while the kidneys and gut each use another 20%. Within an instant of a stressful event, the strenuously working muscles use up to 90% of the blood that the heart is able to pump. Because the heart pumps more vigorously than it did at rest, the muscles are bathed in 18 times more blood than during calm times. In the meantime, the kidneys and gut are only receiving about 1% of the blood during these stressful times. No wonder we don't want to eat during times of extreme stress.

When Sam leaps to his feet, his heart rate increases to pump blood as rapidly as imaginable. As he runs from the tiger, he breathes quickly to oxygenate the blood. The sweat dripping down Sam's body and brow cools him as he runs. His pupils dilate so he can see obstacles in his path; in the dark, he won't trip over a rock. He won't think about anything but running because he is not supposed to stop and ask the tiger if they can settle their differences amicably.

Without the stress reaction, our ancestors would not have survived. But stress has helped us do more than run from tigers. It keeps us alert and prepared. You can be sure that the next time Sam sat down to munch berries, he was attuned to the sounds of brush rustling nearby. That heightened vigilance, caused by low stress levels, can help us today. It's what helps us finish reports and helps our children study when anticipation of a test generates just the right amount of stress.

Few of us need to race from tigers today, but crises, such as violence, war, natural disasters, and major illnesses, require intense efforts for survival. But most of the events that cause stress are not immediately life-threatening—a fight with a spouse, pressure at work, economic worries, or the ongoing challenge of balancing our many roles. Our bodies are not designed to meet those needs day after day. Imagine if they were. Your boss warns that she might fire you. Immediately that part of your brain that stored her favorite joke becomes energized and you retell the joke to lighten her mood, or your emotional centers help you come up with the perfect flattering comment. You need no sleep because you know that your survival at work requires you to clock those 92-hour workweeks. Eating no longer feels necessary because your body has learned to stretch last Tuesday's dinner. You needn't waste any time on frivolous meals!

Let's return to reality. When your boss warns you that she may let you go, your first sensation is that you may vomit because you just ate a huge lunch. Suddenly there is not a drop of blood in your gut. All your blood has rushed to your legs and, for the life of you, you just want to run to escape. But you don't. You stand still because you know that it would be inappropriate office behavior to race out the door.

Your heart, however, beats as fast as it would if you were running. Your breathing intensifies. You sweat and have hot flashes because the adrenaline coursing through your veins is confused about why you aren't listening to it. Why are you standing still when the tiger—your boss—is ready to devour you?

Wouldn't it be great if we had multiple sets of hormones to help us deal most efficiently with each crisis? Hormones that made us regress to lovable 4-year-olds when we have fights with our mothers? Hormones that turn us into study machines with no biological needs—no sleep, no food, no bathroom needs, and certainly no sex—when we have to prepare for examinations? In reality, though, we only have the hormones that prepare us to escape from the tiger and other, more subtle jungle-based problems.

If Stress Is a Survival Tool, Why Is It Eating Us Alive?

When the tiger chased him, Sam had few options. Either the tiger ate him or he escaped. If he had been eaten, he wouldn't have had much to worry about anymore. If he survived, you can be sure that his burst of energy allowed him to outrun the tiger, or at least outrun Zok (his slower friend who never had the chance to become our ancestor because the tiger ate him instead of Sam). In his sprint for survival, Sam used up every hormone, reveled in his success, and in time, his body returned to normal. In the modern world, those same stress hormones remain in our bodies because, unlike Sam, we don't react as fully to our hormonal bursts. We don't sprint away. Instead, our stress hormones continue to circulate, unused and confused—why did my body remain seated when that tiger attacked?

We have more subtle varieties of hormones than those generated during a carnivorous attack. The body's intricate wiring allows us to meet a broad variety of needs. Blood pressure, for example, ranges widely during the day. During sleep, it can be low. At times of crisis or maximum exertion, it can become quite high. When we're functioning in the midst of a hectic day, blood pressure is somewhere in the middle range. Factors that control blood pressure—heart rate, how constricted the blood vessels are, salt and water load—are in a constant dance to meet the body's needs. That dance is carried out through the movements and fluctuations of nerves and hormones, all magically choreographed by the brain. The brain is not an objective choreographer, however. It is heavily influenced by emotion and passion. Sometimes blood pressure goes up because of a real need, such as the need to run or even to stand up after lying down. At other times, blood pressure goes up because of an intense emotion or stays up in a state of vigilance for a coming crisis. Why do poor people suffer more diseases? The answer is profoundly complex. Certainly part of the answer is the pervasive presence of stress in their lives. They remain under constant siege, so their blood pressure remains raised, and high blood pressure leads to disease. It is becoming increasingly clear that childhood trauma, also known as adverse childhood experiences, actually generates "toxic" stress that resets one's hormonal response and neuronal connections for a lifetime. Two other factors explain why stressed people generally suffer ill health. People who are stressed are more likely to do whatever it takes to escape that stress. Many types of escape are profoundly harmful, such as smoking and abusing alcohol and drugs. People with persistent stress also tend to eat more, and obesity leads to ill health.

Let's return to Sam for a moment. Stress helped Sam survive other conditions beyond escaping a famished animal. When Sam was hungry, he couldn't simply drive to a supermarket. Plentiful seasons would be followed by leaner times and sometimes by famine. Sam's body was designed to adjust to a feast/famine cycle. In fact, he could predict when leaner times were likely to come. His body generated just enough stress signals that his metabolism adjusted to store more food as fat to get him through coming shortages. His body produced hormones to increase his appetite so he could eat as much as possible while food was still abundant. Are we surprised that people under low-level but persistent stress tend to overeat? Isn't this level of stress equivalent to a kind of foreboding that our ancestors experienced as they prepared for lean times?

Tying It Together

As you proceed through this book, please keep in mind the following key points from this brief overview of stress:

- Stress is nothing new. We'll always have some degree of stress in our lives.
- Stress is an important tool that can aid our survival.
- The body's reaction to stress is mediated through a complex interplay of sensory input—sights and sounds—as well as the brain and nervous system, hormones, and the body's cells and organs.
- Emotions play an important role in how we experience stress because the brain is the conductor of this system. The way we think about stress and what we choose to do about it affects the impact of a stressful event.

With these points as a backdrop, let's turn the discussion to parenting. Despite our desire to shelter our kids, we cannot completely eliminate stress from their lives. But we can play a vital role in helping them learn to respond to stress in the most beneficial ways. One of those important ways is understanding how emotions help us distinguish a real crisis from a bump in the road. A tiger running at us is an authentic crisis. A hurricane forecast mobilizes us to act quickly and evacuate. An oncoming car suddenly veering into our lane instantly energizes us to steer out of its path.

Milder stressors, such as a test to prepare for or a nagging symptom that requires a doctor's checkup, deserve some extra vigilance. If a young person blows a mild stressor (such as cramming for a test) way out of proportion, she will be unable to prepare well because she will lose her ability to focus. She'll run from that tiger and be incapable of concentrating on anything but escape. In situations like these, parents' subtle (or not so subtle) messages can determine how children define *crisis* and how their stress hormones mobilize. Do you want your child to perceive a B- or a messy room as a major crisis?

I don't want to mislead you. I do not think that parents control their children's worlds and determine entirely how they define crises. Parents can't control poverty, racism, and all the other isms that plague humanity. Parents can't control the weather, disease, random violence, or war. But we can prepare children to navigate a range of crises by helping them realistically assess the immediacy of a threat, develop strategies to deal with and address problems, and have counterbalancing relaxation tools that help them modify the effects of stress throughout their lives. Perhaps most importantly, we can *model* for them how to handle stress in a healthy way.

Building Resilience Videos (www.healthychildren.org/BuildingResilience)

Video 2.3.a Stress Management and Coping/Section 1/Tackling the Problem/Point 1: Identify and Then Address the Problem

To learn about the full offering of* Building Resilience *videos, please turn to page 327.

Ingredients of Resilience: 7 Crucial Cs

Remember when your child was an infant? So helpless and dependent. Most parents hold babies closely, pick them up whenever they cry, and make sure they're always warm and fed and dry. We buckle them snugly in their car seats and strollers. We rarely let them out of our sight. And when we must leave them, we make sure they are safely in the hands of dependable caregivers. We love them so much we want to hold them, tickle them, and make them smile all the time. We know how vulnerable infants are and handle them like fragile porcelain.

Then they grow up. They learn the word "no," start walking away, talk back to us, go to friends' homes for sleepovers, and want to hang out at the mall instead of home. We still yearn to protect them from any possible risk. We know they have to grow up, become independent, and experience the external world of school, peers, and community, but we wish we could wrap them up in that downy comforter, hug them close, and insulate them from every danger.

That natural instinct is bred into our parental bone marrow. But realistically, it is impossible to protect them from everything and probably not wise when carried to the extreme. Why? Because kids *aren't* as fragile as we tend to think. They are born with strengths and abilities to cope with adversity, learn from their mistakes, and mature into responsible, competent adults. Yet they cannot develop and energize their inner resources unless we allow them opportunities to do so.

We don't want children to get hurt, but we also need to acknowledge that they must be exposed to some risk to develop and practice coping skills. If we rob them of opportunities to develop resilience or undercut their abilities by doing too much for them, solving all their dilemmas for them or overprotecting them, we actually send a damaging message—"I don't believe you're capable." This hardly breeds competence or confidence in children. Our challenge instead is to give them some room to err, fall off their bikes and scrape their knees, and at the same time teach them *how* to ride steadily and confidently over the rocky paths that lie ahead.

Throughout this book, 3 essential themes are at the core of how adults affect children's resilience: unconditional love is the bedrock of resilience because it creates security; children meet adult expectations, for better or worse; and children watch what we do more than they listen to what we say. Let's look at these themes more closely.

- Unconditional love gives children the deep-seated security that allows them to take chances when they need to adapt to new circumstances and the knowledge that in the long run all will be OK. Parents' unconditional love and acceptance will be discussed further later. For now, I simply urge you to keep in mind those feelings of protection that you had toward your child when he was a baby. As he grows up and away from you, pushing your buttons and trying your patience, show him your unconditional love. Don't assume that he knows it or takes it for granted. We must never let a child think we don't love and believe in him, even when we dislike or disapprove of his behaviors. Unconditional love doesn't mean unconditional approval. The child is not the behavior. Parents can reject certain behaviors and simultaneously love the child completely. The key is that love is never withdrawn or threatened to be withheld based on a behavior. It is about your child knowing that you are not going anywhere, no matter what. Hopefully parents will be the source of this essential ingredient of resilience, but a grandparent, an uncle, an aunt, a teacher, a health professional, or a counselor can also fill that role. The more supportive adults in a child's life, the more firmly rooted and unshakable his security will be.
- Youngsters live up or down to their parents' expectations. If parents expect the best of their children, kids tend to live up to those standards. High standards really matter, but let me be crystal clear—by high standards, I am not referring to achievements. I don't mean straight-A report cards or pitching perfect Little League games. I mean being a good human being—considerate, respectful, honest, generous, responsible…you know, the qualities you hope your children have. On the other hand, if parents expect children to be lazy, argumentative, selfish, or dependent, kids sense those negatives. "Why," they figure, "should I try to be any different? I guess I'm dumb, a loser, or whatever," and "I have nothing to lose. My parents already think I'm sneaky [or fill in an adjective of your own], so why shouldn't I just lie to them?"

  Young people also absorb messages from outside the family and change their behavior to meet those expectations. Sometimes these messages support the positive image that parents want their children to have of themselves. Other times parents must shield their children from harmful portrayals of youth and low expectations.

- As children's most powerful models, parents are in the best position to teach them about stress and resilience. Whether they're toddlers or teens, children observe parents closely. If we show them negative ways of coping with our own stress, they will follow our example. If we rant at the driver who cut into our traffic lane, our kids will assume that road rage is acceptable. If we binge on junk food whenever we're anxious, they are likely to do the same.

Here is a common example of how a parent unintentionally models negative coping. "Michael, why don't you ever help your mother? Take your dishes to the sink! Pick up your junk! Crap is spilling out of your book bag all over the floor. Why are your shoes on the sofa? Jeez, I want to stretch out and watch TV tonight. I've had a horrible day at work. C'mon, get your stuff out of here.

"Oh, Gladys, as long as you're up, bring me another beer."

Dad has clearly had a bad day, but what lesson does he model for his son? Criticize, vent your anger at others, slump on the sofa, and wash it down with another beer.

On the other hand, if parents talk about their anger or discuss how the day's work was tense and exhausting, they send the message that talking about frustration and stress is a healthy way to vent. They also can demonstrate constructive coping methods by going for a jog after a bad day at work, taking time for themselves to relax before rushing to make dinner, or practicing deep breathing or yoga.

As we show children beneficial ways to deal with stress, we are not only offering them good role models but also treating ourselves well. That's a generous gift to ourselves and our children. We may not think that children always pay attention to what we are doing, but they do. We probably won't be perfect models every time we're stressed, of course, but each time we attempt to offer children a constructive model, we reduce the potential that they will turn to negative ways of coping with stress.

Roots of Resilience

As we've seen, resilience is usually defined as an ability to bounce back or recover from adversity. Resilience has another, similar definition—the power or ability to return to the original form or position. Think of a bent twig. It can be held or tied down, but it will eventually straighten up to its original position. Or compare resilience to those rubbery stretch bands used for exercising. They can be pulled to several times their original lengths, but when you let go, they spring back to their original size. Here's the point: Resilience is a quality that's part of the original. It's already packaged in our kids' makeup. Ann Masten, PhD, one of the leading thinkers on resilience, calls it "ordinary magic." It's not something we need to go out and acquire for them; rather, it is already within them. We just need to nurture it.

It's vital to remember that all children come equipped with assets and abilities, strengths that have been described as "islands of competence," that can become sources of pride and springboards to ongoing accomplishments. Our job is to help children gain appropriate confidence by helping them recognize that they possess various abilities and inner resources. This confidence is an essential ingredient of resilience and can be nurtured at any time in life. Just as we develop and strengthen our muscles by exercising them, we can develop resilience by paying attention to those strengths and building on them.

Seven Crucial Cs of Resilience

To build resilience, it is helpful to begin by organizing many steps into a few categories. A common language about resilience also allows us to collaborate better with spouses, neighbors, and communities as we work together to build supportive strategies for children. I organize the steps and language into 7 integral, interrelated components that I call the 7 Crucial Cs—*competence, confidence, connection, character, contribution, coping,* and *control.* Many of these Cs are borrowed from great thinkers on positive youth development and resilience whose paths have informed mine. The original 4 Cs—*competence, confidence, connection,* and *character*—were coined by Rick Little, who founded the International Youth Foundation.

Each C will be explained in succeeding chapters, but to begin this discussion, I will summarize each component and pose a series of questions about each C. Let these questions rattle around in your mind for a while. Instant answers aren't necessary. The questions are designed only to help you reflect.

Competence

Competence is the ability to handle situations effectively. It's not a vague feeling that "I can do this." Competence is acquired through actual experience. Children can't become competent without first developing a set of skills that allows them to trust their judgments, make responsible choices, and face difficult situations. In thinking about your child's competence and how to fortify it, ask yourself

- Do I help my child focus on her strengths and build on them?
- Do I notice what she does well or do I focus on her mistakes?
- When I need to point out a mistake, am I clear and focused or do I communicate that I believe she always messes up?

- Do I help her recognize what she has going for herself?
- Am I helping her build the educational, social, and stress-reduction skills necessary to make her competent in the real world?
- Do I communicate in a way that empowers my child to make her own decisions or do I undermine her sense of competence by giving her information in ways she can't grasp? In other words, do I lecture her or do I facilitate her thinking?
- Do I let her make safe mistakes so she has the opportunity to right herself or do I try to protect her from every trip and fall?
- As I try to protect her, does my interference mistakenly send the message, "I don't think you can handle this"?
- If I have more than one child, do I recognize the competencies of each without comparison to siblings?

Confidence

True confidence, the solid belief in one's own abilities, is rooted in competence. Children gain confidence by demonstrating their competence in real situations. Confidence is not warm-and-fuzzy self-esteem that supposedly results from telling kids they're special or precious. Children who experience their own competence and know they are safe and protected develop a deep-seated security that promotes the confidence to cope with challenges. When parents support children in finding their own islands of competence and building on them, they prepare kids to gain enough confidence to try new ventures and trust their abilities to make sound choices.

In thinking about your child's degree of confidence, consider the following questions:

- Do I see the best in my child so that he can see the best in himself?
- Do I clearly express that I expect the best qualities (not achievements, but personal qualities such as fairness, integrity, persistence, and kindness) in him?
- Do I help him recognize what he has done right or well?
- Do I treat him as an incapable child or someone learning to navigate his world?
- Do I praise him often enough? Do I praise him honestly about specific achievements or do I give such diffuse praise that it doesn't seem authentic? (More information about praising effectively is in Chapter 7.)
- Do I catch him being good when he is generous, helpful, and kind or when he does something without being asked or cajoled?
- Do I encourage him to strive just a little bit farther because I believe he can succeed? Do I hold realistically high expectations?

- Do I unintentionally push him to take on more than he can realistically handle, causing him to stumble and lose confidence?
- When I need to criticize or correct him, do I focus only on what he's doing wrong or do I remind him that he is capable of doing well?
- Do I avoid instilling shame in my child?

Connection

Children with close ties to family, friends, school, and community are more likely to have a solid sense of security that produces strong values and prevents them from seeking destructive alternatives. Family is the central force in any child's life, but connections to civic, educational, religious, and athletic groups can also increase a young person's sense of belonging to a wider world and being safe within it.

Some questions to ponder when considering how connected your child is to family and the broader world include

- Do we build a sense of physical safety and emotional security within our home?
- Does my child know that I am absolutely crazy in love with her?
- Do I understand that the challenges my child will put me through on her path toward independence are normal developmental phases or will I take them so personally that our relationship will be harmed?
- Do I allow my child to express all types of emotions or do I suppress unpleasant feelings? Is she learning that going to other people for emotional support during difficult times is productive or shameful?
- Do we do everything to address conflict within our family and work to resolve problems rather than let them fester?
- Do we have a television and entertainment center in almost every room or do we create a common space where our family shares time together?
- Do I encourage my child to take pride in the various ethnic, religious, or cultural groups to which we belong?
- Do I jealously guard my child from developing close relationships with others or do I foster healthy relationships that I know will reinforce my positive messages?
- Do I protect my friends' and neighbors' children, just as I hope they will protect mine?

Character

Children need a fundamental sense of right and wrong to ensure they are prepared to make wise choices, contribute to the world, and become stable adults. Children with character enjoy a strong sense of self-worth and confidence. They are more comfortable sticking to their own values and demonstrating a caring attitude toward others. Young people who are future oriented may work harder and make wiser decisions today. Some basic questions to ask yourself include

- Do I help my child understand how his behaviors affect other people in good and bad ways?
- Am I helping my child recognize himself as a caring person?
- Do I allow him to clarify his own values?
- Do I allow him to consider right versus wrong and look beyond immediate satisfaction or selfish needs?
- Do I value him so clearly that I model the importance of caring for others?
- Do I demonstrate the importance of community?
- Do I help him develop a sense of spirituality?
- Am I careful to avoid racist, ethnic, or hateful statements or stereotypes? Am I clear how I regard these thoughts and statements whenever and wherever my child is exposed to them?
- Do I express how I think of others' needs when I make decisions or take actions?
- Do I encourage effort and tenacity? Do I help him think about how delaying instant gratification can pay off later?

Contribution

It is a powerful lesson when children realize that the world is a better place *because they are in it.* Children who understand the importance of personal contribution gain a sense of purpose that can motivate them. They will not only take actions and make choices that improve the world, but they will also enhance their own competence, character, and sense of connection. Teens who contribute to their communities will be surrounded by reinforcing thank-yous instead of the low expectations and condemnation so many teens endure.

Before we can foster this sense of contribution, here are some things to consider.

- Do I communicate to my child (at appropriate age levels, of course) that many people in the world do not have as much human contact, money, freedom, and security as they need?
- Do I teach the important value of serving others? Do I model generosity with my time and money?
- Do I make clear to my child that I believe she can improve the world?
- Do I create opportunities for each child to contribute in some specific way?
- Do I search my child's circle for other adults who might serve as role models who contribute to their communities and the world? Do I use these adults as examples to encourage my child to be the best she can be?

Coping

Children who learn to cope effectively with stress are better prepared to overcome life's challenges. The best protection against unsafe, worrisome behaviors may be a wide repertoire of positive, adaptive coping strategies. Before we begin teaching children the range of coping and stress-reduction skills, some basic questions to ask ourselves include

- Do I help my child understand the difference between a real crisis and something that just feels like an emergency?
- Do I model positive coping strategies on a consistent basis?
- Do I allow my child enough time to use imaginative play? Do I recognize that fantasy and play are childhood's tools to solve problems?
- Do I guide my child to develop positive, effective coping strategies?
- Do I believe that telling him to "just stop" the negative behaviors will do any good?
- Do I recognize that for many young people, risk behaviors are attempts to alleviate their stress and pain?
- If my child participates in negative behaviors, do I condemn him for it? Do I recognize that I may only increase his sense of shame and therefore drive him toward more negativity?
- Do I model problem-solving step-by-step or do I just react emotionally when I'm overwhelmed?
- Do I model the response that sometimes the best thing to do is conserve energy and let go of the belief that I can tackle all problems?
- Do I model the importance of caring for our bodies through exercise, good nutrition, and adequate sleep? Do I model relaxation techniques?
- Do I encourage creative expression?
- As I struggle to compose myself so I can make fair, wise decisions under pressure, do I model how I take control rather than respond impulsively or rashly to stressful situations?
- Do I create a family environment in which talking, listening, and sharing are safe, comfortable, and productive?

Control

When children realize that *they* can control the outcomes of their decisions and actions, they're more likely to know that they have the ability to do what it takes to bounce back. On the other hand, if parents make all the decisions, children are denied opportunities to learn control. A child who feels "everything always happens to me" tends to become passive, pessimistic, or even depressed. She sees control as external—whatever she does really doesn't matter because she has no control of the outcome. But a resilient child knows that she has internal control. By her choices and actions, she determines the results. She knows that she can make a difference, which further promotes her competence and confidence. Some questions about control include

- Do I help my child understand that life's events are not purely random and most things happen as a direct result of someone's actions and choices?
- On the other hand, do I help my child understand that she isn't responsible for many of the bad circumstances in her life (such as parents' separation or divorce)?
- Do I help her think about the future but take it one step at a time?
- Do I help her recognize even her small successes so she can experience the knowledge that she can succeed?
- Do I help her understand that no one can control all circumstances but everyone can shift the odds by choosing positive or protective behaviors?
- Do I understand that discipline is about teaching, not punishing or controlling? Do I use discipline as a means to help my child understand that her actions produce certain consequences?
- Do I reward demonstrated responsibility with increased privileges?

A Web of 7 Cs

Before we consider each of the 7 Cs individually and in depth, I want to emphasize how interrelated they are. Here is a brief, whirlwind description of how intricately interwoven these 7 ingredients of resilience are.

Children need to experience *competence* to gain *confidence.* They need *connections* with an adult to reinforce those points of *competence.* They need *character* to know what they should *contribute* to their families and the world, and *character* is forged through deep *connection* to others. *Contribution* builds *character* and further strengthens *connections.* Children who *contribute* to their communities gain *confidence* as they feel more and more *competent.* All of this leads them to recognize that they can make a difference and change their environments, and this gives them a heightened sense of *control.* Children with a sense of *control* believe in their ability to solve problems so they will more tenaciously attack a problem until they find a solution. This newfound area of *competence* then enhances their *confidence,* which will be used the next time they need to reinforce their beliefs in their ability to *control* their environment. When children know they can *control* their environment, they will more likely use healthy *coping* strategies because the need to deaden the senses or escape reality will be lessened. A key *coping* strategy is turning to people with whom you have strong *connections.* And so on.

As you think about the building blocks of resilience, do not be surprised when you notice that your child is already strong in one or two of these categories and that you need to focus your energies on other areas. Similarly, your community may be expert at supporting some components of resilience and be in serious need of other strategies that will support its young people to adapt and thrive.

Building Resilience Videos (www.healthychildren.org/BuildingResilience)

Video 3.3 A Brief Presentation of the 7 Cs Model of Resilience

Video 3.5 Is It Possible to Give Our Children Unconditional Love While Also Holding Them to High Expectations? Absolutely.

To learn about the full offering of* Building Resilience *videos, please turn to page 327.

Not Letting Others Undermine Your Child's Resilience (or Psych You Out!)

Ask any parent, teacher, or coach—we know in our gut that youth live up or down to our expectations. That's why we went out of our way to catch our children being good when they were 2 years old. They delighted in our pride and kept doing what it took to earn our praise. Teenagers would be no different, but as they grow up they quickly learn that people begin to expect the worst of them. Many parents are too busy to notice the continued miracles of normal development and have just enough time to focus on problems. Society portrays teens as the source of problems, as challenging, even dangerous.

As my twin daughters were turning 13, I experienced an onslaught of warnings from near-strangers and friends alike. "Get ready…just remember they can't help it. It'll get better." I think I got an extra dose because of my well-known respect for teens. "Dr Ken, the world is watching you," was my favorite comment. I heard, "We'll see what you think of teens once you have them," more times than I can count. I smiled because it was easier than launching into my fantasy tirade. "How dare you hold my girls to low expectations!" I wanted to say. "Yes, they will test me and my boundaries. I hope they do. How else will they learn their limits? I know it won't always be fun, but I will not make it worse by fearing them. I will continue to expect the very best from them!"

Media Misrepresentation of Teens

Books that portray how crazy teens are and popular media that emphasize their self-indulgence reinforce the sense of foreboding that parents feel about the arrival of adolescence. Even exciting new medical knowledge about the teen brain is sometimes presented in ways that suggest teens are all impulse and no control and that a part of their brains are missing.

New imaging techniques prove what we have always known: The teen brain is a work in progress. The emotional center of the brain, the amygdala, develops more rapidly than the thinking center that regulates emotions, the cerebral cortex. The brain is not fully developed until about age 25. This does not mean teens are broken. It means we need to nurture them and pay special attention to helping them avoid situations in which they would find it harder to regulate their emotions and equip them with tools that make it easier for them to do the right thing, even when their emotions are spinning out of control. Don't worry, a lot of this book is about just that!

If parents weren't already frightened by stereotypes of adolescence, they receive media and even some public health messages that hype teen sexuality, drug use, and violence—"Crisis in America!" This "Teens at risk!" mentality that promotes the storm and stress of adolescence does great harm to our youth. Beyond increasing parental anxiety, it leads to the negative behaviors we worry about and the counterculture that interferes with youth taking the positive steps they need to thrive.

The offensive portrayal of youth creates a self-fulfilling prophecy for 2 key reasons. First, remember that one of the fundamental questions of adolescence is, "Am I normal?" Teens tend to do what they think "normal" is. If a teen sees a stereotype often enough, she will believe it and might behave negatively just to fit in. The second point follows directly: Because teens live up or down to expectations, they will behave in ways they believe others expect. The more we allow these negative images to circulate, the more youth will do what it takes to match them, the more uncomfortable they will feel with themselves when they don't, and the greater difficulty they will experience navigating peer relationships when they choose to do the right thing.

I have counseled students going to college whose biggest anxiety had nothing to do with academics. Instead, they worried they wouldn't be able to keep up with the drinking. I know countless teens who feel badly about their virginity because they are 16 and know with certainty they are abnormal. I know many who are having sex, not because they are ready but because they think they are supposed to. I watch painfully as youth in underperforming schools don't believe they're supposed to study because they've incorporated a toxic message about their potential to become highly educated into their self-image and have grown to accept that academics are not for them. These under-resourced teens have investments directed toward them in the form of prevention programs but have few enrichment activities. Despite the best of intentions, they may receive a message that the very issues the prevention programs target must be what normal teenagers like them do. If prevention programs were better balanced with strength-building enrichment programs, teens would have positive alternatives clearly defined and a better understanding that they were expected to develop into creative, future-oriented people.

With the best of intentions, public health messages want to illuminate the problems of youth. "Did you know that X% of teens have sex before the end of high school?" "In the city of X, more than X% of teens drop out before graduating high school." "Binge drinking is a growing problem on campuses; X% of freshman say they have blacked out after a night of drinking."

News outlets hype stories of teen crises to draw parents in. Because "dog bites boy" isn't news, they rarely tell the stories of the kids thriving and contributing to society. Instead, lead-ins ensure that parents will tune into the news. "Is your child having sex in your house at 3:00 in the afternoon? Parents, you'll want to hear the startling finding of a new study on teen sexuality, right after these messages." Then the story airs. "Crisis in our community—38% of teens..."

When every expert asks, "Where are the parents?" and talks about "kids nowadays," youth learn that adolescents are supposed to frighten us. The news needs to be reported, of course, but stories should include facts without hype. And wouldn't it be nice if some stories focused on helping teens resist peer pressure by giving them face-saving techniques they can use to leave a risky situation while following their own internal compass?

Countering the Negative News

Social marketing experts understand the power of the media in shaping self-perceptions and behaviors. Jeff Linkenbach, EdD, of Montana State University has created a vigorous response to popular messages about adolescents. With www.mostofus.org, he strives to teach communities and policy makers who drive the self-perception of youth to transform how youth are portrayed. What if the binge-drinking story said, "Although X% of college freshmen say they are drinking to dangerous levels on the weekends, the good news is that most teens are choosing better ways of spending their time." What if the story on school dropouts sounded more like, "Clearly schools in X city are not performing well because some kids are not able to be successful and X% are leaving. The good news is that most teens are working hard to keep their stake in the future." Imagine how much better youth who wanted to delay sexual activity would feel if stories like this ran: "Despite the fact that popular shows focus on teens having sex, in a recent study, fewer than half of teens were choosing to have sex by age X."

So what can a parent do? First, never stop catching your teen being good. Second, set clear, positive expectations. Third, ignore the hype that creates anxiety in you and subtly transmits lowered expectations to your child. Fourth, as best as you can, insulate your children from the negative messages swirling around them by reframing the hype. If the news will not point out that 22% is not a crisis, you do it. Listen to the story and note, "Too bad for those kids, but the good news is that most kids, more than 3 out of 4 actually, are not doing it."

What can a parent do within the community or as a community leader?

- Spread the good news messages.
- Advocate for the positive portrayal of youth in the community. Ask for a shift away from media coverage where only the highest achievers and delinquents get noticed. Make sure acts of generosity and compassion shown by everyday students are noticed as well.
- Advocate for enrichment programs, especially in those areas most at risk that currently only have prevention programs. This doesn't mean you should suggest that risk-based programs (like those for drugs, violence, and teen pregnancy) be cut—they have tremendous value. But we must guard against a situation in which only youth who engage in worrisome behaviors get our added attention and those who don't view themselves as outside "expected" behaviors in their community. Sports, art programs, and academic enrichment activities running in parallel send the message that we expect youth to be creative, have strong bodies and minds, and be prepared to lead us into the future.
- Give youth opportunities to contribute to their communities. When they are serving others, their value will be noticed and they will receive vital reinforcing displays of gratitude.
- Work with parents of your teen's friends and with your community so that more young people have the rules and boundaries you have for your own child. Adolescents who see these boundaries as normal have no reason to rebel against them.

The next time a friend tells you, "Uh-oh, she's 12, put on your safety belt," smile and say, "I'm ready for the ride. There will be some bumps, but I expect her to come through just fine. She has already shown me what a fine person she is."

***Building Resilience* Videos** **(www.healthychildren.org/BuildingResilience)**

Video 4.2 Ignore the Negative Hype About Teenagers: Expecting the Best From Adolescence Will Pay Off

To learn about the full offering of* Building Resilience *videos, please turn to page 327.

PART 2

Competence and Confidence

Competence is ability rooted in experience. Children acquire competence by mastering tasks and facing challenges. Competence is cumulative. The more children master life experiences, the more they realize they can tackle challenges and thereby develop genuine confidence. Along with a strong sense of competence comes tenacity, the ability to stick with tough tasks and solve problems. Safety follows competence because children who trust their abilities have an easier time standing firm in their values and making their own decisions when faced with unsafe situations.

Competence is not a vague feeling that "I can handle this." If it were, it would not only be empty and unfounded, but it could also be dangerous. For example, a 4-year-old who has just learned to ride a "big kid's" bike may *feel* capable of cruising around the neighborhood and crossing major intersections, but obviously she is not yet able to do so. A 14-year-old might argue, "I can take care of myself, Dad. If there's beer at the party and other kids start drinking, I can handle it. I just won't drink." But under pressure to be accepted by friends, young people can become overwhelmed. They often *assume* that they will be able to handle challenges, but they haven't been tested by experience. They haven't developed and demonstrated enough competence—yet.

Competence derives from a wide range of achievements, from almost invisible steps to major leaps. A child becomes competent when she learns to build a sand castle and demonstrates tenacity when she rebuilds it over and over after waves wash it away. A child demonstrates bravery and confidence when she crosses the threshold on the first day of kindergarten and gives her parents a nod that says, "I'll be OK." She knows she is competent when she makes it through the day despite her fears, and she is ready to go back the next day.

The first time a child can cook eggs by himself may be a small deal to adults, but it's a milestone for him. A youngster owns his own sense of competence when, after getting hit in the nose with a hardball, he goes back out and practices fielding until he's no longer afraid to take his position at third base. A teenager experiences a rich, satisfying competence when he is able to stand on his convictions and not shoplift when his friends are doing so.

Competence is the first of the 7 Crucial Cs to consider because it provides the bedrock for resilience. Without genuine competence, it is unlikely the other 6 Cs could be developed. Competence is the largest area to cover in this discussion because fostering competence requires an understanding of several key principles.

- **Getting out of the way!** Normal child development occurs because children are wired to build new knowledge and skills from each experience. Sometimes adults do their best when they get out of kids' way.
- **Play is one of the major jobs of childhood.** It is filled with opportunities for children to discover their competencies. We must allow plenty of time for free child-driven play, the most effective type of play for children to discover their competence in the world.
- **Noticing, praising, and criticizing.** Competence is enhanced or hindered by the ways that we communicate and interact with children. New skills and abilities are reinforced when adults notice and praise them. Criticism, when given insensitively, can undermine a child's ability to become more competent. When criticism is offered as constructive, targeted feedback, it can enhance growing competence.
- **Striving for authentic success.** If we are to prepare children to thrive in the future, we must think beyond the grades and extracurricular schedules that seem to measure success today. We must ask whether children possess tenacity, love of learning, and creativity. We should consider whether they are under so much pressure that those critical ingredients will be stifled.
- **Thinking clearly.** Sometimes the way we think prevents us from recognizing our competence and paralyzes confidence. This is true for children too. To be able to get past difficulties, we first have to be able to stop thinking in a self-destructive manner.
- **No more lectures.** Though our advice is offered with good intentions, it often undermines children's growing competence. In short, lecturing backfires. We need to know how children think so that we can put them in the driver's seat as they develop solutions for themselves.
- **Guiding children to find the right choices.** Parents can use specific skills to steer kids toward making their own safe decisions in the face of peer pressure.
- **Media literacy.** Young people need to be able to sift through media-driven messages so they can be in control of their own opinions and self-image.

Getting Out of the Way

As children develop, they increase their competence over time. Think about your own child and how nearly every day brings new skills and abilities. How parents react to these miracles is key to a child's motivation to continue striving. If a child takes a significant step and no one notices or cares, she learns that her accomplishments don't matter. These achievements are often ignored because parents take normal events for granted—after all, every child learns to walk, to talk, to go to school for the first time.

Think about the biggest challenge of your adult life or your most difficult task at work. I bet it pales in comparison to the huge leap that occurred when you learned to take your first step as a toddler. Children accomplish these tasks all the time, but some parents don't build on the spirit of growing competence innate to childhood because they ignore their child's everyday milestones.

Other parents do anything but ignore their children. They hover, praise incessantly, and protect, protect, protect. While involved parents are more likely to produce motivated kids, we have to find balance. Overly involved parents can unintentionally get in the way of children's acquisition of confidence and drive to achieve new competencies. If we push kids too hard to master the next step, we may push them into feeling incompetent. We also may inadvertently interfere with natural processes that allow them to become increasingly competent.

To foster their competence, we need to recognize when and how our involvement helps or hurts. As situations arise throughout childhood and adolescence, we need to understand when to do the following 3 things:

- Get out of the way.
- Join in and help a child build new avenues of competence.
- Guide a child to think through situations wisely and safely.

Getting out of the way is a tough challenge. We want to help, fix, and guide kids. But we have to remind ourselves that when we just let them figure things out for themselves, we communicate this powerful message: "I think you are competent." When we let them build blocks to their unique specifications, we are communicating, "I think you are capable." When the blocks tumble and they rebuild them without our intervention, we convey the message, "I like it when you try again."

Every time we try to solve problems for them, we undercut their growing sense of competence. If we solve all their problems, they will remain dependent on us. While it may be an attractive prospect to have our children always need us, our job is to create capable individuals. When we support their problem-solving skills by getting out of their way or by offering gentle guidance only when necessary or when they ask for it, we foster their growing sense of self-reliance and independence. When we recognize their capabilities, we diminish the number of power struggles with them. As a result, our children will be more comfortable returning to us for the nurturance and support that has no age boundaries.

The Parent Alarm

Why do many parents have so much difficulty trusting in their children's competence to learn how to face and overcome challenges? It's our *parent alarm*—that menacing feeling that arises whenever we sense that our children might be in trouble. As soon as the parent alarm goes off, we immediately proclaim restrictions that prevent them from getting close to a sticky situation. The alarm is also a major barrier to effective communication.

"Mom, I met this girl..." The parent alarm response: "You're too young to date!" That's a lost opportunity to discuss feelings, sexuality, and respect for others when building relationships.

"Dad, I think the guys on the next block are smoking some weed..." Dad's parent alarm blasts, "Never go over there! Don't you dare hang out with them!" That's a lost opportunity for a discussion about drugs, peer pressure, and especially how grateful Dad is that his son comes to him to talk about drugs.

The parent alarm is an instinctual rapid response we use to steer children away from danger when our sensors shout, "TROUBLE!" The parent alarm is beneficial, of course, when a situation involves danger. Don't worry about building competence at that moment; let the alarm ring and rescue your child. If you have to scream and take quick action to prevent a 4-year-old from toppling a pot of boiling water off the stove, yell loudly! If your teenager is drunk and getting in a car, grab the keys and prevent tragedy at all costs. These are lessons that we cannot afford to let children learn on their own.

Short of scenarios that challenge safety, we should try to let children figure things out on their own. Sometimes doing nothing is precisely what they need. Wendy Mogel, PhD, speaks of this in her aptly titled book, *The Blessing of a*

Skinned Knee. Paying attention but doing nothing to interfere sends children the wonderful message, "I trust you to handle this."

Some problems clearly require guidance. In *Parent Effectiveness Training,* Thomas Gordon, PhD, offers considerable wisdom that can help parents decide when and how to intervene. He suggests that parents first decide who owns the problem at hand. If the child owns it (when the problem is one that a child experiences in her own life independent of her parents, such as a conflict with a friend or teacher), parents can be most helpful if they don't try to solve the problem. They can get out of her way or help her to problem-solve by using techniques like role-playing or choreographed conversations (see Chapter 11). On the other hand, if parents own the problem or if a child's behavior interferes with the parents' lives (such as coming home late and waking parents), the parent has the right to be more directive.

Many parents believe that they know exactly how to get children to figure out what's wrong—they tell them; they lecture about every possible dire consequence of their behaviors. Parents' protective instincts want to steer children far away from dangerous outcomes and toward safer, immediate solutions. What are some reasons that we jump in as soon as our parent alarm rings and try to fix their problems or correct their mistakes?

- We worry that they will not be successful.
- We think that they are not trying their hardest.
- We worry that they will embarrass us or reflect poorly on us.
- We see our children as reflections of ourselves; they become the product we have produced, and we want our work to seem perfect.
- We are uncomfortable when we make mistakes and assume our children share that insecurity. We wish to spare them the same discomfort.
- We have strong standards of right and wrong, and we don't want our children to stray too close to the boundaries of what we believe is wrong.
- We think that criticism is the best kind of guidance, and we offer our judgments as keys to self-improvement.

Interference Versus Getting Out of the Way

Let's consider how parents interfere or get out of the way as a child develops from toddlerhood through adolescence. For each scenario, imagine what your parental impulse would be if this were your child. Then consider whether you could let go enough to allow her to boost her own competence. Look for the subtle messages you might convey with your desire to protect your child.

Eleven-month-old Sophia pulls herself up on wobbly legs and takes her first step. What a wonderful metaphor for life! What's next? She inevitably falls. Will anyone notice her great achievement? Or will the tall people around her ignore this magnificent moment? Will they applaud and encourage her to use her strength and ingenuity to stand back up? Or will they run to pick her up and prevent her from experiencing the thrill of getting back up by herself?

A few months later, Sophia is an avid walker exploring her environment. She wants to climb the stairs and explore the kitchen (with all its electric appliances and other dangers) and the living room (with all its fragile knickknacks). Will her parents get down on their knees to see the world from her perspective and childproof the house so she can move around safely? Will they grab her every time she gets near a breakable object and shout "No!"? Will they let her hold one in her little hands, cupped gently by their own palms, while she observes and touches it? (Afterward, they put fragile items out of reach.) Will they yell at her every time she climbs because they worry that she may fall, or will they stack a pile of pillows on the floor and let her climb and tumble to her heart's content?

At age 4, Sophia is proudly building with blocks. Do her parents praise and encourage her as she adds piece by piece? Or do they say, "That's going to fall down if you don't put the bigger blocks on the bottom"? They're trying to be helpful by teaching her basic physics, but they're sending her the message, "I don't think you're a very good builder."

Do they sit down next to her, join in the project, and ask her where to place each block? If they let Sophia be the construction foreman, they have the joy of playing alongside her while allowing her to experience the wonderful, powerful feeling of control. But if her parents sit beside her and build a bigger house than she could ever build, they leave her feeling somewhat incapable.

At age 6, Sophia paints a picture of a garden under a bright blue sky. She uses vivid colors to paint flowers that are larger than the dog in the corner. Do her parents tell her, "That is the most perfect picture in the whole world," which makes her question their assessment skills? Or do they say, "What beautiful colors," which offers praise that she knows she has earned? Do they tell her, "The flowers are out of proportion to the dog," which shows her they are displeased? Do they encourage her to proceed at her own pace by saying, "I really like your picture. Please draw me another wonderful surprise"? Do they support her creativity with open-ended remarks such as, "Tell me about your picture"? This type of neutral comment opens an opportunity to learn from her imagination and avoids the embarrassment she would feel if they made a faulty guess about the images in her picture.

When Sophia is in fourth grade, she has her first group assignment for science. She and 2 classmates are studying endangered animals, but her partners aren't pulling their weight. Sophia gets frustrated but does her own work well. Do her parents encourage the work she is doing and stay nearby so that they can answer her questions as they arise? Or do they tell her, "We are going to make the most wonderful project in the whole school," and spend the evening completing "our" science project?

When they see her class's completed projects, do they say, "Yours is the best science project I've ever seen!" and sign her up for an after-school science club? Or do they say, "You really did a nice job. I especially liked the piece on the gorilla" (authentic, specific praise) and ask her if she'd like to visit the zoo?

Or do they tell her they like her work, but if she had put in more time, it could have been even better, "like Soyun's," which clearly tells her that her parents are dissatisfied? If they really think she could have done a better job, they might say something specific, such as, "I really liked your section on the red-eyed tree frog. You put a lot of heart into that. I noticed there were other animals you didn't include. Were there any other animals you wish you had more time to study?"

At age 12, Sophia is about to enter that phase of middle childhood that parents dread: the "mean girl" stage. Her best friend abruptly rejects her for "not liking boys yet and still playing with dolls." Sophia comes home devastated, runs to her mother, and cries, "Courtney's telling everyone I'm a baby."

Oh, no! Her mother's parent alarm blares, "I've got to make her feel better." Does she tell Sophia, "This isn't such a big deal," which devalues Sophia's hurt and lets her know that her mother thinks she's emotionally immature? Does she reply, "I never liked Courtney anyway," in an attempt to bond with her daughter? That response implies that her daughter has bad taste in friends. And at some future point, if Mom needs to offer guidance about avoiding negative influence from Courtney, this comment sets Mom up for the retort, "You never liked her anyway," after the girls repair their friendship (which preteen girls do even as we continue to hold grudges for the hurt our daughter has endured).

If Sophia's mother says, "Courtney's mother is my friend, so you'd better work this out," she sends the message that her priorities do not include her daughter. If she says, "I once had a friend who dumped me. Let me tell you how I handled it," that statement translates into, "I have to give you the solution because you are not competent to fix it yourself." Or does she listen to her daughter's feelings, acknowledge how upsetting the situation is, and ask, "How do you think you can handle this?"

Now Sophia is 15 years old and has just broken up with her first boyfriend. She brushes past her parents and says, "You just wouldn't understand." An hour later, she sulks into the living room, cuddles between her mother and father on the sofa, and talks about a fight she and Tyler had. Do her parents say, "What a creep he is! You're better off without him," which prevents her from saying she's still madly in love? Do they say, "If you just lost some weight, boys would find you so attractive"? Do they say, "You were too young to start dating anyway. We knew you'd get hurt"? Or do they listen quietly and help her think it through and communicate with their supportive presence that it's OK to be sad?

Finally, Sophia is a senior preparing for college. Do her parents help her exaggerate her application résumé, which clearly tells her that who she is, the authentic package, is just not good enough? Do they rewrite her essay, sending the unspoken message that they see her as incapable of doing it well enough herself? Do they tell her that she must go to the college that family members attended, or that they have worked so hard only so that she can go to the very best college? Who will she think they're really concerned about? Whose needs and reputation are her parents really looking after? Will she feel like a failure if she doesn't get into her first-choice school? Will she feel as though she has failed this initiation into adulthood because she did not meet her parents' goals?

Or do her parents listen closely to her interests and help her clarify what she is looking for in a college environment? Will they guide her to find the best possible match to meet her interests, needs, and desires?

Like Sophia, all children have almost daily opportunities to demonstrate and shore up their natural capabilities from their first toddling steps to their senior year of high school. As parents, we can support their efforts by getting out of the way.

Sibling Rivalry

It sometimes seems impossible to get out of the way when siblings are squabbling. One whines, "She started it. Punish her!" The other argues, "No I didn't. He did. Punish *him!*"

Sibling rivalry has a bad reputation. But there's a positive side to it. As brothers and sisters argue over everyday issues, they have an opportunity to become competent at negotiating and peacemaking, if we allow them to settle their differences on their own. This means refraining from interrogating ("Who started it?"). It means staying out of fights unless someone is getting physically hurt. Each child usually wants parents to take his or her side. Instead, we can remain neutral and calm. "I'm sure you can both come up with an answer. You might not like it as much as if you got your own way, but I know you can work something out together." Then walk away.

When we don't get drawn into their battles, they are often quite capable of problem-solving on their own. When both work out a compromise, each will be more likely to stick to it because they are invested in it. They have contributed to the solution rather than having it imposed on them. When parental judgments about who is right or wrong are removed from the scene, siblings have less to fight about.

***Building Resilience* Videos** **(www.healthychildren.org/BuildingResilience)**

Video 5.2 The Toughest of Balancing Acts: How Do We Protect Our Children AND Let Them Learn Life's Lessons?

To learn about the full offering of* Building Resilience *videos, please turn to page 327.

The Value of Play

For too many young people, childhood is a time of crammed schedules and heightened pressures. Their afternoons, evenings, and weekends are slotted into tight segments for soccer, drama, homework, music lessons, tutoring, ballet, gymnastics, and more homework. Some children are so busy they give up critical sleep time to complete their schoolwork. Even during the summer, their hours are filled with activities to keep them occupied and safe while parents work.

While most kids thrive, some react with anxiety and other signs of stress. Highly scheduled children have less time for child-driven creative play that is central to healthy development. When adults over-schedule children's free time, it isn't really free at all. Two important elements are forgotten amid these hectic schedules. Unstructured free play (or downtime in the case of adolescents) not only offers protection against harmful effects of stress, but it also gives children opportunities to discover their own interests and competencies. Play allows them to use their creativity while developing imagination, dexterity, and physical and emotional strength. When adults aren't directing or organizing them into activities, kids create and explore worlds they can master. Play helps them develop new competencies that lead to enhanced confidence and resilience. In fact, play is childhood's inborn tool to build resilience—"Me, I'm not scared, I'm the superhero." Undirected play allows children to learn how to work in groups—to share, negotiate, and advocate for themselves. Think of 4-year-olds on the playground and you'll recognize some of the skills that will help them navigate the adult workplace.

When play is allowed to be child-driven, kids move at their own pace, discover their talents and interests, and ultimately engage in the passions they wish to pursue. In contrast to passive entertainment like watching television, play builds active, healthy bodies. Above all, play is a simple joy that is a cherished part of childhood.

Play also offers parents a wonderful opportunity to engage fully with children. Here's an opportunity *not* to get out of the way entirely! The key is to let them choose and direct the playtime activity. We can be on the sidelines and ask how they would like us to be involved, but we have to remember it is *their* play, not ours.

When we observe children at play or join with them, we have a unique opportunity to see from their vantage point as they navigate a world perfectly created to fit their needs. The interactions that occur through play tell children that we are fully paying attention to them. Parents who take the opportunity to glimpse their children's world through play learn to communicate with them more effectively and gain another setting to offer gentle, nurturing guidance.

If we want children to enjoy the many benefits derived from play, we need to make a determined effort to limit the over-scheduled, overstretched atmosphere in many families. We have to make more time for free, exploratory play. Unfortunately, we may feel like we're swimming upstream because we receive carefully marketed messages that "good" parents expose children to every opportunity to excel and ensure that children participate in a wide variety of activities. As a result, much parent-child time is spent transporting children between those special activities.

It is not clear whether this jam-packed routine is offering a developmental benefit or producing children who are better prepared for the future, but it is clear that this lifestyle has repercussions. Many parents feel they're running on a treadmill to keep up, yet they dare not slow their pace for fear that their children will fall behind. We need to take a deep breath and find an appropriate balance between preparing for the future and living fully in the present through play and rich parent-child interaction. That balance will be different for every child, based on individual academic needs, temperament, environment, and family situation.

Children aren't the only victims of over-scheduling and lack of free play. Parents burdened by work responsibilities and maintaining a household find themselves sacrificing their own downtime because they need to arrange activities and drive children between appointments. The pressures they feel to meet every need they perceive their children require to excel make them feel inadequate. Most importantly, parents miss opportunities for high-quality time with children. Some of the best interactions occur during downtime—just talking, preparing meals together, working on a hobby, or being immersed in child-centered play.

When children play alone or with friends by engaging their imaginations and talents in a wide-open arena without hovering adults, they explore a variety of interests and discover what they like to do. The more they enjoy it, the more they do it and the better they become at it. But all too frequently, an adult steps in and says, "I see you and your friends like putting on puppet shows. Maybe you'd like to take a drama class. I'll sign you up."

Before you know it, parents have turned play into "practice" or "lessons." Some children may genuinely enjoy pursuing these interests in a structured way. Others will be turned off quickly. If they'd been allowed to pursue their interests in an unstructured way, they might have enjoyed mastering new skills. Perhaps most important in terms of enhancing resilience, they learn what kinds of activities or hobbies can take them away on an instant vacation as a means to relax (see Chapter 30).

Going With the Flow

Parents sometimes tell me that their children are self-driven in avidly pursuing a sport or other activity, but this may not always be the case. When the drive truly flows from within a child, it should be supported. On the other hand, if a child's drive is motivated more by a desire to please parents than self-satisfaction or joy, this drive can become one more stressor in the child's life. It is far better to let children discover their interests freely, and follow them without imposing too much structure on their activities. We can put a little wind behind children's sails to support them, but the direction should come from them.

Give your child as many opportunities as possible to play freely if you want him to discover his likes and skills. Your child will reap an internal satisfaction from being good at something, whether it's building towers of blocks when he's 4 or staging plays when he's 14. Don't you wish you had more time to play now? Wouldn't your work life be more productive if you had that right balance of work and pleasure? Your child learns this balance by choosing how to spend his unscheduled time while still getting his chores and work done. He will be a happier, healthier, and more successful adult if he learns to mix achievement and pleasure now.

As we reflect on the value of play, we should not forget the school day. Recess is being challenged as a relative waste of time because it distracts from academics. Many communities are cutting down on recess, and some are eliminating it entirely. Poorer children are more likely to have it cut from their school day. Recess is not a waste of time. It helps kids engage in school and offers the "reboot" that allows them to focus better in class and absorb their lessons.

Please don't misread my advocacy for play as anti-enrichment activities or for recess as antiacademic. Enrichment activities and high-quality academics should be available to all children, but children develop optimally when they have a balance of enrichment and play. My concern is that unscheduled, free playtime is considered expendable when different forces compete for a child's time. It is not; it is the work of childhood.

Building Resilience Videos (www.healthychildren.org/BuildingResilience)

Video 6.1 The Importance of Play in Promoting Healthy Child Development

To learn about the full offering of **Building Resilience** ***videos, please turn to page 327.***

Noticing, Praising, and Criticizing

When children demonstrate their competence, we can reinforce it by noticing and praising them, or we can undercut it through inappropriate criticism.

As busy as we are, we can't let ourselves become too distracted or take their achievements for granted. If we have the casual attitude, "Isn't that what 7-year-olds are supposed to do, after all?" we will miss opportunities to reinforce their competence. Perhaps our 7-year-old struggled to read the whole chapter or do that gymnastic flip for the first time. We can help her recognize her own competence in reaching those relatively minor achievements if we use a little praise. "That was a long chapter. You really stuck with it, didn't you?" "I know you've been practicing that flip. You really did it well."

A few words about praise: Don't lather it on too thickly. If we hype an accomplishment like blocking a soccer goal and imply that it's equivalent to winning an Olympic medal, our children won't believe us. They also won't recognize or appreciate an achievement when they do something particularly meritorious because all the praise seems the same.

The opposite—no praise or attention—takes the luster out of achievements and stifles motivation. Genuine praise goes a long way in reinforcing positive behaviors. To do so, praise should be specific. For example, "Wow, you used a lot of great colors in that painting. Look at those bright red and blue birds!" is more specific and authentic than simply saying, "You're a great artist." The first comment shows the child that we're really looking at her creation and appreciating it. The second comment sounds vague and canned. She knows she's not Picasso. It sets a high expectation that a child may feel she cannot meet.

I was reminded of the importance of specific praise by my daughter Ilana when she was 10 years old. In 1 hour, she taught herself to do a flip off the diving board at a community pool. She transformed from a child scared to consider it into a proud girl who could do a well-polished flip and a half. She first let her legs go slightly over her head just before entering the water; she landed flat on her back in pain, but she grinned. Within minutes she taught herself to curl and tuck. I (who can't do a simple dive without belly flopping) stared in amazement. I oohed and aahed sincerely for the whole hour. When she got out of the pool, I burst out, "Ilana, I am so, so proud of you!" She asked, "What are you proud of? That I was able to do a flip? That I tried to teach other kids how? Or that even though I was really excited, I always waited my turn?" (Perhaps Ilana should be writing this section about praise...)

Praise Effort, Not Intelligence or the End Result

If you want your child to reach her potential, one of the most important traits to nurture is *tenacity*—the "I'll stick with it" approach to challenges. Carol Dweck, PhD, professor of education at Stanford and author of *Mindset: The New Psychology of Success,* has proven how well-intentioned but misguided praise can go awry. She conducted a relatively simple experiment that demonstrated the dramatic differences in children's performance based on the type of praise they received. Fifth graders were given a series of puzzles designed so that all children would do fairly well. After the first part of the test, they were told their scores and given a single line of praise. One group was told, "You must be smart at this"; the others were praised for their effort: "You must have worked really hard."

The students were then given a choice of which tests to take for the second round. Students could choose a test that would be harder but from which they'd learn a lot, or an easy test similar to the first. Ninety percent of children praised for their *effort* chose the harder set of puzzles, whereas the majority of those praised for their intelligence chose the easy test. Next, all the students were given a test that was 2 years above their grade level. As expected, it was difficult for all of them, and most were not able to complete the tasks. The students who had been praised for their effort on the first test assumed they simply hadn't worked hard enough. Those praised for their intelligence took their failure as proof they were no longer smart or maybe never were. Their discomfort was visible. Then a final round of tests, as easy as the initial test, was given after the "failure round." The children who were praised for their intelligence initially did worse than their very first attempt, and those praised for their effort showed improvement.

This study suggests that we should recognize the process, not the product, and praise effort rather than grades and test scores. So what does this look like? See the Table on the next page for examples of what to say and what not to say.

Do Say	Don't Say
What did you learn in school today?	How did you do on your test?
How'd you pick up your game?	How many goals did you score?
Were you proud of your piece in the art exhibition?	Did you get the blue ribbon?
I love watching you think. You work so hard to figure things out.	You're so smart.
Tell me about your picture. It seems to have so much feeling.	You're such a great artist.
I think you did well because you really studied. It paid off.	Math sure comes naturally to you.
I really admire how you'll search for the answers and get help until you feel confident.	I'm so proud of your grades.

The Downside of Criticism

All children have their own personal strengths, but too often we overlook them because we're focused on what they do wrong or what their shortcomings are, especially as they grow from sweet babies to independent children and sometimes rebellious adolescents. Instead of noticing, appreciating, and praising their assets, we pay more attention to their weaknesses or faults because we want to improve them. This is where criticism creeps in.

Adults usually criticize with good intentions, but pointing out only their mistakes or what's wrong usually puts them on the defensive. Instead of thinking objectively about what we've said, kids want to defend themselves. Criticism also shames them, which can breed anger and resentment. Criticism can make children feel inept—precisely the opposite of competent.

We must not be afraid to point out how they could do better, however. If criticism is offered without denigrating a child in a personal way, it can be helpful. Two basic points: The most important guideline is that criticism, like praise, must be specific; and when we want to help children get past a shortcoming, it's more effective if our constructive criticism also recognizes their strengths.

Specific criticism points out errors that a child should avoid in the future. But no matter how upset you are by what your child has done, be careful to target the specific behavior and avoid making personal statements about your child. For example, consider the following scenario:

Jordan runs into the house, tracks mud on the carpet, and leaves his rain-soaked jacket puddling on the kitchen floor. It's fine for his parents to say, "You've left a mess all over the place. We expect you to clean it up." It's not helpful to say, "You are such a careless slob." When we need to point out children's errors or shortcomings, it's far more effective to build from their strengths. This is particularly true when they are stuck and don't know how to accomplish a task. Point out what they've done well in the past, ask what they've learned, and invite their suggestions about how they might use past experiences to handle current problems.

If we want to help children build competence, we have to help them develop their own strengths. We need to capitalize on real experiences in which they have learned appropriate skills and allow them to practice those skills and apply them to new settings. When they fall into difficulties, we can help them draw on those experiences as opportunities to learn to avoid or prevent similar difficulties in the future. When we're about to open our mouths and utter a critical comment, we should stop and ask ourselves, "How can I use this experience to help my child learn from this mistake without destroying her confidence or instilling shame?"

Unintended Criticism

Our criticism needn't be blatant or intentional to be harmful. Children sometimes simply don't understand where our criticism is directed. The following example illustrates how these misunderstandings occur:

Thomas, a curious 3-year-old, is playing for an hour by himself. He industriously rearranges some furniture. He moves chairs around his table and cleans up the clutter on the table as he prepares to draw pictures. When he finishes, he wanders over to his blocks and builds a tower. Thomas then demolishes it because he has magically transformed into a pterodactyl whose wings crash into the tower. He stops his pterodactyl noises and rebuilds the tower.

Watching him play contentedly, his mother is pleased by the way he entertains himself. As it gets dark, Thomas notices that a lamp is unplugged. He picks up the plug and reaches toward an outlet, which fortunately has a childproof plug. His mother suddenly shouts, "No! No! Don't do that!"

How does Thomas interpret her message? "I've been bad." He assumes her harsh tone covers all his recent behaviors (rearranging furniture; cleaning up clutter; drawing pictures; building, smashing, and rebuilding towers; creating an imaginary dinosaur; attempting to illuminate the room). He doesn't understand that she thought he was terrific until that one dangerous moment with the electric plug.

Criticism (or directly changing behavior) is necessary whenever there's imminent danger, but we have to be careful in how we express it. We need to be clear about giving kids an appropriate amount of information that they can process. If criticism is not focused and specific, it leaves a great deal of room for misinterpretation. Thomas's mother might have said, "Don't touch that plug!" After he dropped it, she could have reminded him that he'd been told to stay away from electric outlets, then immediately tell him what a good job he had done with his tower and drawings and redirected him to those activities. Because she is human, it is all right that she shouted "No!" loudly. She should be concerned that he might get an electric shock. But after she shouts, it's important that she make it crystal clear that it was only the plug that's forbidden, and that she really liked how Thomas was playing before that moment.

Unspoken Criticism

Not all criticism is verbalized. Sometimes a parent's actions can be unintentionally critical without saying a word. For example, a 10-year-old loved spending time with his father. One of his favorite activities was helping his dad with weekend projects. When a table needed painting, Dad opened a can of paint and handed his son a brush. Sounds easy enough, but as the boy proceeded, he couldn't smooth out the brush marks. The more he painted, the more brush strokes appeared. He grew frustrated and asked his father for help. His father took the brush from the boy's hand and repainted the table himself.

Years later, the boy recalled how insignificant and criticized he felt. His father probably thought he was helping his son, but he really hadn't. By taking over, the father criticized his son's work and failed to help him become more competent—without uttering a word.

A Word on Teens

As our children grow and our family lives become busier, it often seems that teens would rather be with their friends than us. Our time with them is at a premium and we want to make the most of every moment. Sometimes we use these few precious moments to get in all our criticisms and "instructions."

When they were little, we knew that the most effective way to elicit good behavior was to catch them being good, notice their progress, and show appreciation for it. Teens are bigger, but they are no different. Never forget that core point of building resilience: Our children live up or down to our expectations. Couple this with the fact that teens want our attention as much as young children do—though they would deny that emphatically—and you can better understand why focusing on negatives will backfire. Teens will continue to do whatever gets your attention, good or bad.

***Building Resilience* Videos** **(www.healthychildren.org/BuildingResilience)**

Video 7.1 Using Praise Appropriately: The Key to Raising Children With a Growth Mind-set

To learn about the full offering of* Building Resilience *videos, please turn to page 327.

Authentic Success

Our goal has always been to prepare children to thrive and succeed far into the future. Generations of Americans have dreamed that children will have better, more successful lives than their parents and grandparents. For many, that dream became a reality. But today we fear this dream may no longer be achievable. Especially in difficult economic times, we realize our children may have to outperform us just to keep up. We feel the pressure. So do they.

To maximize their chances, we try to instill in them the cornerstones of enduring success—commitment to hard work, tenacity, and love of learning. When possible, we expose them to a variety of opportunities so they will be prepared to flourish. With the best intentions, we begin building their résumés at earlier ages than ever before.

Many young people internalize society's stresses and absorb the pressure to succeed. They believe that they need to become all things to all people to make it. Some children use this pressure as fuel, perhaps even reaching levels of success they may not have attained otherwise. Others become so stressed that they lose the love of learning, and their innate curiosity is crushed. Some create an image or posture that allows them to pretend they just don't care—they walk off the playing field before others have an opportunity to judge them.

Resilience isn't only about overcoming external challenges. Sometimes it is about overcoming voices from within that tell us we are unacceptable unless we consistently perform at the standards that please everybody.

Defining Success

I frequently ask parents and teens, "What is success?" Teens respond, "Having money"; "Getting into the right college"; "Driving a nice car." (In fairness, there are always some teens who talk about their desire to make the world a better place.) Parents speak of the importance of happiness, service, and relationships.

Where did this disconnect happen? Are we raising a selfish generation, or are teens absorbing messages we don't think we are sending?

Let's attempt to define *authentic success.* No one has a corner on its meaning. Every family needs to define it for themselves. I speak as a parent when I say that I will consider my daughters successful adults if they remain happy, generous, and compassionate. Ideally, they will improve our world and maintain their creative potential. I speak as a concerned citizen when I say that creativity and innovation are needed to lead us into the future.

We can be successful and contribute to the world in many different ways. Our challenge is to recognize the gift in every child and create circumstances in which all children have support and resources to reach their potential. While we recognize that many avenues lead to success, this chapter focuses on teens who are likely college-bound and the consequences of the pressure that many feel.

A Choice Between Happiness and Success?

Teens aren't completely off base when they say success is about money, education, and a good job—they're just being honest. But many parents might worry, "If we define success more broadly to include happiness and compassion, might we destroy the motivation and drive that lead to a competitive educational spot and ultimately a good job? If we protect children from pressure, will they languish in mediocrity?"

Today's teenagers have more impressive college applications than a decade ago. On paper they look almost too good to be true—socially committed, brilliant, athletic, musical, artistic, and widely experienced in summer jobs, internships, and community service projects.

But as we prepare these paper-perfect students for higher education, we may be undermining their ability to succeed in life. As we mold them to be "well-balanced," we actually may be making them feel unsure of their own footing. They may be so committed to being perfect that they fear being anything less. In fact, the most worrisome thing about this generation of driven students may be the fear of imperfection that's being instilled in their psyches. This fear can stifle their creativity, impede their innovative potential, and diminish their ability to experience joy.

We must never forget that our ultimate goal is to raise healthy, successful 35-year-olds, not high school seniors whose success is narrowly defined by the college that admits them.

So the choice is not between happiness and success. Happiness leads to success. Pressure sometimes fuels fear of failure, *impostor syndrome* (more about that later), and fear of the B+. All of these can crush healthy risk-taking that leads to new ideas. Young people who believe a B+ is the end of the world will never think outside of the box. Instead, they will make safe, guaranteed choices. They may have the grades, but they are not destined for authentic success.

Isn't It Good to Be a Perfectionist?

We want children to be healthy high achievers who reach their potential, but that's not accomplished by being a perfectionist. Perfectionists are not resilient; they live life always feeling unsettled. Why? The answer lies in the process, not the product.

The product—an A, a piece of art, a perfect score in gymnastics—does not distinguish the healthy high achiever from the perfectionist. It's the process. For example, a maestro who composes the finest symphony may be driven by a healthy desire to achieve or by an inability to accept anything less than a masterpiece. The difference is in how much he enjoys the process, how much he celebrates rather than disparages his creation, and how quickly he may burn out. The end product might be the same, but the process is tortured or exhilarating.

The world is run by high achievers. Many of them describe themselves as perfectionists because they aren't satisfied until they've done their best. But they prove resilient when they fall short of perfection. Healthy high achievers get genuine pleasure from putting every effort into producing the finest-quality product—an effective business plan, an award-winning presentation, a well-designed computer program. They enjoy the process and excitement that bubbles up from within as they work their hardest. They react to deadlines by generating just enough anxiety to stay energized.

Healthy high achievers see a mistake as an opportunity for growth and as an impetus to learn to do better the next time. They see failure as a temporary setback from which they will rebound. They appreciate constructive criticism because it informs them about how to improve.

High achievers have passion, creativity, and flexibility. They excel at something but maintain other interests as well. Every new venture is flavored by past experience because every disappointment was used as a learning experience. They remain open to looking outside the box for the solutions or strategies. They propel colleagues forward through enthusiasm, love of the process, and willingness to take healthy risks.

In contrast to healthy high achievers, perfectionists reject anything less than a flawless product or performance. They don't enjoy the process of creating because they worry endlessly about not performing as well as they think they should. Their fear of failure is greater than the joy of experiencing success.

When perfectionists do well, they may not even notice because they are so worried about mistakes they might make or how they could do better. The perfectionist gets a 96 on a quiz but is frustrated that she didn't score 100. Perfectionists see every mistake as evidence they're unworthy or not good enough. They don't trust others' praise because they see themselves as "impostors" whose faults are just waiting to be discovered. When criticized, they become defensive, embarrassed, or ashamed. They experience constructive criticism as reinforcement of their ineptitude. Perfectionism is a state of unease driven by an intense sense of feeling unacceptable. Perfectionists fear adversity. They lack the flexibility to rebound from difficulty because challenges paralyze them. The thought of not doing something well prevents them from taking chances that successful people take to reach their greatest potential.

Authentic success is rarely achieved because perfectionists become paralyzed before getting there, lest they disappoint the harshest critics (usually themselves). They may be graced with creativity but are hesitant to tap into it for fear that coloring outside the lines will disappoint others. Innovations are too risky.

Young People Who Don't "Live Up to Their Potential" Aren't Necessarily Lazy

Not all perfectionists are high producers. Their fear of failure may prevent them from initiating or completing tasks. They may avoid a task for fear they can't do it well enough. They may procrastinate because starting a project that they fear will have flaws is too overwhelming. They may pretend they just don't care, or they may feign laziness because it is too hard to confess the depths of their anxiety about failing.

If your child isn't doing as well in school as she used to or isn't "living up to her potential," consider that she may act like she doesn't care because in truth, she cares too much. I have known many young people who work very hard to create an image of nonchalance. Lazy is cool. Being riddled with anxiety is not. I've even met perfectionists who use drugs to medicate their stress and support the image of the burnout who couldn't possibly care.

Some of my most inspirational experiences in the practice of medicine have been watching the healing that occurs when a teen who has become a source of disappointment is able to turn to his parents and confess, "I never stopped caring. I care too much."

If you think this pattern may resonate with your child, think about the sources of the pressure she might be receiving. It may be from you, but it could just as likely come from school or peers. Your less-than-enthusiastic child may be reacting to an older sibling's achievement and fear being unable to live up to that reputation. No matter the source, your child needs to learn that she needn't fear being unacceptable—she is loved unconditionally by you.

What Goes Wrong? Whose Fault Is It?

Certain character traits may make people susceptible to messages that they aren't good enough unless they are flawless. But to become a driving force in a person's life, those inherent traits have to be reinforced from somewhere.

There are no villains here, certainly not among parents. All parents want the best for their children. So how do parents know if a child is self-driven or if it is a parent's fault? That was a trick question. Give yourself a break and delete the word *fault* from your vocabulary. If a child is experiencing too much pressure and some of it came from you, certainly you applied that pressure with the best of intentions. What may feel like helpful encouragement to one child may be experienced as overwhelming pressure to another. In fact, what feels like encouragement to one person may feel like pressure to the same person at a different time in a different mood. This is why we need to take the scrutiny off ourselves and look at our children. Are they thriving or struggling? Do they relish their achievements or fear their inadequacy? Whether or not parents are part of the problem, we certainly can be part of the solution.

If your child has studied her hardest and comes home with a C, you should be proud. Children need to be encouraged to put in a good effort, not to strive for unattainable goals. If you show dissatisfaction with a grade or project when your child has tried her best, you are setting her up to never to be satisfied with her *efforts.* If your child sees a B as adversity or failure, how will she ever learn how to face real challenges?

Do not lead the battle for higher grades. If your child comes home with a B and you think she deserves or, worse, *needs* an A and you go into battle with her teacher, you will be harming her in 3 ways. First, you have made clear that nothing short of perfection is acceptable. Second, you have communicated that the prize matters more than how the game is played. Third, you have impaired her ability to be successful later in life. When she is 32 years old, will you call her employer and demand that her job evaluation be upgraded? In the real world, grades don't get changed. People work harder to attain greater successes. And they find the resilience to do this by using their creativity, ingenuity, and tenacity—all driven by passion for what they do.

It might seem that we should simply urge children to "just try your best." But teens tell me that this statement drives them crazy. This generation is largely motivated by the D word—fear of *disappointing* parents. No one ever really does their best, so they always feel they are underperforming. Instead of the general statement, "Do your best," keep your feedback and encouragement more targeted and understand that someone can try really hard yet perform very differently in 2 different subjects. Talents and strengths are uneven (more on this later). For example, instead of saying, "Don't worry, I just expect you to do your best," a parent might say, "All I can expect is that you put in a good effort. It is not your grades I care about; it is that you are learning. I'm good at some things, and with a decent effort I will always score high—for you, that's math. In other subjects you might work hard and still not get the grade you wish. But all I want from you is to stretch yourself; it's not the grades that matter. I know writing is hard for you; just keep working on it."

Finally, allow yourself a moment of self-reflection. In this age of overstretched adults, many of us see our children as a product that, to some degree, reflects our success as human beings. This may be particularly true for parents who are highly prepared for the work world and have given up that world temporarily for child-rearing, or who are still working but apply the same standards of productivity and performance to home and family as was learned for the workforce. When we do this, our children's successes or setbacks become markers of our own. When they learn somehow that they are our products, it sets them up to want to be perfect to please us. This is not good for children or our relationships with them.

Overstretched Children

Some young people may have jam-packed lives and flourish. They are driven to succeed and relish their accomplishments. They remain joyous and self-confident. Others exhibit signs of weariness or stress, but their parents may see it as the price to be paid for success. As long as grades remain high and they continue to be involved in many extracurricular activities, their parents believe they must be doing well, regardless of outward or inward signs of stress. They believe that happiness sometimes needs to be sacrificed in the name of accomplishment. (From time to time, it may be useful to reread Chapter 6 to remind ourselves of the value of play.)

More parents need to understand that while some children say they are fine, their stress often manifests with physical concerns such as headaches, fatigue, insomnia, dizziness, and belly pain. To evaluate whether children are moving toward authentic success, we need to look less at their accomplishments and more at the kids themselves.

A College Admissions Process Gone Awry

The college admissions process has generated the myth that only perfect, well-balanced, brilliant candidates are worthy of admission, as proven by thick applications with high SAT scores, grade point averages, class rankings, and a lengthy list of extracurricular activities—even better if candidates have built a water purification system in a South American village or organized a fund-raising event for earthquake victims.

People who mistakenly believe that success is tightly linked to only select colleges will do anything—or pressure their children to do anything—to grasp that precious acceptance letter. But the truth is that success is linked to the individual. Higher-profile colleges may help a graduate get his first job, but most people stay at that job only a couple of years. Their performance in that job leads to the next one. In other words, if pressure produces individuals with perfect résumés but crushes their creativity and interferes with healthy development of their interpersonal skills and capacity to rebound from setbacks, their long-term chances for success are seriously harmed.

Let's look at some myths that drive the frenzy of the college admissions process.

Myth no. 1: The SATs or ACTs will determine your life. If you score well on this single test, life will be handed to you on a silver platter. It is worth forgoing pleasure in the present to prepare for this test that hands you the future.

The truth is that no single test determines anyone's life. All of life requires hard work and tenacity. That's why each day should be a balance of work and pleasure. Never avoid living in the present to prepare for the future.

Myth no. 2: Successful adults are good at everything. That is why you must prove you are brilliant in all subjects, a gifted athlete, a talented artist, and a great humanitarian.

How many adults can honestly say, "I'm good at everything"? The truth is that successful people excel at something. What makes them interesting is that they also do other things that challenge or intrigue them. Colleges know this; that's why there are various majors. We must apply pressure back on colleges to stop making teens believe they need to wear a cape, mask, and tights to be worthy of their school. Unrealistic expectations foster the drive toward perfectionism that is bound to crash-land.

The college admissions process has had a trickle-down effect. Parents pressure schools to perform, and in turn schools pressure teens to get into top-rated colleges to demonstrate the school's excellent preparation. They do this even while knowing that each teen needs to find the right match for herself, not the highest-rated school.

Peer groups also generate anxiety in a climate when success is defined by college stickers on parents' car windows. Teens pressure each other about which colleges they're applying to and which accept them. Guide children to keep their grades, awards, and college acceptances close to the chest. Not only will it tone down the competition, it will teach them humility.

A Toxic Society

We live in a culture that reveres success and barely notices regular people doing their best. When we know the names of sports stars and great actors but forget to acknowledge the generous acts of our neighbors, are we teaching children that to be noticed you have to be a star? Who can remember a bronze medalist from the last Olympics? What does it mean when third best doesn't count? To be noticed, you need the biggest prize. And what happens when someone does become a star? How quickly do we jump on their first transgression, and for how long are we captured by the media frenzy? What does it do to children when they are raised in a culture where, to be noticed, you have to be the very best? And to be destroyed, you need only be caught making a mistake. In case the big stories are missed, commercial media subtly and not-so-subtly communicates endlessly, "To be successful, you need to look this way, talk this way, own this, dress this way."

The Fear of Creating Pain for Parents

Sometimes perfectionism has nothing to do with internal or external pressure. Instead, it stems from an intense need to spare a parent. For example, if your children sense that you have been through so much, perhaps because of an illness, divorce, or stress at work, they will do anything to spare you more pain. They will try to be perfect children. Of course, this is exacerbated if parents make statements like, "Do you think I need to worry about you with everything that's already on my mind?" But chances are you don't have to say a word. If your child knows you are suffering, she will do anything not to add to your burden. She'll strive to get straight As to make you proud and keep her anxieties a tightly held secret, always showing you her best face.

If this discussion hits home for you, help your child understand that there is nothing more important to you than being a good parent. Tell him that he does you no favors by protecting you. Here is an example of a helpful statement. "You know I'm going through a lot, but you're always the most important thing to me. Please don't spare me by holding back the details of your life. I'm your [mother/father]. Please give me the chance to do what I care about most—being your parent."

The Solution Starts With Parents

"I never asked you to be perfect." Most parents firmly believe that they never said anything to their child to imply that they expect perfection. Many are adamant that their words always reinforce the importance of happiness. Certainly most parents do send the right verbal message of unconditional acceptance. For many children, perfectionism derives from other forces in their lives.

But we need to consider the possibility that some children pick up parental signals different from those spoken aloud. Ask yourself the following questions, but be gentle on yourself if some of the answers make you realize that you might be part of the perfectionism problem:

- Are you a perfectionist yourself? Are you highly self-critical? Has your child seen you accept your own flaws?
- Do you judge people easily? Your other children? Neighbors? Teachers? Might you have communicated that you can be highly critical? Is it possible your child will do anything to avoid your judgment?
- If you and your spouse or ex-spouse fight frequently, might your children act "perfectly" to prevent you from fighting?
- Are you so busy that you forget to notice your children's achievements unless they get a trophy or an A?
- Are people in your home uncomfortable with expressing emotions? Or do they recover easily, even have healthier relationships after expressions of emotion? Is the only way to achieve harmony in your home to suppress problems and pretend that everything is just wonderful?

Expanding the Definition of Success

Make it clear to your children that your definition of success includes happiness. Show them that you appreciate it when they challenge expectations and are willing to color outside the lines. Let them know a creative spirit is one of the greatest predictors of success. Help them understand that the best ideas are usually rejected at first and that everyone fails sometime, but truly successful people can learn how to do better next time.

You define success, but please include some of the following worthy contenders:

- Happiness; finding meaning in what you do
- Resilience
- Generosity
- Compassion
- Desire to contribute
- The capacity to build and maintain meaningful relationships; the ability to collaborate

- Commitment to hard work, effort; tenacity
- The ability to take constructive criticism
- Creativity or innovation

Recognizing Real Heroes

Do you only notice champions, or do you acknowledge others who have played a good, fair game? Do you admire the runner-up who overcame huge challenges? Who are the heroes spoken about in your house? Sports stars? Oscar winners? Please notice the teachers, doctors, nurses, police, firefighters, military service people, and social workers in your community. Applaud the woman who has sacrificed so she could care for her mother with Alzheimer disease, or the man who spends his weekends mentoring disadvantaged boys.

Opportunities for Self-discovery

Many parents assume that more is better—more activities will "perfect" their children. Enrichment activities are good, but we need to consider the kinds of activities, how many are really good for our children, and who is choosing them. As discussed earlier, child-driven play is vital. Downtime is critical for young people to discover who they are. If they participate only in adult-directed activities, when will they learn what they might choose to do?

Young people's self-acceptance is fostered when they trust that they are competent. If they believe in their ability to manage their own problems, trust their own decision-making capabilities, and develop their own solutions, they needn't catastrophize their mistakes. We nurture their competence by getting out of the way and by encouraging them to take control of their own lives. We want them to discover that they each have a compass and can follow its direction.

Building Spikes

Nobody excels at everything. Successful people are great at something. They usually also can work with other people. What makes them interesting is that they dabble in things that they are not particularly good at but genuinely enjoy (their hobbies). Knowing this, our goal is to allow our children to reveal their "spikes"—areas of excellence from which they will make their unique contributions.

Too often, we tell kids to find their passion. For some kids this feels like an added pressure, especially if they think they need to find it in time to write a standout college essay. *Finding our passion is a process, not a moment.* Many people don't discover theirs until later in life. Instead, we should be telling kids to notice what they are both good at and enjoy. Perhaps most importantly, they need to discover what areas motivate them to keep learning. Which ones make them want to dive deeper and strive to answer the unasked questions?

If we are to support this process of revelation, we need to allow some downtime and some pruning. When kids have every moment planned, they'll lack the time for reflection and will never learn how they would choose to fill that time. Some parents who have been able to bless children with opportunities for participation in a myriad of activities are disappointed when a child wants to "quit" one. Teens especially may be told, "I didn't invest all of this time and money just to raise a quitter." If you find yourself in this situation, you may need to reframe how you experience your child's decision to cut back on activities. If your son wants to quit everything, consider that something serious might be going on, like depression, substance use, or a new crowd's influence. But if he wants to quit lacrosse so he can better focus on schoolwork, theater, or soccer, congratulate him. Don't think of it as quitting; think of it as "pruning"—removing extraneous branches so the strongest shoots can grow stronger. In fact, this mirrors the adolescent brain. The teen brain is losing extraneous connections between brain cells precisely to make communication between neurons faster and more efficient.

If we want our children to discover their spikes, we need to celebrate their unevenness. When we say, "Just try your best," they worry we mean, "Try your best, and I'm quite sure you'll get all As if you do." This leaves them feeling anxious, especially in those areas that don't come naturally. Instead, tell them that you want them to put in their greatest effort, and then pay attention to the inevitably varied results. Explain that everyone deserves the satisfaction that comes from a good sweat and that we never trust results—good or bad, successes or failures—if we haven't applied ourselves to our potential. When we trust that we have put in a reasonable effort, we'll celebrate our successes and won't judge ourselves for our unevenness.

Try explaining to your child

- If something comes really easily and you get top grades but it's not that interesting to you, you should accept the grade but learn that this is not the career for you. You might be tempted to do what comes easily, but you'll get bored if you're not interested.
- If you are good at something, you love doing it, and when you struggle with it you want to learn more, you've found your career. Careers are about loving what you do and working hard to become even better so you can make your greatest contribution.
- If you are not so good at something but find it fascinating and are always

trying to improve, you've found your hobby.

- If you are not good at something, don't find it interesting, and took the necessary steps to learn it (for example, got help from teachers and friends), then forget about it. Just learn it well enough to be able to be well-rounded and participate in conversations. (For example, you don't want to go out to dinner with your new girlfriend's father, who is an engineer, and ask him what kind of choo-choo train he drives.)

Dialing Down the Competition

The first step toward authentic success is redefining success. Once you have done that, you've clarified that your child is living for herself, not to become a product you can display. When parents reject anything less than the perfect product, they promote perfectionism. When they suggest that their children "just beef up" their activities a bit, they are making a statement that their children are not good enough as they are. If a parent treats a rejection as an unmitigated disaster, how will a child feel about being accepted "only" by her second-choice college? Won't she feel that she has failed? She will feel rejected and unaccepted twice, most importantly by the people whose acceptance really matters most—her parents.

Professional Help

A child's anxiety or drive for perfection may make him so uncomfortable that he needs professional help to unlearn his catastrophic thinking patterns and replace them with healthier ones. Professional therapists can be very helpful in this regard; an investment now in your child's emotional health will pay dividends of happiness, contentment, and success throughout his life (see chapters 9 and 39). Ask a school counselor or pediatrician for a possible referral.

Unconditional Acceptance

Perfectionism drives people toward exhaustion for fear that anything less than the best makes them unacceptable. We must look at our children and notice how they are experiencing the process rather than push for a result. If they are driven to achieve to please others, we need to consistently reinforce that they are acceptable to us just because they are ours.

Changing a perfectionist's style is not easy. A perfectionist has a lot invested in being flawless. Giving that up brings the risk of failure or a conflict that the perfectionist is trying so desperately to avoid. A parent's job is to let children know they are adored regardless of their accomplishments. If you directly criticize perfectionists for being hard on themselves, they may just use this as more fuel to reinforce their sense of inadequacy. It is better to notice that they seem uncomfortable or are struggling more than they should. "Darling, I see you're really worried about your grade in English in a way that seems really uncomfortable. It makes me sad to see you this upset. Can we talk?"

Remember, the most essential ingredient in raising resilient children is an adult who loves or accepts them unconditionally and holds them to high but reasonable expectations. High expectations are not about grades or performance. They're about integrity, generosity, empathy, and the traits our children need if they are to contribute to the world.

When you think you should comment about how your children could do better, base your statements on the fact that they *already have* done better. Use an example of past successes to remind them that they're already equipped with the talent, experience, and resources to address new challenges. Remind them of some obstacle they overcame or a problem they worked creatively to resolve for themselves.

Parents must be cheerleaders. We get excited when our children win, but we have to learn to encourage and praise more effectively. We usually tend to praise an outcome or accomplishment—"I am so proud of your blue ribbon!" The unintended message is, "I wouldn't be as proud if you had come home without a blue ribbon." Instead, we have to encourage the *process* and display our pride over how they are playing the game of life with integrity, effort, and, yes, joy.

Accepting Yourself

Self-acceptance is a basic ingredient we all need if we value ourselves. We accept that we are still basically good even when we don't hit the ball out of the park. We remain worthy of others' love even when we are in a foul mood. We feel good about our efforts even when the guy across the hall received more recognition. We are OK because we see ourselves as more than a package of achievements. We don't have to be the best all the time, and we're comfortable that no one can be a star on every stage.

As you struggle at work, let your children know how you are trying a new strategy. And when you don't succeed the first, second, or seventh time, model how you learned from each new effort. You are not destroyed or worthless. You do not become paralyzed. You become energized! You take disappointment with grace and good humor. Your B- at work is not a catastrophe.

One of the greatest gifts you can give your children is to accept yourself. Perhaps the largest contribution to their achieving authentic success is seeing it in you.

***Building Resilience* Videos** **(www.healthychildren.org/BuildingResilience)**

Video 7.1 Using Praise Appropriately: The Key to Raising Children With a Growth Mind-set

To learn about the full offering of* Building Resilience *videos, please turn to page 327.

Thinking Clearly

The way children think about challenges can undermine the confidence they need to tackle adversities. On the other hand, young people who use their thought processes to address issues realistically and resolve them wisely can enhance their growing sense of competence.

Understanding how thinking patterns affect kids' capability of dealing with difficulties is essential to your ability to support their natural resilience. Some of the best studies that demonstrate the importance of thinking patterns began with the Penn Resiliency Project, headed by Martin E.P. Seligman, PhD, of the University of Pennsylvania. After many years of studying abnormal psychology, Dr Seligman came to understand the importance of looking at what makes people resilient in the face of difficulties. He mentored several leading experts in resilience, including Karen Reivich, PhD. Dr Seligman, Dr Reivich, and their colleagues worked with hundreds of schoolchildren and their families and demonstrated that children and adults can become more resilient, more optimistic, and better able to cope with life by changing the way they think about problems. People don't have to remain stuck with their first impulsive, negative thoughts when they become frustrated, disappointed, anxious, or sad. They can use their cognitive abilities to rethink the situation, reframe it, "decatastrophize" it, and find workable solutions. Rather than feeling defeated or depressed, they can find a path that leads to optimism and greater resilience. They can reduce their stress levels and become more effective problem-solvers. Ultimately, they become more confident about facing the next obstacle.

All children can benefit from becoming resilient thinkers, but if you believe that your child's way of thinking is rather negative or creates unnecessary anxiety or sadness, I suggest you read *The Optimistic Child* (Seligman, Reivich, Jaycox, Gillham) or *The Resilience Factor* (Reivich, Shatté). These works can be helpful in preventing young people from becoming self-defeating thinkers. *The Resilience Factor* is not just directed toward children; it is also designed to help adults become more resilient. Because children learn most from observing parents' behavior than words, adults who want to model resilience will find this book a wonderful start.

Some key points of Reivich or Seligman's work include

- Children come up with their own explanations of why they succeed or fail. This is called their *explanatory style.* The essential question that they need to answer in response to failure is, "Why?" In arriving at an explanation for why, children are likely to weave a story. How that story unfolds makes a big difference in the way they respond to failure. Will their story generalize the disappointment and paralyze them from taking further action, or will it be used as a springboard from which they will try again?
- The first part of the answer to why lies in who is to blame. Is it the child's fault or someone else's? If children always blame themselves for problems, they will tend to see themselves in a negative light.
- The second part of the answer lies in "How long will it last?" The answer may make a big difference in their chosen responses. If they truly believe the causes of their problems are going to last forever and are outside their control, they are more likely to give up.
- Children use the third part of their story to explain how much their failure has affected them—is it a small bump or a catastrophe? Children who catastrophize are much more likely to become anxious and feel incapable of coping with the situation.
- It is important for parents, teachers, and coaches to help children correctly assess their successes and failures. A first step is having an accurate, rather than a catastrophic, story line. Resilient people can realistically distinguish when they have control over a situation and when they do not. They gather their resources for situations in which they do have control and conserve their resources when they do not. They can assess when something will pass easily and quickly; they're able to talk themselves down when they start to magnify events in their story lines to catastrophic proportions.

As we interact with the world, automatic thoughts fly through our minds and influence how we respond. Four steps to taking control of these thoughts include

1. Learn to recognize your negative thoughts when you feel your worst. Dr Seligman, Dr Reivich, and their colleagues call this *thought catching.*
2. Evaluate these thoughts for accuracy.
3. Develop more accurate explanations or story lines when bad things happen.
4. Decatastrophize to let go of particularly harmful thoughts that can make you worry that a small mistake or failure is leading to inevitable disaster.

Drs Seligman and Reivich use a cognitive technique originated by Albert Ellis, PhD, a renowned expert on cognitive behavioral theory, called the

ABC technique. The A refers to the *adversity* itself. The C refers to the *consequences* that flow from the adversity. B is the connector, and it is critical because it stands for the *beliefs* and interpretation about the adversity. These beliefs determine how a person reacts to adversity and therefore produces the consequences.

Much of cognitive behavioral therapy works by identifying beliefs that are not accurate. Dr Reivich points out that in conversation, especially those that adults have with children, we tend to focus on the A ("What happened?") and C ("How do you feel now?" or "What are you going to do?"), while ignoring the B connectors. We need to help children hear that silent voice in their heads (sometimes called *self-talk)* that explains their beliefs, forms their interpretations of events, and guides what will happen next. We can begin helping children get in touch with their beliefs by first verbalizing our own beliefs. Talking out loud can help them see the connections.

A good time to help children listen to their self-talk is when you notice a sudden shift in their mood. This may be a clue that they have experienced something stressful and that their beliefs about it are in process. At this time, you could simply ask, "What are you thinking about?"

Whether we're trying to help children hear their self-talk or listening to our own, here are some primary points to consider.

- Identify the adversities that consistently push your buttons; notice which negative emotions and behaviors they trigger.
- Watch your patterns of reacting. Do you usually blame things on yourself or others? Do you tend to see problems or their causes as permanent or temporary? When you observe your reaction patterns, you'll probably notice a theme. Perhaps you fall into certain traps or ways of instinctively reacting in negative ways ("Why do I always do that? I'm so dumb." "It always happens to me.").
- Once you recognize your habitual reactions, you can pull them apart and think of alternatives. If you always magnify the possible outcomes of a situation and expect a disaster, you can train yourself to look for other ways to balance that negative tendency. Rather than blame yourself as usual, you might ask yourself, "What did I do well in that situation? What good things came out of it? How much of the difficulty was caused by me or someone or something else?" You may not have all the answers or solutions, but you can begin to break your pattern and stop reacting reflexively.

Dr Seligman suggests that we ask children leading questions to help them understand the complexity of problems rather than jump to a quick, emotional response. Children think in concrete terms, as I will discuss in greater detail in Chapter 10. They tend to see problems as entirely their fault or never their fault. By posing leading questions, we can guide them step-by-step through a series of possibilities so that they arrive at the realization that yes, perhaps they contributed to the problem, but it may not be completely their fault. Or there may be an entirely different way to interpret the situation.

Take the following problem as an example: Derrick frequently comes home with bruises, scrapes, and torn clothes, and he complains about the school-yard bully. "Frank is always picking on me. He always starts these fights. It's his fault I get sent to the principal's office."

By asking leading questions, his father helps Derrick see a pattern: Derrick rises to the bully's bait by arguing with him, but Frank is at fault for hassling Derrick first. Once Derrick recognizes the pattern, he is able to think of ways to respond differently, like walking away from Frank, defusing the situation with a joke, or hanging out with another group of kids.

Children also tend to make excuses when they feel defensive ("My teacher hates me." "You just don't understand."). This defensive thinking pattern can be redirected if we help kids pull a problem apart and think it through one step at a time. Instead of lecturing children or denying their feelings or statements ("Your teacher doesn't hate you—don't be silly."), we can listen calmly and non-judgmentally before we speak.

To listen effectively, we need to be quiet and *not* formulate our responses while children are speaking. If we're focusing on what to advise them, we will miss their message. But if we listen silently with an open mind, children will know that we care about what they're saying. Only then can we move ahead to ask questions that give them an opportunity to think about the situation in a new way. ("Why do you think your teacher hates you?" "Maybe I don't understand. I'll try if you'll tell me more about it.")

Building resilience in children involves more than helping them change their thinking patterns. Specific social and problem-solving skills are also required (see chapters 11–13), as well as coping strategies (see chapters 27–30). But the first step is to help kids think differently and break the pattern of negative emotional reaction. If your gut says that your child suffers from negative thought patterns in a way that interferes with his happiness or success, start by reading one of the books referred to in this chapter and speaking with your pediatrician or school counselor about a referral to a cognitive behavioral therapist.

***Building Resilience* Videos** **(www.healthychildren.org/BuildingResilience)**

Video 9.1 The First Step of Managing Stress: 3 Critical Questions

To learn about the full offering of* Building Resilience *videos, please turn to page 327.

No More Lectures

It's so easy to slip into a lecture when we notice children's shortcomings. We want to offer sound advice based on our life experience and wisdom. We want to solve their dilemmas and prevent future problems. Our intentions are good, but lectures just don't work—they backfire.

When we launch into a lecture, children tune out before our second sentence is complete. We can list 20 reasons why they should get to bed by 10:00 pm ("You were up too late last night talking on the phone. You'll be too tired to pay attention in class. Why don't you listen to me? I know what's best for you."), but all they hear is, "Waaa...waaa...waaa."

We need to shorten our speeches, be direct, and get kids involved by asking them to make a choice. "Do you want to finish your homework before dinner so you can watch your favorite show, or do it after dinner and skip TV?" Short, sweet, and simple. The child hears your parameters and has a choice, which gives him some control of the situation. If he doesn't finish his homework before dinner, he can't watch television. He determines the outcome.

Lecturing doesn't work for other reasons. As soon as we sense a problem, the parent alarm goes off. We think we must provide an instant solution, so we jump in and start lecturing. But the child rarely has a chance to express his concern, so he feels cut off, unheard, disrespected, or even shamed. When adults lecture, children often feel stupid. No wonder they tune out. Who wants to listen to someone who disrespects you or treats you as though you're brainless? Kids not only tune out, but some become hostile or defensive.

Many parents believe reasoned explanations that link all potential consequences with each choice will teach a child to do the right thing. But too often, parents talk to children in ways they don't understand. This undermines competence. ("I don't get it. I must be stupid. I can't do it.") To appreciate why children don't get our reasonable cause-and-effect lectures, we need to understand how they think. Children think *concretely*. Concrete thinkers don't think about future consequences, only how a behavior affects them *right now.* Ask a

5-year-old whether he'd prefer using a dollar to buy a chocolate bar or invest the dollar for his college education. (It may be worth $3.37 in 15 years!) He'll take the chocolate bar.

Children also think egocentrically. "What will she do for *me?*" They see the world as it revolves around them. They observe and interpret human interactions in terms of what people will do for *me,* to meet *my* needs. They see people as good or bad, depending on whether those individuals give them what they want. This makes children vulnerable to exploitation because bad people can easily convince kids, with ice cream or a few choice words, that they are good people.

As children grow, they become more open to abstract concepts. Abstractions are possibilities, ideas they do not have to see. Abstract thinkers can imagine the future and recognize that choices they make will lead to different outcomes. Most late adolescents are abstract thinkers, but it is important to know that some people will never get there. It is also critical to understand that *all* people think concretely during times of extreme stress.

How does this transition from concrete to abstract thinker occur in children? During adolescence, the brain transforms as new brain pathways are activated that allow young adults to process information in new ways. Do you recall from your own adolescence when you suddenly just couldn't stop thinking? Things began to make sense in ways they never had before, but you also realized that some things made no sense at all. "OK, if the universe goes on and on, it is infinite. But how can something be infinite? It must stop. But if it stops, then what's there?" Your head spun with confusion and excitement.

Something else happens to transition youth from concrete to abstract thinking— experiences teach consequences. With each consequence, the young person begins to get it. ("Oh, so that person is manipulating me." "Oh, because I did X, then Y happened the next day." "I never even imagined that could happen." Or "He said we were best friends, but he was just using me so I would get caught instead of him.") We learn through our mistakes, especially those that bring hurt or pain. Kids learn about their own ability to screw things up and the bitter consequences. Perhaps more importantly, they ultimately learn that people are far more complex than *good* or *bad.* They can be manipulative; smooth, flattering words can mask an ulterior motive. This new cynicism leads to a protective understanding of how consequences follow behaviors. As abstract-thinking adults, we desperately wish to protect our children from learning the hard way. We know mistakes lead to pain. We know how manipulative people can be, and we want our kids to learn as painlessly as possible.

Childhood is potentially dangerous because kids can't think about the far-reaching consequences of their actions and can easily be fooled by ill-intentioned people. So we watch children as closely as possible. We try to explain to them—often emphatically or dramatically—all the future consequences of their behaviors. And we easily slip into the lecture mode.

Let's break down a typical lecture. "What you are doing now, let's call it behavior A, will very likely lead to consequence B. What were you thinking? And then consequence B will go on to consequence C, which almost always ends up with D happening! Look at me when I'm talking to you! At this point, you'll almost lose control—here comes consequence E. Then, depending on several factors completely out of your control, consequence F, G, or H will happen. No matter what, we're talking disaster! You might even die!"

With the best of intentions, we lecture children to spare them the fate of learning through painful life lessons, but we need to pay attention to 2 points. First, sometimes kids have to learn from mistakes, and this kind of learning is very effective. We hope they learn from their minor, less dangerous mistakes while we steer them away from the major ones. Second, we have to lecture wisely. That means taking a completely different approach. No more A leads to B, which leads to C, and so on. The typical lecture has a somewhat algebraic pattern—variables affect outcomes in all sorts of mysterious ways. But there's a reason why algebra isn't taught to preadolescents—their brains aren't ready for abstract thinking. If we lecture them in an algebraic cadence, it only frustrates them because they're not yet capable of following it. When we lecture that way, kids hear our anger, condescension, and threats, but not the content of our message. Just like in the *Peanuts* comic strip, adults sound like, "Waaa waaa, waaa, waaa, waaa."

Before puberty, children think in a more concrete, mathematic cadence. They grasp simple math, like 2 plus 2 equals 4. If we switch to a simple mathematic cadence, they'll get the content of our reasoning. Even a 4-year-old can grasp simple math—one thing added to another can make something different happen.

Our challenge is to put kids in the driver's seat so they can figure things out themselves. If we learn to use a simple mathematic cadence, children can follow and understand what we are saying. Our words need to promote their growing competence by guiding them to discover for themselves how to be wiser and safer. We have to move away from the lecture that undermines developing competence, shames kids, and creates anger within families. Yes, anger. When children, especially adolescents, feel parents' passion, understand their fear, but cannot grasp the content of their words, they feel stupid and incapable, which makes them act out. Parents who passionately communicate from their hearts to protect their kids become frustrated and hurt when they are ignored, often causing them to react with fury.

Another significant reason to stop lecturing in the traditional way is that it may make children do exactly what we dread. This is particularly true of teenagers, who try desperately to prove to parents (and more to themselves) that they control their destinies. Younger children do it as well. When they think parents believe their decisions are wrong or dangerous or that they are naive or stupid, kids have a lot invested in proving parents wrong. If a lecture makes them feel incompetent, they want to prove they are competent. And the result may be the opposite of parents' intended message. Unless we guide them to come to different conclusions by giving them some choice and control, they will go to great lengths to follow through on their original plans just to show parents that their dire predictions were off base.

A Better Way

What's a more effective way to get our points across without lecturing in the tired, old way? How can we break the cycle? Let's first look at an ineffective lecture.

Carl got a D on a history test and is in danger of failing unless he buckles down to study. He finds it easier to say, "History is boring," and refuse to study than to face his fear of failing the class. His father launches into a typical lecture. "You won't study? What are you, crazy? You think I work hard so you can become some dropout? You'll only be able to get a lousy job, living paycheck to paycheck! Then what happens? Your job gets moved overseas. You'll be on the street. No son of mine will be a failure!" Does Carl get the message? Hardly. He's not studying because it's an easy way out in the present moment. He doesn't even follow what his father is thinking. How does not studying for tomorrow's test make him a bum later in life? Carl says to himself, "I know lots of dropouts who have jobs and own their own cars. My father is lame. I'll prove it and he'll tell me he's sorry in 10 years."

Then there's the lecture that ends with the favorite hysterical saying, "But I know this—you are going to *die!*" In the following typical lecture, a father catches his 11-year-old son smoking:

"What? You put that trash in your lungs with my money? If you start smoking, you'll get addicted. Then half your money will be spent on your habit. You'll stink. Your teeth will be yellow. And yes, then you'll get lung cancer or heart disease. If you smoke, you'll *die!*"

What does his son hear? "Waa, waa, waa, waa, *die!*" He understands that his dad considers him naive at best, foolish and incapable at worst, but he misses the point because Dad's reasoning was too abstract. The son feels stupid and frustrated. He knows his father usually trusts his judgment but has lost faith in him. He thinks his father is making a huge deal of nothing. His father just doesn't get it. He is more motivated to do what he initially wanted to prove Dad wrong. Besides, smoking is a sign of growing up, and his father is still treating him like he's a little kid. His father's intervention has backfired.

If parents shift from an algebraic to a simple mathematic cadence, their children can follow their reasoning. Instead of a string of abstract possibilities (A to B to C to D), parents' reasoning needs to be broken down into separate steps. "Did you see how A could go to B? Do you have any experience with something like that? Tell me about that experience. Do you see how B might lead to C? Have you ever seen that happen?"

We need to speak in ways young people understand—short, concrete phrases—then listen to their responses before moving to the next step. This approach makes kids feel competent because we're asking them to go through possible consequences step-by-step with their own ideas rather than those we dictate. They learn the lessons well because *they* have figured them out. They learn by breaking problems down in multiple steps, and they no longer have to learn only through experience. They have no need to rebel, only to listen to their inner wisdom.

To learn about the full offering of* Building Resilience *videos, please turn to page 327.

"I Get It!"

Once we stop lecturing and learn to talk to children in ways they can clearly grasp, we need to teach them specific skills to make wise, safe decisions. This chapter offers several approaches designed to put children in the driver's seat and headed in the direction of reaching their own well-thought-out conclusions.

The Cognitive "Aha!"

When a child sees a solution or finds an answer by thinking through a situation, it's like a cartoon lightbulb turning on above her head. I call this the *cognitive aha!* experience. Suddenly, a child realizes, "I get it."

The cognitive aha! is our goal in guiding children through the process of absorbing the information we want to teach. We want them to comprehend and internalize that information and make it their own. When we steer them through real and hypothetical experiences, we help them break down abstract concepts into concrete, understandable steps. We guide them down the path, but they themselves take each sequential step until they reach the end of the process and suddenly they get it—aha!

Using the previously explained simple mathematic cadence (in Chapter 10), we can present one step at a time in a logical sequence so that children can follow us. They figure things out on their own so they don't have the conflict that comes with our telling them what to think or do.

Choreographed Conversations

An effective way to teach problem-solving and build competence is to stage a *choreographed conversation.* This is a casual conversation between parent and child, but the parent has a hidden agenda—to steer the child through a problem so she can come up with her own sensible solution. Choreographed conversations are best held during a relaxed time, not in the heat of an argument or confrontation.

Here's an example: Dad has heard rumors that older kids are dealing prescription medications to younger kids. He's sure his fifth-grade daughter isn't involved but wants to prepare her for the possibility of being approached. As they're driving to a movie, Dad raises the subject in an offhand way.

"So, Michelle, I heard at work that somebody's teenager was stealing his little brother's ADHD medicine and selling it to kids in middle school."

"Oh, yeah?"

"Do you think it's true?"

"Maybe. I don't know, but I've heard some stories."

"I heard that the older kids start offering free pills to younger kids. Why do you suppose they do that if they aren't getting any money?"

"Maybe to be nice, or make friends?"

"I wonder. You know how the corner store sometimes gives out free samples of candy or chips?"

"Yeah, Dad, I get 'em sometimes."

"Why do you think the store owner gives them away for nothing?"

"'Cause he's nice. He likes his customers and wants to keep them happy."

"I think you're right. He does want to keep them happy, but when he stops putting out free samples, what then?"

"I guess the customers will buy the same candy or chips because they liked them."

"You got it! He's a pretty smart businessman, right?"

"Yeah. He'll start selling 'em and make more money."

"Do you think that's something like the older kids who hand out free samples of pills to younger kids?"

"Sure. They're not going to keep giving away freebies to be nice. They'll start charging money. I wouldn't fall for that."

This father has carefully guided his daughter through a series of ideas and questions that lead to her recognizing the reality of a problem—"aha!" If Dad had simply proclaimed, "I forbid you to take drugs from anyone, ever!" or lectured about their danger, Michelle may have heard the words but not absorbed the message. Michelle is too young and inexperienced to think logically and in an abstract manner about the ulterior motives of older kids. By choreographing their conversation, Dad asked leading questions that guided Michelle to reach her own sensible conclusion. Because she walked through the scenario, the lesson at the end was meaningful to her.

One or two choreographed conversations will not guarantee that Michelle will never try drugs in the years to come. But if her father continues to use choreographed conversations to raise issues of potential harm, he will reinforce lessons that Michelle can understand and internalize. At the same time, he will enhance Michelle's competence to anticipate and deal with challenges.

Role-playing

We can also role-play to get children to the aha! moment. This strategy allows children to explore hypothetical situations and grasp how certain decisions or actions will determine outcomes. Think of it as a rehearsal for real life.

I use the term *role-play* loosely. It doesn't mean that you have a script. It's simply a way to spin out a what-if situation and see where it leads. If it doesn't lead to a successful conclusion, that's OK. In fact, it may even be more effective than a happy ending because it can show your child the various possible results of unwise decisions and actions. When you role-play, keep the following suggestions in mind:

Try to set up a role-play casually. Don't make it obvious or announce, "Let's role-play. I'll be your friend. What are you going to say if he asks you to help him cheat on a test?" If you do that, children will groan and roll their eyes. Instead, be subtle and relaxed. Work "what if..." and "what'll happen when..." scenarios into conversations. When you start a role-play, use neutral situations that don't involve your child or her friends directly because that approach makes children feel defensive. They will think you are being nosy or trying to find out about their friends. This will take their attention off your central message. Instead, spin the role-play around television characters or fabricated strangers, such as the nieces and nephews of a coworker. Keep the tone light and avoid confrontational dialogue. Regardless of where the role-playing leads, stay calm so your child can think instead of react. Don't jump in with answers. Let her fill in the blanks with her own suggestions or solutions. Use short phrases and let her do most of the talking. You can nudge the conversation along if it's stalling by inserting, "Uh, huh...I see...OK...I hear you...then what?" Don't try to sound like a cool kid yourself. If you sprinkle phrases like "My bad," or "Awesome, dude," into the conversation, your child will see that you're trying too hard. Truly cool parents don't talk in kid speak or have to wear nose rings; they respect children and don't try to act like kids themselves or be their best friend.

You can begin role-playing almost anywhere; a car ride, waiting in line, a movie, or watching a television show. "What would you do if you were in that situation?" As your child steps into the role, you can take another part, such as the best friend. As you would in a choreographed conversation, walk your child through various scenarios with a series of what-ifs.

If you use a television program as a chance to role-play, you could start with something like this: "If Brad does X, how do you think Jenna will react?" You are in effect playing the Brad role by tossing out possible actions and suggestions that he might make. "What other choices does Jenna have? What else could she say or do? How could she get out of that situation?" Have some fun with these role-playing activities. Don't make them drip with heavy meaning. Listen carefully to your child's responses and take it from there. Perhaps your child will suggest an action that you know will lead to embarrassment or failure. That's OK! You're just role-playing. When that disaster occurs in a role-play, no one gets hurt, but your child will recognize that specific actions and choices can lead to the misguided end. By acting it out, your child learns a lesson far more effectively and safely than if you had lectured to make the same point.

In another twist on the role-playing technique, you technically don't take on roles but consider real situations and foresee possible outcomes. Mom and daughter are shopping for back-to-school clothes. The dressing room is a wide-open space where curtains divide the changing cubicles. As her daughter is trying on another pair of jeans, Mom notices a group of girls whispering nearby. For a half-second, she wonders why they are wearing baggy jackets in May. Then she sees one girl layer a sweater over a sweater over a blouse and finally zip her jacket. Mom nudges her daughter and whispers, "Look over there."

The daughter responds, "What?"

"See what those girls are doing?"

"Oh my god..."

"What do you think will happen?"

"I bet they'll try to sneak past the cashier."

"Then what?"

"The guard at the door will probably catch them when the security tag sets off an alarm."

"What will the guard do?"

"I don't know. Call their parents?"

"Maybe he'll call somebody else."

"Oh, yeah, the police. Will they have to go to jail?"

In the car, the daughter revealed that some of her friends shoplifted makeup from the local drugstore, but she hadn't. Mom replied, "I bet those girls wanted you to steal some makeup too. It must have been hard to resist their pressure, but you made a good decision. You can be proud of yourself."

"Yeah, I know. But I really liked that mauve eye shadow!" her daughter laughed.

What happened here, and what didn't? The mother could have ignored the shoplifters or lectured her daughter. ("Don't ever try anything like that! I never want to have to bail you out for shoplifting!") Instead, she took advantage of a situation and used it to walk through the consequences of shoplifting. By discussing strangers instead of her daughter or her daughter's friends, this mother prevented her daughter from needing to become defensive.

By calmly steering the conversation along, she got her daughter not only to think about those situations but also to open up and talk about her friends. When Mom learned that her daughter's friends had shoplifted, she remained nonjudgmental and praised her daughter for making a good choice. She sent her the clear message, "I trust you. You make good decisions."

Learning to Recognize a Line

Ordinary events can be great teachable moments precisely because the focus *isn't* on your own child. For example, Dad walks into the living room and notices an about-to-get-steamy scene on the television screen. He sits down beside his daughter and watches silently for a while. At the commercial break, he asks, "Why do you think that girl fell for that guy's line?"

"What line?"

"When he said, 'If you really love me, you'll show me...'"

"Oh, I don't know. I guess he was trying to get her into bed."

"Yeah, and she fell for it. What could she have said instead?"

Television programs are great opportunities to springboard into conversations. The story lines are usually predictable, so it's easy for parents to plan their questions and comments. When talking about fictional characters, parents can use a confrontational or critical tone ("How could he be so stupid?") that would send kids into a defensive frenzy if it were directed at them or their friends.

Television offers ample opportunity to teach kids to distinguish a line. Adults are used to hearing lines. The telemarketer tells us we'll get all sorts of free gifts if we sign up right now by charging it on a credit card. We know there's a catch. But children, and even teens we think are sophisticated, often don't see a line for what it is—manipulative. This father used the television opportunity to open a discussion with his daughter about recognizing a line. When the program ended, he asked her several hypothetical questions that could occur in real life. "What would you think if your friend said X, Y, or Z?"

By using a television program that presented a dilemma, at a calm time when there was no pressing conflict with his daughter, this father wisely set up an opportunity for her to problem-solve in a safe, objective way. If he continues to teach and reinforce problem-solving skills, he will help her rehearse and prepare for challenges that undoubtedly will arise in the future.

Picking Times and Places

The car is a great place to launch a choreographed conversation or role-play. You have a captive audience in your 2-ton moving vehicle. You pass various scenes that can spark a discussion, which allows you to bring up tough topics without having to talk about your child or her friends. You'll drive by kids smoking, kids being disrespectful to adults and each other, inappropriately dressed kids, children out alone when they shouldn't be, children being bullied, and kids making out. Maybe most importantly, you will be able to talk about those significant topics while avoiding eye contact. This can be especially important for boys. It is usually difficult to sit down with your son, look straight into his eyes, and say, "Tell me how you FEEEEEL." It's easier to bring things up sideways and keep the conversation laid back. Let him stare out the window. All the while he will look like he doesn't care, but you will be talking about important matters. A cautionary word if your teen is driving and you're in the passenger seat: It is vital that he keep all his attention and focus on the road. Teens don't have enough experience to engage in thoughtful conversation while driving.

As you look for teachable moments with your child, here are 3 general guidelines.

- Keep your tone relaxed. Children are more likely to listen and even be curious about what you're about to say if you open with offhand questions like, "What would you do if…?" If your child doesn't respond with interest, drop it. Other opportunities will pop up.
- Avoid end-of-the-world scare tactics. Whether you're talking with your child about actual events or hypotheticals, don't overdramatize. She'll never take you seriously if you say, "Smoking will kill you by the time you're 30." First of all, kids don't think about being 30, 40, or 50 years old—it's far too distant and abstract. Secondly, they'll conclude you're trying to scare them because they know smokers who have lived into their 80s. Even if you use scare tactics they might believe, they will react emotionally or defensively rather than think about possible consequences. Scare tactics only increase children's stress; they don't help them problem-solve.
- Avoid hurtful criticism. When a child has done something foolish or harmful, parents tend to blurt out phrases like, "How could you be so stupid? Why didn't you think first?" Labels, sarcasm, and shame put children in the position of having to defend themselves or retreat into anger and resentment. Even worse, these negative criticisms make children feel inept.

These strategies may prevent many behavior problems. But trying times will inevitably arise, no matter how diligent you are. When your child has a behavior problem, you'll want to be prepared to deal with it. The starting point is an understanding that behavioral change occurs in sequential steps.

To learn about the full offering of* Building Resilience *videos, please turn to page 327.

Changing Behavior Step-by-step

If we want children to become more competent, we need to understand that behavioral change is a process that takes time and practice. We guide them through this process so they will become more responsible for their choices and therefore more competent to handle other challenges.

Whether we want to prevent a problem, redirect negative behavior, or promote an entirely new, positive behavior, we need to steer children through 5 related steps in the following order:

1. Become aware that a problem exists.
2. Recognize that the problem affects them so that they become motivated to change.
3. Acquire the skills to find a solution.
4. Weigh the costs and benefits of changing the behavior.
5. Make a decision to change and commit to it.

Behavioral change is a step-by-step process, so you need to give targeted guidance tailored to where your child is at the moment. If you offer guidance that's too many steps ahead of what he's ready for, he will become frustrated and you'll stifle his progress. If your guidance is a few steps behind where he is on the behavioral change spectrum, he won't benefit because he has passed beyond your suggestions. The goal is to recognize the stage where your child is right now. Then he will be comfortable, and you can guide him to the next step.

For children who don't even see the problem (not even at step 1), offering information makes a lot of sense. At some point, though, you'll find that your child does know there's a problem (step 1). He knows the problem affects him and wants to change the situation (step 2). He doesn't yet have the skills to change the situation, however, so he's stuck. This is where you can step in and teach him skills to find a solution (step 3). You may use choreographed conversations or role-playing. Once he has some skills to address the problem, he needs to weigh the benefits and disadvantages to changing the behavior (step 4). Then he has to decide which direction to take—to change the behavior or continue it. If your child has coping skills, such as those offered in Part 4, he'll be more likely to move forward. Many negative behavioral choices function to manage stress and will win the day when a young person considers life without them. If, however, he has learned positive coping strategies, he can replace the negative behaviors more comfortably and will therefore more easily choose to do the right thing. Your child's ability to maintain his behavioral choices will be reinforced or undermined by important influences in his life like parents, peers, teachers, and the media.

If the problem is drinking at parties, for example, 15-year-old Camela is at step 2. She knows there's a problem because she has gotten drunk, thrown up, embarrassed herself in front of friends, and her parents have caught her staggering in after her curfew. She may want to refuse to drink, but she doesn't have the skills to change her behavior. At step 3, her parents need to teach her those skills. Even after she acquires them, she may not be sure that changing her behavior is worth losing the acceptance of her partying peers. She will have to weigh the benefits against the cost of alienating friends (step 4). If she does decide to stop drinking at parties, she will have to commit to her decision and stick with it (step 5), which will require the ongoing support of her parents and nondrinking friends.

Because Camela is at step 3, her parents can use role-playing or choreographed conversations to help her figure out ways to refuse alcohol at these parties or find other alternatives, such as hanging out with a nondrinking group of friends. Here's another skill-building technique they might use.

Decision Trees

A *decision tree* can break down vague lessons ("Don't drink—you're too young, it's illegal at your age, and you can get in big trouble...maybe die.") into concrete segments seen on paper. Remember, Camela is 15 years old. She may not yet be thinking abstractly. While her parents talk with her about drinking, they sketch out various possibilities that Camela suggests in response to their leading questions. Some branches of the tree may lead to dead ends or unwanted results. Others may produce viable solutions.

Camela's parents begin in the present.

"OK, your friends tell you there's a party next Friday at the Williams' house." They draw a little square at the bottom of the paper. "What's going to happen?"

"Everybody will go," Camela immediately replies.

"Will Mr or Mrs Williams be home?"

"Probably not," Camela answers sheepishly.

Her parents sketch a line from the box and write in "parents not home." They ask her what would happen next. As she suggests various possibilities, such as, "James brings a keg," "More kids show up," and "We don't know some of them because they're from another school," her parents write down these events in a sequence. Her parents easily foresee alarming scenarios—a raucous party, neighbors calling police, arrests for underage drinking, date rape, alcohol poisoning, rushing to the hospital—but Camela doesn't acknowledge these possibilities until she sees them sketched out on paper. She begins to see how A (no parents home) can lead to B (lots of underage drinking) to C (arrest or worse).

Her parents don't just leave it there with a scary outcome. They then lead Camela along other tree branches and suggest other possibilities.

"What if someone called the Williamses to see if they'd be home? What if the Williamses are home, but older kids who drive have alcohol in their cars and kids sneak outside to drink? What if you're uncomfortable and want to get out of there? What if someone offers you a ride home and you know they've been drinking?"

As they sketch their way through these possibilities, Camela begins to see that there are alternatives to going along with the crowd, which was the only path she imagined before this decision tree exercise. Her parents ask, "What else could happen? What other choices do you have?" This leads to other tree branches. "Maybe I could skip the party and go to another friend's house overnight." (This friend isn't in the drinking crowd.) "Or maybe I could tell my friends that I have to babysit that night because I need the money for our class trip. Or maybe I could stop by the party for only a little while and then say I have to get home because you've lowered my curfew."

As Camela comes up with these alternatives, her parents sketch them on the decision tree and connect them to the ultimate goal: Camela doesn't get drunk, comes home safely, and doesn't lose face with her peers. She has a concrete lesson, in black and white, on paper. She can see how the dots connect. She now knows she has choices. She sees how each choice can lead to a certain outcome. She is now competent to make wiser choices than drinking with the crowd.

But will she? The next step (4) in the behavioral change model is to weigh her options. Is she willing to risk friends' disapproval or rejection if she chooses not to drink? Does the chance of getting home safely outweigh the chances of getting into a car wreck or swept up in a police raid? If she makes the less wise choice, her parents will have to continue to work with her on problem-solving skills. But if she makes the smarter, safer choice, her parents will still need to be involved in a supportive role because new challenges will inevitably arise to test her resolve.

As you use decision trees, if your child gets stuck or suggests an unwise or impractical action, you can redirect the discussion back on point with comments like, "Uh-huh. Let's see. I worry that might be a mistake to try that. Let's think about this and see what could happen if..." Guide your child along with specific questions but don't supply the answers. Remember, this is an exercise on paper. Your child can always retrace his steps or turn in another direction if he makes a poor choice. Decision trees are most effective if not used too often. Save them for major issues.

Decision trees can work with younger children too, as long as you keep the discussion at a level your child understands. In the next example, the behavior problem is fighting.

The teacher called 8-year-old Eric's parents to report that he is often getting into playground and school bus skirmishes. First his parents want to be sure Eric is aware of this problem, so they say in a nonjudgmental tone, "Your teacher called last night to say that you've been having some problems on the playground and bus." Notice that they don't grill him or make an assumption of guilt. Their even tone allows Eric to open up and say that, yes, he'd gotten into a couple of push-and-shove matches because he felt bullied by classmates.

His parents take it to step 2 to see whether he's motivated to change. "So, do you like fighting?"

"No, it stinks," he answers. "I don't like getting shoved around in front of my friends, but I don't know what to do about it. Two of the guys are bigger than me." Eric has recognized the problem, knows it certainly affects him, and wants to change the situation. He has the motivation to change, but he isn't at step 3 because he doesn't have the skills.

At this juncture, his parents step in to sketch out some decisions he might make. They walk Eric through a series of events one at a time. One branch of the decision tree leads Eric to more fights, a black eye, the principal's office, and eventually suspension from school. Another branch leads to avoiding the bullies by sticking close to a group of friends. Another branch points to sitting near the driver at the front of the bus instead of the rear where the bullies sit. Still another branch leads Eric to defusing these confrontations with self-deprecating humor whenever the bullies approach him. Yet another leads to taking karate lessons so he becomes more confident (but not aggressive) about facing them.

More Skills for Your Repertoire

When we think about the skills needed to promote safe behaviors or move toward a successful future, there's almost no end of desired skills. Let's focus on skills needed to navigate the suggestions, pressures, and influences of their peers. These potentially life-changing skills can be broken into 3 categories.

- Learning to say no
- Recognizing manipulation and responding to it
- Shifting the blame to save face

The Unique Power of "No"

It is unrealistic to expect young people to stand up to their friends and say, "No, I won't do that. It's just not right." It is equally difficult to expect them to say no effectively to a peer or refuse to go along with the crowd because the very word *no* has become so overused and weakened. Many parents say, "No, you can't have that toy," when a child begs at the checkout counter. The child whines and the parent replies, "No, I said NO! OK?" OK? Is it really necessary for a parent to ask a child's permission?

Many children grow up hearing wishy-washy noes. They learn early in life that if they stick to their guns, continue to beg and argue, and wear us down, they can turn our initial no into a "Well, maybe," and finally a "Yes." To compound the problem, many parents overuse no. If we use the word no less frequently, children learn that we mean it. Learning that "no means no" in their early years can make it easier for preteens and teens to understand that message clearly when they have to say no themselves. I urge parents to feel comfortable saying "Maybe," or "I'll have to think about it," instead of a spontaneous no, when they don't really mean no.

I have learned from many of my teenaged patients that equivocal noes lead to conflicting double messages, particularly in sexual circumstances. Although gender roles are certainly changing and girls are more forceful in pursuing boys than in past generations, the following example is still a common situation:

A boy comes on to a girl, flatters her, pressures her to have sex. She finds him attractive and says no with a smile or giggle. He doesn't hear no in a manner that prompts him to walk away; he hears, "Maybe. Keep flirting with me, keep asking." Such mixed signals could lead to date rape. Girls and boys need to say no like they mean it. Too often, I have heard girls explain that they don't like to say no because "it sounds mean."

We need to teach how to say no in a clear, firm tone and make it nonnegotiable. An ideal way to teach this lesson is through a role-play. For younger children, you could set up a role-play around almost any issue for which you want them to be able to refuse a behavior. Take stealing, for example.

Aneesh and his father notice a skateboard that someone has left near the sidewalk. Dad sets up the role-play by saying, "I bet somebody will be tempted to steal that. What if some kid asked you to take it?" (Here, Dad steps into the role.) "'Let's take it. Nobody will know.'"

"I'd tell him, 'Somebody might see us,' because I really don't want to steal it."

"'Nobody's around. C'mon, let's take it. Don't be a wuss, Aneesh.'"

"'Well, I don't know. No, I don't think we should.'"

"That doesn't sound like no to me. Can you say it like you mean it?"

"I guess I could say..." (Aneesh's voice gets stronger.) "'No, I don't want to take it because I already got a skateboard,' or 'No, I saw someone looking out a window and they'll tell on us.'"

"Right, that's good and clear. You said it strongly enough that you made me believe you."

Dealing With Manipulation

Adults have a distorted view of peer pressure. We tend to imagine that it comes from a sinister child or teen who threatens our sweet, innocent child. In fact, peer pressure is much more subtle. Words are not even exchanged most of the time. Peer pressure usually is internally driven. "If I wear a bike helmet when none of my friends do, I'll look like a mama's boy." "If I just take a drag of this cigarette, the sixth graders will think I'm cool enough to hang out with them." "I better not hang out any more with Susanna because then Emily will think I'm not good enough to be her best friend."

There's no magic way to prepare children to manage this internally driven peer pressure. The best we can do—and it does make a big difference—is to help them develop strong character and always be available to listen to them when they need a sounding board.

Although most peer pressure is internally driven, young people still do receive pressure-filled, manipulative messages from peers. Some of these messages come from "the group"; others come from individuals. Much of childhood, and particularly adolescence, is spent figuring out who we are, so kids tend to know which groups they fit into and which they don't. Quite a bit of child culture is defined by telling kids why they are out and what they must do to get in. "We all have our ears pierced. If your mom doesn't even let you do that, then you couldn't have any fun going to the mall with us. We don't go to little kid shops," or "I really like hanging out with you, but it's just that after soccer, the 5 of us go out to the field and slam back a few beers, that's all."

The best a parent can hope is that their child is so bathed with security and so solidly clear about his values that he won't stray too far. It's also helpful for a child to have more than one circle of friends (see Chapter 20). If he has only one circle and that group moves into behaviors beyond his comfort zone, he'll become isolated if he doesn't go along with them. But if he has other sets of friends, he can turn to them for other options.

Parents can prepare children to handle another kind of peer pressure, the type that comes in the form of manipulative messages from someone who tries to get a child to do something he wouldn't choose to do on his own. It's rarely delivered in a rude or confrontational tone; rather, it's couched in friendship, even love. It says essentially, "C'mon, haven't I done enough for you already?" and includes lines like, "I really love you and I want to be able to show you," or "I want to hang out with you, man. I just really, really want to get high too." With younger kids, it sounds like this: "C'mon, I'm your best friend, aren't I? I just really want you to..."

A commonly taught way to deal with these manipulative lines is to first recognize a line and then to respond by pushing the pressure back on the other person. For instance, "I really love you and I want to show you," would be countered by, "No, you don't. If you really loved me, you would wait!" Or, "C'mon, we're buds, let's get high. Everyone does," would merit a response like, "Well, I'm not everyone, and I don't need to be your friend."

I believe this push-back approach is seriously flawed because it ignores the fact that kids, especially preteens and teens, want desperately to be loved and accepted. So while they understand this push-back technique, they may not actually use it in the real world. I realize that many parents want their children to stand up to and abandon friends with riskier behaviors, but I'm afraid it just won't happen.

A more effective way to handle this kind of pressure fits into youth culture and allows kids to keep their friends while controlling their own actions. This technique has 3 stages.

- First, kids need to be able to recognize a line. You can help even younger children to recognize manipulation by pointing it out on television, in the neighborhood, or wherever you see it. "My goodness, he sounds like he wants to help me, but I know that he really wants me to..."
- Second, children need to be taught how to state their positions clearly, with no ambivalence, in a direct way that isn't argumentative, accusatory, or self-righteous. "I don't want to steal that." "I won't cut school with you." "I'm not ready for sex." "I'm not doing drugs." "I'm not cheating."

- Third, they quickly offer an alternative that allows them to maintain the relationship on their terms but doesn't end the friendship. "If you want to come over to my house instead, I've got a new game we can play." "But I love you too, and I still want to be with you and have fun in other ways." "I won't get high, but if you aren't too wasted, I'll shoot hoops with you later." "I won't cheat, but I'm not bad at math, so if you want, I'll help you study."

The best way to prepare kids to learn these strategies is by role-playing, as discussed earlier. But be subtle; if you practice role-playing about how to say no to sexual advances before your daughter's first date, she will be mortified. Remember to look for external situations to teach these skills.

To learn about the full offering of* Building Resilience *videos, please turn to page 327.

Shifting the Blame to Save Face

We can further strengthen children's competence in dealing with peer pressure and other negative influences if we teach them skills to reject certain behaviors or get out of jams without losing face. This is particularly important for teenagers. We often believe that they will do the right thing based on their own moral compass or our best parental advice. But if their decision doesn't play well in teen culture, they often choose not to follow a well-thought-out strategy. The following techniques are designed to offer a way out while still fitting in. But don't wait for adolescence. Even if your children aren't yet teenagers, you can prepare them at a younger age. They will be able to use some of these techniques before they hit double digits.

Code Words

You and your child choose a code word or phrase that will only be used in an emergency and not shared with friends. Make sure you agree on what an emergency is. Your child may assume it means, "I'm in a burning building. Come rescue me." You may assume it means anytime your child needs to be pulled out of a risky social situation. Discuss what you mean and reach a clear understanding. Then rehearse how to use the code word in future situations.

When I discuss the use of code words with my patients and their parents, I describe an emergency or dangerous occasion as any situation in which a child feels uncomfortable or at risk and can't get out of it safely on his own. For example, 12-year-old Andre is at a friend's home when other kids show up with bongs. Andre has never tried marijuana and he feels on the spot. If he turns it down, his friends will think he's a wuss. He's uncomfortable and doesn't know what to do.

If he and his parents have already agreed on a code word and rehearsed how to use it, Andre can get out of the situation. He tells his friends that he has to call home or "my Dad will be really angry." He phones (or texts) home in front of them so they can clearly hear (or see) his end of the conversation.

"Yeah, Dad. I'm over at Sandy's. We're doing homework. I'll be home as soon as I can. But I didn't have time to walk Shaggy. Can you walk him for me?"

Shaggy is their code word. When Dad hears it, he knows his son is in a tight spot, so Dad raises his voice loud enough for the friends to hear him yell through the phone, "You're already late! I told you to be home by 8:00! Get home this minute or else!"

If Andre thinks he can leave immediately and still save face with his friends, he will say, "OK, Dad. I'm leaving right now," slam down the phone, and complain to his friends, "I gotta go or my old man will kill me." If it's too far to walk or he can't get a ride home, he can ratchet up the phone conversation to let his father know he needs rescuing.

"What do you mean, I have to come home this minute? I'm staying. I don't have to listen to you!" That's the warning sign to his father that Andre needs to be picked up. So his father yells—again, loudly enough for the friends to hear—"What's Sandy's address? I'm coming to get you right now. You'd better be waiting at the door when I get there." Then he whispers, "If your friends need a ride, I'll take them too!"

Andre can then turn to his friends and complain about what a pain in the butt his father is. Andre has gotten himself out of a potentially risky situation without losing face or wimping out. In fact, his friends sympathize with him. When they get home, Andre's father doesn't blame him for getting into a tight spot or hanging out with bad friends. Instead, he praises Andre for using their code word effectively. Andre has mastered this skill and is prepared to use it again the next time he's in a difficult spot.

A code word can also be used to help children face uncomfortable social situations because they know that can always call on a parent to get them out of the predicament without embarrassment. A shy child, for example, may find that going to your office party with you would be overwhelming. To make her more comfortable, you could say, "You know, all you have to do is tell me that you have homework to do [or you forgot to feed the fish—the phrase doesn't matter] and I'll make sure we leave." That will make her feel brave enough to know she can handle the party.

Using a code word is an ideal addition to the Contract for Life promoted by Students Against Destructive Decisions (SADD). In that contract, the teen promises to call for a safe ride if there are any substances that might decrease the driver's focus. Ideally teens will call readily because they value safety so highly and trust their parents. But that is a gamble not worth taking. If a code word is added to the contract, it makes it easier to call home.

Another common situation that creates anxiety in children is the roller-coaster friendship ride—the shifting status of *best friends,* especially among girls. It's difficult to repair friendships after an argument. Parents can help by first listening to their child's hurt or angry feelings and then using a choreographed conversation to help her think about how to face the friend the next time they meet, such as at a sleepover next weekend. The final step, which lets her know in advance that she can handle anything no matter what comes, is having a code word to use if she becomes uncomfortable and wants to come home early.

Just Blame Me

A similar technique teaches children to blame parents to get themselves out of a tight spot. Tell your children that it's perfectly fine with you if they want to paint you as the meanest parent in the world. You're happy to be the bad guy if it will help them stay away from risky behaviors or situations.

Many young people want to avoid or stop negative behaviors of their peer group but are afraid that rejecting these behaviors will cost them friendships and acceptance. So shifting the blame to their nagging, ridiculous parents is an acceptable way to avoid those behaviors. Other examples of how kids can paint parents as the enemy to get them out of a jam or protect them from risky behaviors include, "My parents are so mean, they'll ground me for a month if I don't get home on time," or "I can't smoke weed with you because my mother sniffs me when I get home. She actually smells my clothes and stares into my eyes."

Create a Rumor

A similar strategy is to suggest that your child create a rumor or spin a tale of what will happen if she does something you won't approve of, such as, "My parents said they'll take my phone if I do that again," "They'll send me to another school if I get caught cutting classes again," "They won't let me get my license if I don't study," or "If I get one speeding ticket, they said they'll take my license away."

Your child can also blame someone else, such as a principal or guidance counselor who "will expel me if I cut class again" or a doctor who tells her not to smoke. ("I have asthma and my doctor says I could end up in the hospital if I smoke.").

You may never have threatened to take away the phone, send her to another school, or deny her license, but these white lies are an effective out for children or teens who are in situations in which they want to avoid trouble or change a behavior but still retain standing with their peers.

I know this may make some parents uncomfortable because on some level I am advocating lying. Ideally, all children would have the ability to handle everything—they would never be frightened of a new situation or in danger of succumbing to bad influences. They would say, "I disagree. I won't participate." But I know that they cannot, even if they have a full rational understanding of the consequences. Peer culture can be so tough to navigate that if they don't have a face-saving maneuver that allows them to make a sound decision and do the right thing, they often will take risks rather than confront or lose their friends. So while lying is not consistent with the values we want to teach children, living up to their own standards definitely is a major value we hope they hold. These techniques make this possible. Above all, it reinforces the parent as the person they can always rely on to get out of trouble.

To learn about the full offering of* Building Resilience *videos, please turn to page 327.

Media Literacy

To be competent in today's world, children have to deal with many powerful influences. They need to understand the motivations of people who try to affect their behavior or the way they think. We've addressed some ways to prepare children to evaluate peers' motivations, control their own choices, and form their own values in the face of peer pressure. But there is another strong and sometimes dangerous influence on our children—the media.

In the 21st century, the media have an ever-present effect on how children view the world and perhaps even themselves. We need to prepare our children to be media literate so they can properly understand, interpret, and reject media messages when necessary.

Kids spend more time in front of a screen than ever before—television and movies screens, computers, video games, and all sorts of handheld devices, including cell phones with pictures, e-mail, and easy Internet access.

The Henry J. Kaiser Family Foundation conducted 3 studies between 1999 and 2009 that revealed a dramatic increase in the amount of time children and teens spend with entertainment or electronic media. With technology allowing around-the-clock media access, young people aged 8 to 18 years spend an average of 7 hours and 38 minutes a day—more than 53 hours a week—using computers, televisions, cell phones, video games, and other electronic devices. And much of that time they are multitasking—texting and listening to music while watching television or surfing on the computer, for example—so they're actually cramming 10 hours and 45 minutes into those 7 hours and 38 minutes each day.[1]

Don't assume that all of this is bad. Some media exposure is preparing children to navigate an increasingly wired and computerized world. However, once children begin communicating primarily through texting and social networking, they do less face-to-face interacting; therefore, be sure your child knows

[1] Information from *Generation M²: Media in the Lives of 8- to 18-Year-Olds,* The Henry J. Kaiser Family Foundation, January 2010.

how to have a polite interaction and deal with people before entering the cyberspace world. Also, all of this multitasking may not be producing people who are actually better able to multitask. People who spend their lives doing 2 or 3 things at once tend to genuinely believe they're adept at this juggling and can stay focused on each task at hand, but research proves that this is not true. In fact, teens who consistently multitask are found to lose focus with straightforward tasks because they get bored.

Almost 70% of US children have televisions in their bedrooms, and solid research shows that televisions in bedrooms affect school performance. Many kids also have DVD and video game players in their bedrooms. Still more kids now walk around glued to computer screens on their smartphones. Newer technologies (which children "absolutely need") are rolling out faster than we ever imagined.

In addition to hours and hours of screen time, children are exposed to scores of advertisements each day, from the logos on T-shirts to ads on billboards and buses. They are also inundated by messages in the music they listen to and magazines and Web sites they read.

These powerful influences often don't project the values we want children to hold. I'm not just talking about violence or sexual activity. In an attempt to promote certain products or simply keep the child consumer tuned in, many media messages target a child's insecurity. These messages imply that the child isn't slim, good looking, cool, or rich enough because he doesn't eat certain snacks or have the "right" sneakers, clothes, phone, backpack, or even car.

Have you noticed how many commercials include children who, of course, cannot even use the advertised product? Advertisers aren't just interested in making children consumers themselves; they're attempting to turn them into little lobbyists who will influence parents' buying habits.

If children accept these media messages at face value, how will they ever become competent to stand up and say, "No, I don't need to buy that," "I don't want to do that," and much more importantly, "I am OK the way I am," and "I am happy with what I have"?

Isn't contentment a piece of happiness and resilience? Is it possible to feel content in a world that says you never have enough? No one can have everything, but what does it do psychologically to children and families who can't afford what most middle-class families can buy? And how does this never-enough advertising blitz affect middle-class children who are led to believe that they won't be good enough unless they are affluent?

We need to raise media-literate children if they are to rise above these dangerous messages and feel satisfied with their own capabilities and identities. I strongly urge families to put the television in one room of the house where they can watch together and ban televisions from children's bedrooms. Televisions have become so ubiquitous that they are even used as babysitters or entertainment on family car trips—kids watching televisions in the back seat while Dad or Mom are up front, talking on a cell phone or listening to the radio or a CD. This hardly promotes family connection.

I am not suggesting we ban television altogether; there are ways to control its influence and enlighten children. We can begin immediately by watching television with kids and discussing commercials. I started this with my own daughters when they were about 3 years old. At that age, children can't yet tell the difference between commercials and programs, but it is important that they begin to understand when the program stops "because right now someone is trying to sell you something."

As you watch television with your children, ask questions like, "Why do those people do that? Do you really think other kids will think you're a superstar if you wear those sneakers? What is behind those ads? What do the people who made the commercial want you to think or do?" By asking leading questions and listening to your child's responses, you can guide your child toward the conclusion, "They're out to sell me something. I have choices. I don't have to be manipulated."

When a toy is promoted through a television commercial or used as a tie-in between a fast-food purchase and a movie, ask, "Why do you think they're advertising [or selling] that toy right now? Is it to get you to go see the movie? If kids have already seen the movie, do you think they'll want to buy the toy?" Even 7-year-olds can understand marketing manipulation when you guide them along. That doesn't mean, of course, that they'll say, "Don't buy it for me. I won't cave in to such a manipulative, commercial scheme!" They'll probably still want the toy, but they'll start to become more media literate. If you continue to reinforce these messages by raising similar discussions over time, they will integrate the message, "I have choices here."

With children approaching adolescence, it's important to begin contrasting the truths of heavy alcohol and cigarette use with their media exposure. The next time you see a beer commercial or billboard featuring a handsome guy with perfect abdominal musculature (his own 6-pack!), lifting a beer with beautiful, unnaturally thin women at his side, ask your son if your heavily drinking neighbor resembles the guy in the ad. I'm guessing your neighbor probably doesn't have 6-pack abs or beautiful women hanging on him. He's more likely to have a normal-looking wife who begs him to drink less and pay more attention to her. Your son will get the picture.

As children mature and become better able to distinguish between programming and commercials, encourage them to be more discriminating about what they watch. By asking leading questions, you can steer them toward judging whether a program is engaging and thought-stimulating or mindless drivel. Ask them questions like, "What did you like about that program? Could you figure out what was going to happen? If you hadn't watched it, do you think you would have missed something important?" You can help your kids become competent television critics while keeping your own opinions to yourself.

Teaching opportunities don't always have to spring from a television commercial. They could arise from a video game. Video game makers want children to buy more video games, so they make the games fast-paced and often incorporate violence to capture children's anger, aggression, or desire for control.

Talk to your children about how they feel when they play these games. Help them recognize the underlying motives of the game makers. Explain that sitting in front of a game and pretending to kill people desensitizes some people to real tragedies. In my experience, kids always tell parents that this won't happen to them. You can reassure them that you don't believe they will become desensitized, but as a matter of household policy, you can limit the amount of time they are exposed to violent material. While you should limit screen time altogether so children will find more creative, physical, or intellectual pursuits, you can be more lenient with nonviolent video games. Your kids may not swear off playing video games forever, but hopefully they will find alternatives to offensive games.

Not all media are manipulative. Some are educational, informative, and purely entertaining. (I have discussed how media offers a prime opportunity to engage kids in role-playing or spark a choreographed conversation.) But even educational or nonentertainment media, notably the news, can have a profound if unintended effect on children.

As much as we worry about children becoming numb to violence through movies and video games, we also need to monitor their exposure to the news. Some families leave the television on continuously. Sadly, we can become numbed by the tragedies of the world—famines, wars, acts of terror, and disappearances of children. Limit the around-the-clock reporting of huge stories like terrorist attacks, hurricanes, plane crashes, kidnappings, and abductions. That repetitive exposure can sear images into the consciousness. Many younger children are terrified by nightly news stories but will usually not tell their parents because they see the parents watching the news so passively—it all seems so normal.

Don't assume that older children and teenagers can handle the news without being deeply affected. They have a greater understanding of what is happening and may have lingering, unstated worries. It is important for older kids to know what is happening in the world. As with all media, the amount of exposure should be monitored and parents should help them process it.

Media Dos and Don'ts

The following Table includes some ideas that will build competence, others that will foster important family connections, and still others that are just good parenting:

Do	Don't
Read to and play with your child every day.	Let your infant or toddler be exposed to television and computer games.
Expose your children to a wide variety of ways to entertain themselves.	Let your children think there is nothing to do except watch television or play video games.
Watch television with your children and use it as a tool to explore values and human interactions.	Watch your show in another room because the kids are watching "some nonsense."
Have media-free family dinners together.	Read, talk on the phone, or watch television during meals.
Enjoy family time together (sometimes) with media, but limit your home to 1 or 2 televisions.	Have a television in every room.
Encourage good study and sleep habits.	Allow television in bedrooms. (It interferes with sleep.)
Help children with computer-based homework (and monitor the sites they visit).	Allow computers in kids' bedrooms. (It interferes with sleep and is harder to monitor for inappropriate use.)
Discuss the motivations of advertisers.	Leave the news programs on, assuming it's "just news."

Do	Don't
Help children to understand that no one can be as perfect as the people on commercials (even if they do use that breath-freshening, tooth-whitening, cavity-fighting toothpaste!).	Let children or teens keep cell phones in their rooms after bedtime. (They will receive texts all night. Instead, have a mandatory recharging dock in the living room.)

To learn about the full offering of* Building Resilience *videos, please turn to page 327.

Not Being Broken

In any discussion about competence, some parents worry, "My child has a learning difference (or a limiting chronic illness). What if she never becomes competent? Will she never be resilient?"

In the 21st century, we seek perfection and quick fixes that will make every child fit snugly into an idealized mold. When a child doesn't fit into that mold, we look for a label and solution. I am thrilled by the progress we have made in diagnosis and early intervention. I strongly support asking a child's pediatrician and teachers when parents are worried about a child's delayed developmental milestones or sense that she's not performing as well as she should or is having social and school adjustment difficulties. My biggest worry, however, as we identify more children with learning differences (differences, *not* disabilities), is that we will see them as somehow broken or in need of fixing.

We forget that there are different kinds of thinkers and learners. Some of us learn best visually, others through listening, and still others by tackling a problem with our hands. Most of us are flexible and can learn fairly well by using a combination of our senses. Some of us find it particularly challenging to integrate one of those senses well enough to learn when information is delivered primarily through that sense. For example, people who have difficulty with visual processing won't be able to learn best by looking at pictures. Some of us focus well, despite lots of distractions, and others lose focus on the task at hand and concentrate instead on the distractions. Different ways of thinking, different ways of being.

Each of these different styles may be balanced by enormous strengths. Children with learning differences in one area are sometimes gifted in another. We all know people who didn't do well in school but are masterful with their hands, and others who were brilliant in the classroom but can't use a screwdriver. We know individuals who are too fidgety to read a book but whose creativity and passion for the expressive arts are inspirational.

It is important to be able to function in school because school is where society teaches children. The problem is that schools are generally designed for people who fit into a particular mold—those who can sit still and focus for hours and learn by hearing and seeing—which brings me circuitously back to our caveman ancestor, Sam.

Hunters and Lookouts

When Sam needed food, did he go to the supermarket, stroll down air-conditioned aisles, and peer through plastic wrap for the best cuts of meat? No, he hunted while other tribe members foraged through shrubs and fields for berries, herbs, and roots. Sam and 20 caveman buddies prepared for the great hunt, sharpened their spears, and planned how they'd track game. Intent on finding a herd of deer, they entered the forest knowing they could not survive the coming winter unless they brought home some meat. Twenty-one men focused on the deer...what happened? Did they kill the deer? You bet they did. That was a lot of human concentration focused on one goal. The tribe ate through the winter. But what else could have happened?

The forest is also home to lions, tigers, bears, and snakes. If all 21 were focused only on the deer, some would have become prey themselves. Some of them needed to serve as lookouts. Generations later, the scenario still applies. We need lookouts, people who are easily distracted by the rustling brush, a distant sound, or an unusual smell. We can label people who have trouble focusing and are easily distracted, and we should help them to learn more effectively in school. But we dare not see them as broken because it may be precisely their differences that ensured our survival. The lookouts may have trouble focusing on the blackboard or textbook, but their distractibility and great attention to their environment can be important strengths.

There is a full life ahead for children who are now labeled as *distractible* or have other learning differences. If this speaks to your child, I suggest that you get extra tutoring (especially the kind focused on organizational skills), consider medicines, explore early interventions, and allow your child to burn off that "lookout energy" with exercise. Ask your pediatrician to join you in maximizing your child's chances of learning as much as she can in her own way. But trust in your child's wisdom that she will find a career path that uses her strengths.

Children with learning differences are not broken. If parents view them as in need of fixing, their learning differences will hold them back. If parents find appropriate interventions while celebrating and supporting their children's strengths, they will thrive. For parents who are worried about competence and resilience in children with learning differences, I suggest thinking again about what resilience is—bouncing back, overcoming difficulty. If you refuse to see your child as broken, if you recognize and build her strengths, you will help her overcome hurdles and she will indeed become a master of resilience.

Chronic Conditions

Chronic diseases do bring limitations that can affect some capabilities, but that doesn't prevent children from becoming resilient. Children with chronic diseases are often blessed with particularly strong characters and competencies that healthier children could only dream about. If they are treated as fragile, their conditions can affect their resilience because they will never know how to take a chance or believe in themselves. When parents can overcome the challenges and fears that come with raising a child who has a chronic condition and see the whole child, they can help their child become highly resilient.

I've had the privilege of taking care of hundreds of children with chronic diseases. I can assure you that they are often remarkably mature, insightful, and committed to contributing to the world. When parents recognize their kids' strengths (and contain their own anxieties about the disease), children learn to view the ailment as a challenge to overcome. They are deeply resilient. They have character traits that often surpass their chronologic age. Children with chronic conditions often have a well-honed sense of what really matters. They understand the importance of family and health. This strengthens their character. They've often developed tremendous competencies to compensate for their challenges. This builds confidence to meet or overcome other, unrelated struggles they may face. They are certainly not broken.

I would add that parents of children with learning differences or chronic conditions can use the same competence-building strategies discussed earlier. You may need to adapt role-playing or choreographed conversations, for example, to your individual child's age and ability level, but like all children, they too need parental guidance in these areas.

A Competence Recap

As you work on competence-building skills with your child—and it will be work, although it will have its humorous and joyful moments, I promise you—notice your progress and hers. You will become a better communicator; you will lecture less; you will notice and praise your child's assets; you will become more adept at guiding your child to become a problem-solver; and you will show her how to break apart complex, often confusing challenges and take them one step at a time.

Your child will become more competent because you are guiding her with a supportive hand and specific skills. As she practices these skills, she realizes that she has a variety of alternatives. Your child can make choices; she is capable; and she is competent. By helping her increase her competence, you are boosting your child's resilience. As she recognizes and uses her competence, she will be more confident, which leads straight to the next chapter.

To learn about the full offering of* Building Resilience *videos, please turn to page 327.

Building Confidence

Confidence is rooted in competence. Children can't gain genuine confidence without experiencing their own competence. They have to manage challenges to know they are able to succeed. Only then will they be truly confident.

Why is confidence so important? It feels good, of course, to know that you can do something well. But confidence is especially critical to children because it is necessary to navigating childhood and adolescence successfully and safely. That journey involves taking risks at every step of the way—risks in walking into a new school for the first time, trying to make friends, or not making the team. Without solid confidence, children won't take necessary risks. If they have an unrealistic, hollow sense of confidence, they may take chances recklessly. But authentic confidence, which they have earned by demonstrating competence, assures children that they have some power over their environments. They are more likely to persevere and have an optimistic outlook instead of feeling passive or powerless. Confidence earned during childhood and adolescence will be a springboard toward success in adult life.

Before discussing confidence in more detail, I'd like to clear up some misconceptions. When I use the word *confidence,* I do not mean the same thing as the overused, feel-good term *self-esteem.* For about 30 years, a self-esteem movement has urged parents and teachers to build a child's self-esteem as if this quality can be bestowed by piling brick on brick. That external approach presumes that adults can construct a child's self-esteem by telling him 3 times a day that he is terrific, beautiful, or brilliant. If every child in the class wears a sticker proclaiming, "I am special," all are supposed to soar up the self-esteem scale. If all 25 children are special, how can each one be special? Kids aren't dumb. They quickly figure out that empty words and labels are meaningless. Don't get me wrong—I want children to have a high degree of self-esteem. I just want it to be authentic. All children are indeed special, but I want them to learn that with genuine, targeted information that helps each child know why he is unique and valued.

I have another problem with the way self-esteem is often reinforced. When we are so concerned that children "feel good," we emphasize their moods over their experiences. Watch how this typically happens.

Marcus is learning to ride a 2-wheel bike. He's been practicing with training wheels until he feels ready to pedal without them. His mother unscrews the training wheels and Marcus bravely takes off. He immediately begins to wobble. Neighborhood kids start laughing and calling orders to "steer straight." Marcus naturally becomes flustered. He zigzags a few feet, veers over the curb, and falls off. His mother rushes over, checks for scrapes (there are none), and pours out a litany of, "You did great! Look how far you went the first time without training wheels! Don't look so sad!"

Marcus's mother is doing what many well-meaning parents do. She's so focused on his feelings that she isn't thinking about how to promote resilience—in this case, Marcus's ability to get back on the bike and practice until he masters the 2-wheeler. Instead, she wants to make him feel good. Most parents worry terribly when children fail at something or feel sad and discouraged, so we respond by saying and doing *anything* to brighten their moods. We deny it was a failure. We tell them that it was a wonderful success. We blame someone else or reassure the child, "It just wasn't your fault." We try to deflect their feelings by cheering them up: "Let's forget about it. Are you in the mood for a hot fudge sundae?"

Responses like these are dishonest and misguided because they send the message that feeling bad is wrong. This can be a setup for later problems because sad, uncomfortable, or anxious feelings take on disastrous meanings: "I'm supposed to feel special. What's wrong with me because I don't feel happy now?"

Rather than trying to cheer up a child every time he experiences failure or disappointment, we should focus on resilience. We all have failures. Resilient people learn how to do better the next time. They are persistent. They use those sad feelings to motivate themselves a little more.

Emotions like sadness are beneficial when based on an authentic event. They exist for a reason. If we paint over those emotions with a "feel better" approach, we do not support resilience. We want children to feel good as a result of what they have done, not believe naively that they will do good things because they feel good about themselves.

How could Marcus's mother have better responded to his bike spill? She might have strolled over less dramatically, asked him if he was hurt, and said, "Well, that was your first spinout on a 2-wheeler. Do you know how many minutes you stayed up before the fall? How do you feel? Yes, it's a bummer. Ready to try again? I like the way you keep trying even when things are hard."

These responses don't deny the failure or his feelings. She simply reflects on what happens, acknowledges that he's disappointed ("Yes, it's a bummer."), and shows him that she is proud of his efforts. She doesn't dwell on his feelings or smother him with cheerful words.

Real confidence, as opposed to self-esteem or "confidence-lite," fosters resilience because it results from demonstrated, proven competence. A child knows in his bones that he has mastered a task, so he believes in his ability and is truly confident. Adults can certainly nurture his confidence by teaching problem-solving skills and providing safe opportunities to practice those skills. We can recognize children's assets and help them use those strengths to overcome difficulty and bounce back. It is not enough simply to tell them they're terrific or dress them in "I am special" T-shirts.

As we teach children a repertoire of skills and they become more competent at making good decisions and solving problems, we cannot assume that they will automatically overflow with confidence. Even when they are in the process of becoming more competent, they may feel uncertain that they really are capable. Confidence needs support and reinforcement. We can do this in 3 basic ways: catch them being good, offer genuine praise, and set reasonable expectations.

Catch Them Being Good

We do this all the time with very young children. We make a big deal of every developmental milestone and minor accomplishment. "Ooh, you ate all your cereal! You're such a big girl to brush your teeth all by yourself!" Fast-forward to age 12 or 14: "Why can't you ever pick up your things? Why do I have to remind you every morning not to forget your homework? Are you *ever* going to finish your chores?"

What has happened in the intervening few years? We stopped being thrilled by their good behaviors and achievements. Why do we become so focused on what's wrong with them? We should still try to catch them being good by reinforcing their good behaviors, kind gestures, and unprompted acts of kindness by offering a few words of appreciation and praise. It's just as important to older children as it is to toddlers. Never forget, they still crave our attention and approval.

Offer Genuine Praise

Effective praise was discussed in Chapter 7, but I want to relate it here to confidence. The best way to praise children is not with vague words ("You're wonderful!") but with words that show children we really notice and appreciate what they have done. "It was so thoughtful of you to help Grandma carry her heavy grocery bags." "You really make me happy when you help get dinner without my having to ask you first." Remember also to focus your praise on effort, rather than performance or product. This has been proven by Carol Dweck, PhD, who used it to create the "growth mind-set" linked to success.

If we want to support and reinforce a child's sense of confidence, our praise must be genuine. Excessive praise won't ring true any more than false praise will, but try for a balance. Look for one or two things *every day* that your child has done that are worthy of a verbal pat on the back. Praise is a powerful way to encourage positive behaviors. If you want your child to continue a good behavior, pay attention to it.

Sometimes we get so caught up in our love for our kids that we heap enormous amounts of praise on them and tell them how perfect we think they are. On some level we may do this in hopes of creating a self-fulfilling prophecy. "If I keep telling him how spectacular he is, he will become that wonderful person." On another level, we do this to build a child's self-image and, we hope, self-confidence. "You are the kindest child in the world. You don't have a mean bone in your body. You're the perfect child I'd always dreamed of."

Well, no one is perfect, even your child. And if anyone knows your child isn't perfect, your child himself does. It is difficult living on a pedestal. A child (or an adult) can become too hard on himself. If a child is told he doesn't have a mean bone in his body, how will he feel when he's angry at someone and wants to strike back? It's a setup for denying emotions or anxiety when upsetting emotions surface. Taking it a step further, a young person can consciously or unconsciously decide to jump off that pedestal to show the world he isn't perfect. It can be much harder to bounce back after a failure because perfect people aren't supposed to fail. It's OK to tell your child something like, "You are the perfect child for me," as long as it's combined with clear messages that no one is truly perfect and that you love him unconditionally.

Set Reasonable Expectations

Children live up or down to our expectations. I repeat this frequently because it's so easy to forget. As children's competence and confidence grow, we need to continue to hold up high expectations to keep them moving in the right direction. I don't mean unrealistic expectations. The NBA or WNBA will not draft every young basketball player. Not every child can get into an elite college. We cannot expect children to be perfect, but we can expect them to be honest, caring, and responsible. We can hitch our expectations not to their achievements but to their human qualities.

You may be thinking, "OK, I get it. Hold them to high expectations for their human qualities, but what about the day-to-day accomplishments—don't I have to keep holding the bar just above their reach?" I have no simple answer because the answer has to be individualized for your child's temperament. Children gain confidence through their successes, and that gives them the push to test whether they can master more challenging tasks. If the next task is far more difficult than they can handle, they will undoubtedly fail and perhaps lose confidence. They may tie that failure to your high expectations. They are struggling to please you, so their failure is magnified. If this is the case, they may experience shame, which can prevent them from reaching for achievements they would be able to master.

Our challenge as parents is to monitor children's responses to achievement and failure and have a handle on their capabilities. Some questions to consider include

- Does a particular achievement seem like a stepping stone to the next one?
- Is your child energized by a failure to try again, or does he become frozen by that failure?
- After a success, does he like to stay on that level for a long time until he feels comfortable enough to move forward, or is he eager to proceed quickly to the next level?

When your child is ready to try the next challenge, see where he would like the bar to be set. Support him to determine what he can handle. If you set the bar too high, he will fail you (emphasis on *you*). This has to be about him, not you. If you set the bar too low, he will think you haven't been watching him closely enough to know his capabilities.

Most importantly, react supportively when your child does come up short. It's crucially important for children to know that we all fail, we can recover, and those people who are successful are the ones who try again. Thousands of opportunities will arise to support your child to try again—the first time he walks and falls, when he misspells words on a test, when his art project ends up in spills and splatters. Numerous opportunities also arise during your child's growing years for you to model how you try again without shame and with good humor when you haven't always succeeded. I believe we have just defined resilience again.

De-emphasize Incompetence

In this discussion of confidence, I want to mention *in*competence. One of the greatest ways to destroy confidence is by emphasizing incompetence and shaming children. First we return to the lecture. As soon as we fall back into an old pattern of lecturing, we undercut children's sense of competence and confidence. As discussed previously, lecturing robs them of opportunities to make decisions and learn from them. It is often triggered by something they have done wrong. Lectures do damage by making them feel small, inept, stupid, unheard, and shamed. Lecturing is not the only tool we use as we try to change children's undesirable behaviors. Sometimes they make us so angry or worried that we focus only on what they are doing wrong. We want to shout repeatedly, "Stop that, you fool!" in the vain hope that they will come to their senses. It doesn't work.

Some adults blindly assume that kids will change when they become aware of all their dangerous behaviors or human frailties. I work with a lot of young people who engage in worrisome behaviors like drugs or early, unprotected sex. I watch as adults, parents and professionals with the best intentions, point out everything these youth are doing wrong. As the adults get frustrated with the young people's inability to change, they begin pointing out every character fault. I call this *mudslinging.* It usually sounds something like, "Maybe you're not ready to quit drugs because you have no motivation. You're too lazy. How can I trust you, even if you say you're going to quit? You're really shaming your mother and me." Mudslinging creates a series of blots on young people's self-image and robs them of the confidence they could have used to rise above a challenge.

Youth will never have the confidence to change when they feel denigrated or are made to focus repeatedly on their faults. They know they can change or improve when they are reminded that they have, in fact, already done better. They have more than enough strengths and capabilities to overcome their mistaken choices.

The best way to promote positive behavior is by accentuating existing strengths. If we want young people to rise above negative behaviors, their chances of success will be much greater if they have developed confidence. It takes confidence for anyone to change direction or alter habits, stop a dangerous but comfortable behavior and move toward something safer but less familiar. Confidence comes from knowing that success is possible. This strength-based approach allows us to build on something. Simply being highly aware of our problems and faults can lead to paralysis, but a ripple of positive energy can flow from each strength, each island of competence. When we allow that to happen, problems begin to disappear amid a sea of success.

Know your children so well that you see all of their wondrous accomplishments and good traits, and allow yourself to be constantly reminded of why you are so crazy about them. This knowledge will serve you well when you need to redirect their behaviors back to something that will make you proud.

Playing to Strengths in the Midst of Problems

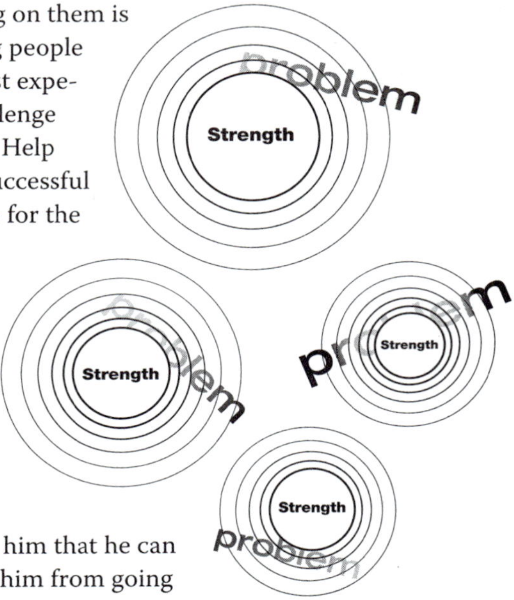

Recognizing strengths and building on them is particularly important when young people are having difficulties. Look for past experiences when they overcame a challenge or dealt with a problem effectively. Help them go back and draw on those successful experiences and use their expertise for the difficulties they now face.

A child who procrastinates about homework will not respond to "You are so lazy!" or "You can't go out with your friends until you finish your homework." He may be paralyzed by anxiety or feel that the task is insurmountable. Being called lazy only shames him and certainly doesn't convince him that he can handle the homework. Prohibiting him from going out won't help if his roadblock is anxiety. If his problem lies with his organizational skills, keeping a child inside may prod him to take the right direction. It's more likely to be effective if he is reminded how overwhelmed he was last week when he couldn't organize his social studies report. But once he got started, he felt much better because he divided the large assignment into small sections and tackled them one at a time.

When children are engaged in worrisome behavior, look for the good that also exists. Children who act out in class may be bored because they are so far ahead in a lesson. Adolescents doing drugs often have a deep sensitivity that they are trying to deal with, albeit in a troublesome way. A 4-year-old who hits her 2-year-old brother may be frustrated that he's not following the rules that she has learned so well. She needs to learn not to slug her brother, of course, but punishment alone will not teach her how to channel her energies. After she is told clearly that hitting is inappropriate, she could be reminded of how proud her parents are that she cares about the rules and how well she follows them, and she could be encouraged to teach her brother the good behaviors she knows. The goal is to create a ripple of confidence that flows from a child. When she knows she's competent, she can build on those positive attributes and move away from negative activities.

I used a strength-based approach with Rita, a 14-year-old patient, when she started smoking marijuana and her grades began to slip. Rita used to talk about wanting to go to nursing school to become a pediatric nurse. When her mother took a second job to save for her education, Rita had to watch her younger brother and sister in the afternoons and evenings. She had less time to study and became anxious. "To chill," she said, she began smoking weed "only after they went to bed. I never smoked in front of my brother and sister."

I could have reprimanded her or given her 40 reasons not to smoke marijuana. I could have begun mudslinging and challenged her character, lack of resolve, or failure to appreciate her mother's sacrifice. All of this would have increased her stress, leading directly to increased marijuana use. Instead, I listened silently to her story. I didn't interrupt or criticize. By listening to her intently, I discovered all the things she was doing right. When she finished talking, I simply said, "We need you to be a pediatric nurse. Look how good you are with little kids. You get your brother and sister's dinner. You make sure they're safe. You bathe them and put them to bed. You're really responsible. You've already proven how good you are at caring for people." After speaking to her strengths, I said, "I'm worried, though, about how much marijuana you are smoking and how that may interfere with your future plans. Can we talk about this?" We talked about healthier ways to chill (relaxation techniques are discussed in chapters 28, 29, and 30) so that she would be less anxious and better able to cope with her schoolwork.

I often use the following pattern or choreographed conversation:

Step 1: I notice what you are doing right. (I demonstrate that I have noticed by reflecting it back.)

Step 2: I am worried about you.

Step 3: Can we address this problem?

It is so much easier for young people to deal with why we are worried if we first note their successes. And when we get their permission to address the problem, we get buy-in and offer them the kind of control they need to be willing to consider taking steps to change.

Confidence is the key ingredient that allows a young person to take those chances needed to excel and be brave enough to take the first steps toward positive behavioral change. Confidence derives from trusting in one's capability, knowing that one has strengths. Many adults undermine young people's confidence by focusing on their risk-taking, faults, or mistaken behaviors. Although they may do this with the best intentions, they undercut the potential for progress and feed into the cycle of shame, hopelessness, and powerlessness that prevents children from recovering from mistakes. Just to drive this critical point home, look again at the 5 steps of behavioral change described in Chapter 12. Those steps are a simplification of many existing behavioral change theories, but I think they are missing a key point. People do not even allow themselves to get to the first step—to become aware—unless they have the confidence to believe they can change. Focusing on problems alone instills shame, undermines confidence, and therefore impedes progress.

Children will make mistakes. Our job is to set them straight, not make them feel good regardless of their behaviors. But if we focus only on what they do wrong, it's as if we're attaching weights to their legs that make it harder for them to bounce back. If we recognize their strengths and remind them of their abilities to succeed, we energize them to transform failure into a learning experience from which they can rebound.

Children get constant messages about their capabilities and deficits from teachers, coaches, and peers. We cannot protect them from all of the messages that lower their confidence, but we can ensure that their connection to us remains a protective force that emphasizes their competencies and builds their well-deserved confidence.

To learn about the full offering of* Building Resilience *videos, please turn to page 327.

PART 3

Connection, Character, and Contribution

Connection

Human connection provides reassurance that we'll be OK despite tough times, and it gives us deep-seated security that convinces us we can take chances. Connection to other people tells us, "We can get through this together." We support others during their troubles, which helps us realize we have a place to turn when we need their support. Human connection allows us the luxury of being weak at times and letting others care for us while we reenergize. During times of crisis, we turn to people with whom we share our deepest connections to regroup and remind ourselves that we're part of a family or community and that our purpose in life remains intact.

Connection isn't just about getting through hard times, however. It also lets us experience a higher level of security that gives us joy and a comfortable base that permits us to take chances that allow us to come closer to our potential. When we forge a secure connection with our children, they have absolutely no doubt that we're crazy in love with them. From this solid base, they will connect with others more comfortably. Those without this secure base may turn inward and focus more on their own needs or do whatever it takes to connect with others, even if it is not in their own best interest.

How well connected to other people are most children today? Yes, they live in families, some with 1 parent, others with 2. Children of blended families may have 3 or 4 adults in a parental role. They may have other familial connections with siblings, grandparents, uncles, aunts, or cousins. They have friends and classmates, teachers and coaches. For a great many children, though, connections to others are weak or limited. Weak because families are so busy and have so little time together; quality time is hurried and often scribbled on a calendar to squeeze in next weekend. Limited because families move frequently, which requires children to leave friends behind. Extended families are spread around the country. Many children see grandparents only a few times a year, if at all. Other adults pass in and out of their lives on an irregular basis.

Instead of having strong ties to a network of relatives, friends, and adults in the community, many children are increasingly isolated and disconnected. Even in their own homes, family members may pass each other like ships in the night. Each has a separate thing to do or place to be. As pointed out earlier, children average more than 7.5 hours a day watching television, using computers, downloading music, and instant messaging. For most of that time, each child is unconnected to other people. Electronics and media are not substitutes for human relationships. As soon as we no longer need each other's company to avert boredom, the connection to family begins to wear away.

In this increasingly tech-driven world in which social media dominates interactions, youth are in some ways more connected than ever before. These connections have no geographic boundaries. This can be wonderful for a youth who may have concerns not shared by many in his community and for others, such as children in military families, who move frequently. Will these connections offer better support or further dissolve the need for authentic human connection? Time will tell.

Independence or Interdependence?

Children who have strong resilience are self-sufficient and independent, but they also are *inter*dependent with other people. It's unrealistic and probably undesirable to expect children to be highly independent until they reach adulthood. We want them to exhibit gradually increasing independence, especially as they move through adolescence. But we don't want to send the message that independence means isolation or disconnection. As independent as we want them to become, we also want them to recognize that the healthiest adults remain interdependent on family, friends, and community. After the throes of adolescence, when independence is demanded but *inter*dependence is secretly craved, young adults become more comfortable restoring a warm, secure connection.

The Security Connection

Close bonds to people who provide stability and attention are essential to healthy child development and fostering resilience. One adult can make this critical difference in a child's life. Resilience research consistently demonstrates that guidance and support from a caring adult are pivotal in determining whether a young person can overcome challenges. Hopefully, children will have several supportive people in their lives—parents, relatives, peers, teachers, and clergy.

Connection gives children an essential sense of belonging, from infancy when parents are the center of their world to an ever-widening circle as they grow and step into a larger community. Most parents recognize the significance of infant-parent bonding, but we may forget that forging new ties to other people is important throughout childhood and adolescence. These connections are necessary to develop trust.

When children know that other people care for them and will support them through thick and thin, they gain a strong sense of security that is essential if they are to be resilient. Without that social foundation, kids are reluctant to test themselves and try new ventures. If they won't take such risks, they may remain isolated and timid. They won't move forward to develop new competencies and confidence.

Children need multiple circles of connection to feel secure and protected at home, at school, and in the community. We don't want them to form these connections naively because some people aren't trustworthy. However, we must be very cautious to not instill stranger anxiety in our children. When we teach children they mustn't talk to strangers because they can be dangerous, we limit their ability to reach out for that instant connection they may need one day. The truth is that it's likely they'll need to turn to a stranger for help if they are ever lost, being followed, being chased, or even hurt. We harm our children if we instill a fear that prevents them from seeking needed help. It is better to give them clear instructions on when and how to reach out to adults at the same time you teach them how to avoid danger. Most parents tell children to find a police officer if they're in trouble. That is good advice, but an officer is usually not in view. So teach children to turn to a woman with children if they don't see a police officer. Gavin De Becker offers other safety strategies in his book *Protecting the Gift: Keeping Children and Teenagers Safe (and Parents Sane).*

The Starting Point

Empathy is an important ingredient in making human connection. Empathy isn't sympathy or feeling sorry for someone else. Empathy is about trying to imagine what a situation feels like from another's perspective. It is about not judging before thinking about what it would be like to stand in someone else's shoes. It is not "understanding"; sometimes we'll never understand. But at least we can try to grasp that an issue has a special personal meaning to another. Sometimes saying, "I can't imagine," with warmth and honesty is more effective than pretending to understand. It can be especially effective and sincere to say, "I'm trying; please help me to better understand."

When we have empathy toward our children, we let them know that their experiences and perspective are important. Too often, parents see children as extensions of themselves, problems to be managed, or little creatures to be trained. Sometimes parents can't imagine that their children have significant problems. "How can a silly fight with a friend be compared to my struggle to earn a living? How can a scraped knee produce such a flood of tears when my friend is dealing with cancer?"

We are tempted to say, "Get over it," but children's problems and emotions are real. If we belittle or dismiss them, we generate shame and prevent them from coming back to their most valuable resource—us.

Children need to be heard and understood on their terms. Adults need to grasp that childhood has its own share of turmoil. Children deserve empathy to feel listened to and respected; they also need to see parents project and model empathy to grow up and become caring young people and adults. Without developing an ability to see and feel things from another's point of view, it will be harder to forge positive relationships in the future.

Empathy is protective and preventive. When we are empathetic toward children, we create an emotional safety net. They feel secure in coming to us with problems. When they're in trouble, they know we will listen without criticism or blame. When they make a mistake, they know we'll help them correct it without condemnation. When they come to us with problems because they know we'll be empathetic, they are more likely to let us guide them toward solutions, and they will feel safer in working out their own strategies to prevent the problem from becoming worse.

A Special Mention About Boys

I must make a special plug for allowing boys to have and express emotions. You might think that our gender-enlightened society would have put this issue to rest by now, but studies show adults continue to react quite differently to little boys and girls from an early age. Girls are held more. Boys are wrestled with to make them tough. Boys who cry are told, "Don't act like a little girl." This attitude flies in the face of empathy. Adults who say this not only fail to see the problem from the boy's viewpoint, but they also shame him for having unhappy feelings. If we cause boys to become disconnected from their real, justified emotions, we deprive them of an important tool they need to connect with other people and recover from difficulties later in life.

Boys sometimes behave in a way that feeds into our expectation that their emotional lives are less rich or intense than that of our daughters. Girls may talk passionately about the drama in their lives, whereas boys may pretend not to notice. Girls in our home assert their growing independence by challenging our authority directly (eg, yelling, fighting), whereas boys seem to just not care very much (eg, becoming silent, deaf ["Wha-a-at?"], and very, very tired). Of course, generalizations about gender are always wrong, but when we do see these patterns it can reinforce in us the false belief that boys have fewer feelings than girls.

In fact, research has demonstrated that the rich inner life of boys becomes increasingly stifled as they move through adolescence. The work of Niobe Way, EdD, has demonstrated that middle school boys talk about the depth of their friendships and even describe the love they have for their friends. They speak of being listened to and the importance of having someone who knows everything there is to know about them. As they get older, though, they speak more about buddies and describe their friendships as more centered around activities than meaningful relationships. In fact, they have grown to view the kind of relationships they had earlier cherished as being somehow feminine.

I dream of a world in which we will not socialize boys to believe that shutting down their feelings is a sign of manhood and where sensitivity is seen as an essential element of masculinity that prepares young men to be better lovers, husbands, coworkers, and fathers. Such a world would have men be able to benefit more fully from the protective elements of enduring and growing connections. It also would position men to be more resilient in the most challenging of times because they would more comfortably reach out to others for the support that can literally make the difference to survival.

None of us can change the world on our own. We may not even be able to single-handedly protect our children fully from society's gender role stereotypes. But each of us can absolutely ensure that we create a space where our children can fully express their emotions. A starting point is for us to know that the emotions are there, even if they are not palpable on the surface.

Your son has a deep inner life, even if he is not showing it. Your knowledge of his depth will stem your frustration with his (occasional or frequent) silence and change your perception from "he doesn't care anymore" to "he's creating a space to process." Your understanding will allow him to build his emotional resilience, rather than reinforce in him that feelings are not something men are supposed to acknowledge. All of this will protect your connection with him.

If you have a son, I suggest that you read one or more of the following books to reaffirm your sense that young men have rich inner lives. If you or your spouse doesn't have time to dive into a book, may I suggest you watch the 1986 classic *Stand by Me,* directed by Rob Reiner. I promise you that reading these books or watching that film will make you want to hug your son.

Real Boys: Rescuing Our Sons from the Myths of Boyhood, by William Pollack, PhD (1998)

Raising Cain: Protecting the Emotional Life of Boys, by Dan Kindlon, PhD, and Michael Thompson, PhD (2000)

Deep Secrets: Boys' Friendships and the Crisis of Connection, by Niobe Way, EdD (2011)

Our Responses to Children's Emotions

Children pay a great deal of attention to how we respond to their emotions. How often have you seen a child take a mild tumble? Usually he has 1 of 2 reactions. If the adults around him get hysterical, he cries. If they calmly reassure him he's OK, he gets up and goes on playing. When emotions are real and deep—let's say his best friend has made fun of him and he's completely disheartened—and adults lack empathy, ignore him, or denigrate his feelings by saying, "It's nothing," or "It'll be OK," he may not let himself feel those emotions again. He may not trust his own feelings. He may not go to adults the next time he's sad or worried. He has lost a profoundly important coping strategy for dealing with challenges when he no longer feels emotions or goes to others to process them.

If we cause children to be disconnected from their emotions and therefore not share them, we deprive them of an important tool that they will need later to recover from adversities. We know that people who have experienced tragic events recover best when they hold deep connections to other people.

People who grow up in a caring environment learn to be caring. They measure the "caringness" of the environment by whether they are listened to and whether adults pay attention to or deny their emotions. A simple, "I really want to understand how you're feeling now. Please tell me so I can try to understand," can go a long way toward preparing children to use other people as a support system throughout their lives.

Useful Unpleasant Emotions

There's yet another reason not to let children become ashamed of their negative emotions. Even unpleasant emotions are useful because they inform us when we should be cautious. Anxiety tells us that we have stepped outside our comfort zone and may be approaching danger. Sadness reminds us how much we care when we experience a loss and teaches us that we need to appreciate what we have. Fear teaches us to be vigilant. Anger tells us that someone has stepped over our boundary zone, and we may need to defend ourselves.

When we empathize, children learn to listen to their own emotions. When we help them name their feelings, their frustration lessens because they can express themselves, better inform us when we should worry, and show us how we can offer support. When we allow them to process real versus perceived slights or dangers, we support them in becoming more emotionally mature and healthy. But if we don't listen with empathy or belittle their emotions, they learn to suppress feelings and perhaps lose some of the protection those emotions provide.

***Building Resilience* Videos** (www.healthychildren.org/BuildingResilience)

Video 3.5 — Is It Possible to Give Our Children Unconditional Love While Also Holding Them to High Expectations? Absolutely.

To learn about the full offering of* Building Resilience *videos, please turn to page 327.

The Art and Importance of Listening

"My parents never listen to me." More than anything else—more than a trip to Disney World—kids want parents to listen to and respect them. They crave our attention, even when they seem to be pushing us away. Listening is the starting point of every good human interaction. We may think we're listening to children when we are only hearing their chatter. Hearing the noise and listening to the meaning in their words are entirely different.

Parents tell me they often don't know what to say to their kids when their children are troubled. They worry that they'll mess up by giving the wrong advice. My response is consistent. "Don't worry, just listen. If you can be a sounding board, you will help him figure things out."

This may be the most important chapter of this book because nothing else will work if you don't become a good listener. Give yourself the gift of losing the fantasy that you're supposed to have all the answers. Free yourself from the myth that says good parents always have ready solutions. If you believe that myth, you'll never feel adequate as a parent because no one has all the answers. Instead, know that if you listen well, your children will always have someone on their side to help them unload their worries and develop their own solutions. Sometimes there are no solutions and only time will fix the problem; even then, listening offers the gift of unconditional respect.

Earplugs

We need to recognize and overcome barriers to listening because we miss so many wonderful opportunities for the frank, deep discussions essential to strengthening family connections. One of those common barriers—the earplugs that keep us from listening to our children—is jumping in with our parental wisdom too soon. This only stifles the conversation. Here are 3 earplugs we need to remove.

- *The parent alarm.* "My child is in trouble!" We jump in with a solution before the child finishes a sentence. "Mom, Brian was caught cheating in—" "I told you he was a bad influence. I'm calling your teacher. I want your desk moved away from his." This is a lost opportunity to talk about honesty, the value of hard work, and the satisfaction of accomplishing something yourself. Perhaps it's even a lost opportunity for your son to say that he considered cheating and feels bad about it. You'll never know.
- *Our discomfort with silence.* Most of us have been taught that silence is supposed to spark further conversation, but we still find silence awkward. When children are groping for the right words, struggling to tell us something that's bothering them, or simply thinking about what to say next, we tend to fill the silence with our own words of wisdom. It's better to give children time to put their thoughts into words. If they seem to be struggling, use some brief coaching words like, "Hmm, you're really thinking."
- *Discomfort with kids' mistakes.* Most of us are uncomfortable when children make mistakes. Instead of letting them think things through, we wish to correct their ideas before they get out of hand. So we start telling them how to prevent or correct mistakes, instead of listening as they try to figure out their own solutions.

How Do We Know When Children Want to Talk?

If only children held office hours. If only we could have time delegated for deep discussions. (Wednesday from 8:00 to 9:00 pm would work perfectly in my schedule.) If only kids would start conversations with, "I'd like to talk now. Do you have some time?"

Children are rarely direct when they want to talk. They don't come to us with a well-organized agenda of concerns. Instead, they approach us in as many different ways as there are children and temperaments, often depending on their mood at the moment. Sometimes they come to us in silence, perhaps with a furrowed brow that says they're upset. At other times they feign indifference with that "What, me care?" look to see if it sparks our interest. Or they may open with an "I have a friend who..." story so they can seek advice without making a confession.

There's the one-step-at-a-time approach: They reveal just a small piece of the story to test how we'll react. If we leap in, criticize, or give lame advice, we fail the test. Then, of course, there's the bombshell: "Take this, Mom and Dad—what are you going to do now?" If we jump in with punishment, we have lost an opportunity to understand what the bombshell means.

Rage is the most difficult approach of all and is common in adolescence—red-hot anger that blames parents for the problem. Why us? Because we are the only safe people to blame, the only ones who will receive their rage and still love them. Let them let it out. Tell them if they have been inappropriate, but stay calm, don't punish. Say something like, "You seem to need to get that off your chest. I'm here to listen." Other times you may need to give yourself a time-out before being able to remain calm and nonjudgmental. That makes you human. You could say, "I hear your anger, but if I just get angry, we won't get anywhere. I'm going to take a walk; when I come back, I'll be ready to listen." You've prevented an escalation and modeled a healthy coping strategy.

Next Step: Availability

If you are alert to the wide range of clues your children offer, you will have taken the first step toward becoming an effective listener. The next step is availability. The timing of children's needs usually doesn't meet our schedules, so flexibility is key. No matter what you planned, listening becomes the most important thing you can do. Of course, children have to respect your schedule. You don't need to allow them to interrupt your phone calls, for example. You might say, "Hold that thought. I'll be off the phone in 3 minutes." It's not always realistic to be flexible at every moment. When your sensors are raised but the world gets in the way, explain that you know he needs your time and attention. Then tell him precisely when you can give it to him. If you know he has something on his mind that you've put off discussing, call him during the day (after school or at the sitter's) to let him know you're thinking of him.

Spontaneous Opportunities to Listen

Family meetings provide a time for adults to listen to children and offer a great way to work on issues that can improve connection. Realistically, a child's need to talk usually doesn't coincide with scheduled meeting times. Some of the most fruitful conversations may occur spontaneously when you're building a model together, baking birthday cupcakes, or riding in the car. For boys in particular, who are somewhat more comfortable talking about their feelings when they can look around and act like they don't care, car rides are opportunities for conversations, as are spur-of-the-moment talks that arise while throwing a ball or playing a game. Remember, many boys don't do as well with those eye-to-eye, "Tell me your feelings" conversations.

Quantity Versus Quality Time

In our over-scheduled lives, we often talk of making *quality time* for our children. I agree—a few moments, when parents are truly present and undistracted, can be most meaningful. At the expense of saying something unpopular, though, *quantity* matters too. All parents are stretched to fulfill multiple obligations, but we need to make available as much time as possible for our children. To some extent, the quality of our time with them is influenced by the quantity of that time. I'm not suggesting that you quit your day job. I am saying that there will be more opportunities to listen if we spend more time with our children. We won't always be there for the crises or heart-to-heart moments, but the more time we spend with them, the more likely we will be available to listen during a significant moment.

Curb the Interruptions

We interrupt children for 2 reasons. The first is that most of us find silence uncomfortable. The second is that it's difficult to withhold our parental wisdom. So rather than listen in silence, we blurt out our opinions. We may not think that we're voicing our views directly because we may make comments just to keep the conversation going. But children are hyperalert to our views and attitudes, especially our critical opinions, and their antennae pick up even the smallest clues about how we feel.

We can learn to limit blatant criticism for the big issues, but we are frequently unaware of how loud our subtler messages can be, even when we are trying to be supportive listeners. In routine daily conversations, we drop clues that we're judging, moralizing, minimizing, negating, catastrophizing, belittling, and shaming. The following example illustrates how a parent's various responses may be interpreted by a child:

Nine-year-old Madeline comes home from ballet class with eyes brimming with tears. Gradually, she reveals pieces of the story. Her teacher has said she's improving but may never learn to plié well enough for the recital. A parent's comment like, "What does she know?" will undermine Madeline's confidence in her teacher, belittle the problem, and hardly support her in trying to improve her pliés.

If her mother says, "Sweetheart, you will be the star of that recital," Madeline will question her mother's grasp of reality, feel more pressure to perform well, and conclude that her real fears are not taken seriously.

If her mother suggests, "Fine, quit ballet if that's what you want," she is turning the situation into a catastrophe that doesn't exist.

If she says, "Oh, don't cry, darling. It's not that bad," she minimizes a problem that is really upsetting her daughter.

If she says, "Your teacher has no right to say that to you!" she creates a moral judgment and prevents further discussion, especially when Madeline thinks her teacher is wonderful.

Keep the Ball Rolling: Encourage Them to Talk

The key to getting a child to open up is to say very little. Simply use short phrases that prompt more conversation. This is particularly important at the beginning of a conversation because we want children to reach a point where they're comfortable enough to express whatever is on their minds. To reach this point, they must know that we are paying attention and have only their agenda in mind.

The following manner of talking seems stilted on first reading. It requires some practice to sound authentic rather than like someone trying to impersonate a therapist. (Therapists are trained to withhold comments because it makes people feel listened to and accepted despite whatever they have to say. This keeps them comfortable enough to continue disclosing their thoughts.) Trust me that this is important. I suggest that you practice this technique with another adult until you can do it in a natural way that makes conversation flow.

First point: Remember the power of silence. Saying nothing, while being in the present moment, sends a loud message that you are accepting of the person who is talking. This doesn't mean that you approve of everything he says; it means only that you are glad he's saying it.

Second point: As your child gets comfortable talking about an uncomfortable subject, listen attentively and silently. When you feel you will burst if you don't utter something, feel free to nod and say, "Hmm," and "I see." When you are about to spew forth your wisdom, refrain! Just continue to give brief statements that let your child know you're impressed that he is talking and you are eager to hear more. Some examples include

- "Tell me more."
- "Wow, you have quite a story to share."
- "Please keep talking. I'm really interested."
- "It sounds like you have a lot on your mind, so I'm glad you're talking."
- "I love that you're so open and honest with your feelings."
- "It means a lot to me that you feel comfortable talking to me."
- "You're doing a great job of describing what happened."
- "Could you repeat that? I want to be sure I understand what you're going through."

You'll know when your child has unloaded. He finishes what he wants to say and feels an emotional release. The pace of his conversation may slow. His body language may soften. He may even blow you out of the water with, "What do you think?"

When that happens, be certain you are completely clear that you have gotten the story straight. If you aren't quite sure, you might say, "This is what I heard. Did I understand you correctly?" or check his emotions by saying, "It seems that you are feeling.... Is that right?" or "When something like that happened to me, I felt like.... Do you feel a little like that?" We know that when 12 people hear the same story, the result is 13 different interpretations. It is important that we understand our child's interpretation because that is what matters here. He will greatly appreciate that you want to understand it correctly and that you've listened so carefully to his story that you can recount it.

How to Respond

Sometimes, there may be absolutely nothing else we should do but be fully present as a sounding board. At other times, though, a child needs direct guidance. The best way to figure this out is to ask: "How can I be most helpful to you?" When you sense your child needs guidance, you may not think your ideas can actually help him get out of a jam. But you can take the first step by starting with, "Hmm...how are you thinking of handling this?"

Children occasionally come to us for advice. When that happens, go ahead and give it, following this approach. Always try to avoid lecturing and critical judgment. Break your wisdom into separate digestible servings by speaking in a tone and cadence that your child understands. If you offer 10 brilliant pieces of advice in one broad swoop, you may overwhelm or confuse your child and he'll miss much of what you are saying.

Mind Your Body Language

Parents can master all the effective listening skills previously discussed and still blow it if their body language projects a different attitude. A frown, rigid posture, or furrowed brow doesn't indicate a willingness to listen without judging.

If a child is trying to talk about a worrisome situation, it is difficult to listen without tensing up. We tend to concentrate on our words, not our body language. Off-putting body language can stop a conversation as easily as insensitive spoken words. When a child senses that a parent is angry or fearful of the subject, he will clam up.

- If you tell your child you have time to listen, show it. Sit down. Get down to your child's eye level instead of hovering over him. Eliminate distractions. Turn off the television and cell phone. Just be there.
- Take deep, soothing breaths to turn off those surges of adrenaline that make you perspire or make your legs tremble with anxiety. Fool your body into thinking you are relaxed. This helps you think more clearly and prevents outbursts that could stop the conversation. Sometimes deep breathing won't work, especially if your child's concerns generate fear or anxiety in you. In that case, step away and run in place. Remember, stress makes you feel like you're being attacked. Sometimes, you just can't think until you've run from danger (see Chapter 29).
- Watch the defensive postures that say you're uncomfortable with the subject under discussion. Avoid folded arms, finger tapping on the table, or leg shaking that convey anxiety or annoyance.
- Make sure you give lots of hugs because they make everyone (you too) feel better. Children receive hugs as the ultimate sign they are safe and protected.

In my experience, nothing is more important to being an effective parent than making children know they are truly heard. This doesn't mean we have to agree with everything said or condone every behavior. But before we can impart any useful guidance, we have to send the clear message that we're really listening to the words and trying to grasp the emotions beneath them. In communicating with kids of any age, we need to create a zone of safety that makes them know we are trustworthy. Otherwise, they are likely to shut down, tell us nothing, or lie to defend themselves and get us off their backs. Whether they come to us with serious troubles or everyday matters, we can create a safe zone by listening patiently and nonjudgmentally, without interrogating them or interrupting with a solution or advice. This projects a clear message that we love them unconditionally. We're not going anywhere. There are no requirements to receive our love.

To learn about the full offering of* Building Resilience *videos, please turn to page 327.

Strengthening Family Ties

Listening is the best way to connect with children. How else can we strengthen our connections within our families?

Deepening Parent-Child Connections: Low-Yield Time Gives the Highest Yield

When our children are young, we ooh and aah to their every antic. We celebrate them at play and revel at the miracle of their development. Then, as they get older, we tend to have a bit less time and they *sometimes* seem a bit less cute. They are especially uncute when they shower us with messages that they'd like to spend less time with us. As a result, we try to maximize the time we do have together by having those "high-yield" conversations that focus on grades, scores, and results. This is one of the biggest mistakes we make as parents.

We push our children away when we cram more into less time. Making our limited time high yield makes it anxiety provoking. We want our children to enjoy the time we have together, not dread it. When we focus on what our kids produce, they begin to feel like a product. You'll know how they are performing but not how they are feeling. You'll know their scores but not their struggles. You'll miss out on the opportunity to parent in the active sense of the word.

When I speak to young people, they often complain that their parents only care about their grades or performance and no longer seem to care about *them*. I'll then ask them how much of themselves, beyond what they produce, they share with their parents. The usual response? "That's pretty much all we talk about. My personal life is my business." Get it? This is a cycle. First, we try to maximize our moments together by focusing on the "important stuff." Then, kids think that is all we care about, so they don't talk about anything else. As a result, we feel badly they are not sharing their lives. And so on. To parent our kids, we must know them. For us to know them, they must reveal themselves.

I tell young people that they are largely in control of breaking this cycle. If they give their parents the time they (secretly) mutually crave and fill that time with real discussions, their parents will likely come through. If they only share their grades, they really have no right to expect their parents to see them in the rich context of their lives.

While you do want to know your child's grades, it is more important that you know your child's internal life.

Don't worry about sacrificing your effectiveness to guide them. When the time you have together is time you both look forward to, you'll find yourselves with more time together. Some of that newfound time can be used to address school and other important topics, but most will be spent just staying connected. If you're worried that you'll waste critical time you could be using to help your child achieve success, let me assure you that the unconditional nature of your love is precisely the ingredient your child needs most to be launched toward a successful future.

Creating Family Rituals

Even when our time is limited, we can create special times and establish simple, regular family rituals. We don't have to spend 2 hours a night or all weekend on togetherness projects, but we can get into the habit of doing routine events together on a consistent basis, such as preparing meals, walking the dog, or doing chores like laundry. We can use these occasions as opportunities to listen to our children, encourage them to talk to us, tell us jokes, sing songs, dance around the kitchen—whatever you both can enjoy at the moment.

You can enhance family connection by eating at least one meal a week together, though more is better. Choose an evening the coming week when your family will all be present. No matter how busy everyone is, set a firm date. Be respectful of your teenager's social schedule by being flexible about the day and time, but plan in advance and stick to it. Attendance is required (dress, optional). Take no excuses, no last-minute "But I have to go to my friend's house," or "I forgot." If you're especially busy, prepare something in advance or bring in takeout, but make the weekly sit-down dinner a routine. You may want to turn off phones during dinner or light candles on the table, but make it an event.

Other valuable family traditions include reading bedtime stories, sharing hobbies, and spending regular special time with children, as a group and one-on-one. You can designate 10 or 15 minutes each evening or alternate evenings to spend separately with each child. This may sound counter to family connection or togetherness, but the point is to devote individual attention to all your children one at a time. Avoid sibling rivalry by helping each child to understand that just as you're spending special time with another on Tuesday, you will spend the same amount of time with him or her on Wednesday.

This special time with each child was especially valuable in my family because we have identical twin daughters. We split up and had an Ilana-Mommy and a Talia-Daddy day (or the reverse) about every 2 weeks. This allowed us to focus on the uniqueness of each child. While this may be particularly important in a household with twins, many parents tell me that when life gets chaotic, their children blend together—bad for children, bad for parents, and a setup for sibling rivalry.

Specific Techniques for Connecting

When your children were babies, you probably had certain rituals like the evening bath and bedtime story. As they grew, they took their own baths or showers and read themselves to sleep.

I have a suggestion: Reestablish that ritual with a twist. Children may feel too old to be read to, and they don't need your help with a bath when they're 10 or 11 years old. Do something together each evening, even if it takes only a few moments—a guessing game, telling jokes, or singing a song—and make it a routine event. And *always* say good night to each child or have her come to you to say good night before she goes to bed. This is particularly important when she becomes a teenager, so I strongly suggest you establish this pattern as early as possible.

The *nightly check-in* is a technique that I have been promoting for years with preteens, teenagers, and parents. It is not meant to be punitive, but it works as an effective disciplinary tool with adolescents because it ensures a safe return home when they have been out. Here's how it works.

Make sure your child understands that you expect her to come in and tell you when she gets home. Even if you are asleep, she is to wake you up and tell you she's arrived safely. Ask her to talk with you for a few moments. Don't ask for details about the evening—she will see this as interrogation—but remain open if she wants to share details. Tell her you're happy to listen to her no matter how tired you are.

Be firm and don't permit any exceptions or excuses like, "I didn't want to wake you because I knew your were tired," or "I forgot because I was so sleepy." If you establish this rule early and hold your child to it, she will understand that there will be a predetermined consequence or loss of privilege if she breaks the check-in rule.

The rule has several benefits. It is an effective way for parents to monitor adolescents. It reduces your worry that your teen is drinking or using drugs because you will be able to determine her coherence as soon as she gets home.

It also gives her a great refusal skill to use with her friends. "I can't smoke weed with you because I have to check in with my parents as soon as I get home. They smell me!" Their friends will sympathize and reduce the peer pressure because of your "stupid check-in rule." Essentially, it is a great tool to allow her to self-monitor and create her own boundaries with peers.

If you use the nightly check-in in a loving spirit, as in, "I'm glad you're home safe. I need to know you're OK. I love you," your child will view this ritual not as controlling but as caring. She will see your concern as positive attention, not interrogation or distrust. This, in turn, helps her feel even more connected to you.

Fun and Games

Play provides one of the best ways for parents and children to connect. Parents pressed for time may think they have little opportunity to play with their children. But kids never outgrow having fun with their parents, even when they become adolescents. If you have time for only a short, simple game, try to squeeze in some fun with your child. You don't have to take her to a professional ball game and spend 4 hours and $200. Free, unstructured, spontaneous play is cheaper and usually more fun.

There's a lot more benefit to playing with your child than getting to know her better and watching as she builds her competencies and resilience. There's the pure joy of play. When children play, they remind us of a very basic lesson: Make the most of every moment and appreciate what we have.

I was reminded of this when we were on a family vacation. It was time to pack up and drive to the next spot, but my daughters were enthralled with a sandy hillside that they had transformed into a sliding board. They wanted to keep sliding. I kept rushing them. Then I suddenly caught myself—why was I so worried about where we should be in the next hour, when they were having such a good time now? My needs were instantly put into perspective and were insignificant in comparison to the joy my daughters were experiencing.

We adults are always so future-oriented. Think of a road trip with the family. Sure, kids are always asking, "Are we there yet?" But wherever they are, it is good to learn *they are there!* Every stop seems like the best. They can't imagine going to the next site and leaving that most perfect sliding hillside behind. Parents, with our adult minds, miss out on the present because we are focused on the future ("How long will it take to get there? Where will we stay? When will we be able to clean all this trash out of the car?"). We have lost the ability to relish every moment. We hear all the folk wisdom ("Take time to smell the roses!") that tells us to slow down and cherish the beauty and pleasure we usually overlook, but children really get it! If only we allow them to do so.

Children and adults who can draw pleasure from the little things will find it easier to spring back from difficult challenges and misfortune. We're all surrounded by inspiration, if we only choose to see it and allow it to rejuvenate us when things get us down. When we play with children, we're reminded of this essential truth. When we meet them where they are—on their playground, governed by their rules—and we don't force them to change, they'll retain this protective approach to life. And our own adult resilience will be enhanced as we learn to find little vacations everywhere.

Siblings: Part of the Family Team

Volumes have been written about sibling rivalry. I won't attempt to repeat that advice. In the context of strengthening connection as a building block of resilience, this point is basic: Sibling rivalry is not only inevitable, but it also serves a purpose by giving kids a chance to work out differences and practice negotiating skills in the safety of their families. Sparring with a brother or sister is a normal way to test strengths and weaknesses and define separate identities. In other words, a child can practice individuality and independence while still being part of the family team.

Of course parents get headaches from sibling fights, but if we avoid taking sides or assigning blame and strive instead for fairness, we can encourage siblings to work out their differences. This builds their competence at problem-solving and encourages family cohesiveness.

Susan Beris, MD, coauthor of *Beyond the Visit: From Pacifiers to Piercing, Toilet Training to Tattoos,* shares some advice that she frequently gives parents: Each child in the family should be encouraged to excel in, or at least love, something different. A son may love photography; a daughter is at her peak on the soccer field; a younger son adores baseball. They may all share the one interest, such as swimming. But if they also have separate interests, they are less likely to get entangled in the negative aspects of sibling rivalry. A younger brother won't have to go through years of insufferable comments like, "When your big brother was on my team..." (which he interprets as, "You'll never live up to him."). Encouraging different interests also gives each child an experience of being a star in her own arena. It gives other siblings a chance to cheerlead for the one currently in the spotlight.

Keeping Adult Connections (Including, Especially, Your Spouse)

We are so child focused, especially when we feel guilty that we are not giving them enough, that we sometimes allow our adult relationships, including those with our partners, to lapse. Remember 2 key points so that you will understand the importance of maintaining meaningful adult interactions generally and specifically with your life partner. First, ultimately, those are the relationships you will be left with when your children grow. So if you have young children and you and your spouse skip "dates" because you just have more fun with the children, reverse course. Cherish and honor your adult connections. If I haven't convinced you yet, perhaps because it sounds somehow selfish to you, remind yourself that you are raising a child to be a happy, successful 35-, 40-, and 50-year-old. We are not making adulthood look attractive when we are so child-focused that we forgo rich adult relationships. For the sake of your child's future, care for those relationships with the same focus you have on caring for your child.

To learn about the full offering of* Building Resilience *videos, please turn to page 327.

Widening the Circle

Outside the nuclear family, children need connections to multiple groups of friends, relatives, community, and the world. Think of it as a chain of strong interlocking circles—the more circles build the chain, the more they feel a sense of belonging and support.

Friendships

Circles of friends shift like the tides during childhood and adolescence. School friends move away or get dropped for cooler peers. Neighborhood friends go on to different schools and cliques. Preadolescent girls in particular seem to change friends almost daily. On Tuesday, Tasha is your daughter's inseparable best friend forever. By Friday, Tasha won't talk to her and moves on to a different group that excludes your daughter. By next Wednesday, Tasha will be back at your house.

I know it sounds sexist to ascribe this pattern to girls, and generalities are always wrong. However, boys seem to work out their differences with name-calling or a shove and get over it quickly. Ten minutes later, they're skateboarding or tossing a ball around together. Some girls tend to hurt each other with psychologic weapons, such as gossip and nasty remarks, and weep over it for days.

Children can be deeply hurt and isolated—left unconnected—when suddenly dumped by a close friend or group. In the worst-case scenario, they may do whatever it takes to fit in again rather than risk isolation. To avoid the perils of social isolation, it is important to ensure that they have more than one circle of friends—some at school, some in the community, and others through scouts, sports, or religious organizations.

Relatives and Neighbors

Relatives form another strong link in the chain of friendships. Cousins in particular can offer a child good role models and guidance. If your child is having a problem with friends or at school, he may be more willing to open up and discuss it with an older favorite cousin. Older neighbors can also be good models for your children—perhaps the 19-year-old college student down the street who holds a part-time job and plays in a band, or the babysitter who volunteers at a homeless shelter. If you ask these young people simply to keep an eye out for your child, to inquire how he's doing from time to time, you will be offering both a valuable opportunity. For the older ones, it's an opportunity to be influential and have someone look up to them. You're letting them know you have respect and confidence in them. For your younger children, you're expanding their circle of connections and exposing them to examples of healthy teens.

Multigenerational relationships also strengthen a sense of connection. A doting grandparent, a favorite aunt, or a cool uncle gives children valuable support and makes them feel part of something bigger than themselves. For centuries, children grew up amid many generations. They worked on a family farm or in a family-owned business alongside grandparents, parents, and other relatives. As they grew, they developed increasing abilities and took on more responsibilities that prepared them for adulthood. As adults, many took over those family enterprises.

Today, it is rare for a child to grow up in a tight-knit family environment. We cannot recreate the family farm or open a general store with Grandpa behind the counter, but we can try to strengthen family ties for our children's sake, whether our extended families are large or small. Today, we can encourage them to e-mail Grandpa on the other coast. We can encourage young children to make drawings and small gifts to send to relatives and write thank-you notes when they receive gifts from them. The more family connections children have, the more security will envelop them, the more content they'll be, and the better equipped to spring back during rough times.

Adolescents and Connection

Relationships with people outside the family can come in particularly handy during adolescence. Preteens and teenagers go through periods of hating their parents, or so it seems. This is an upsetting but normal part of their growing independence. It is helpful to remember that much of their reaction stems from how much they actually *love* their parents. To figure out who they are and who they want to become, adolescents need to reject almost every idea their parents have and try out a few new ideas of their own. But rest assured, they don't hate everybody.

If parents have wisely supported adolescents in forging a variety of positive connections, teens will turn to other trusted people for guidance during that period of mid-adolescence when everything parents say is ridiculous.

Be subtle about fostering these other connections. If they seem forced or directed, teenagers may think these other people are your stooges and their views will be seen as tainted. So don't suggest, "Why don't you hang out with that mature college kid down the street?" Instead, set up situations in which someone like this model neighbor can interact spontaneously with your teenager (maybe drive him to the mall), and let the relationship develop from there. If your child has a favorite older cousin, aunt, or uncle, make it possible for your teen to spend more time with him or her.

Community Connections

When children are old enough, they need to gain a sense of broader connections beyond their individual families. By belonging to sports, civic, and religious organizations, children learn that they have a place in the larger community. And that community—a team, the Boys & Girls Club, church, synagogue, mosque, or temple—values them as members. These connections show children that they're part of a safe and supportive community. If parents locate or help their children join organizations that promote the same values they cherish, parents' efforts to instill these values can be reinforced by those groups. Children who participate in these organizations learn that parents aren't the only ones who expect them to play fair, be honest and loyal, and show responsibility. Others also expect these standards. As discussed in the next section, connections like these contribute to a child's character.

Many children do not feel connected to people outside their immediate family. A lot of kids don't even know their neighbors. After school, many children return to empty homes and stay indoors. Whether they live on city blocks, rural farms, or suburban cul-de-sacs, they are physically isolated—disconnected—from people nearby. One way to foster some connection is setting up a safe house with neighbors so children know where to go if their parents aren't home or they feel any danger. If they know the retired fireman who lives across the street is usually home every afternoon and they can always ring his doorbell, they'll feel more securely connected to their neighborhood. Setting up safe houses in your community is similar to practicing a home fire drill. Be clear about where to go or when to call, and make sure your children know where those phone numbers are posted in your home.

You will undoubtedly think of other ways to create and support relationships between your child and other people in your community. In our harried and often chaotic world, it is more important than ever for young people to have as many adult connections as possible.

Who's Watching the Kids?

That answer may seem all too obvious—it's the parent's job, of course. But all adults have responsibility to watch out for the children being raised in our communities. I was privileged to see how well community involvement in child-rearing can work when I lived on the Cheyenne River Sioux Reservation in South Dakota. Outsiders used to pass through Native American communities quickly and draw the erroneous conclusion that no one was watching the children. Kids wandered throughout the community, well beyond the boundaries of their homes. So who was watching the children? Everyone was. They were everyone's responsibility. Each adult in a parent's generation was regarded as an aunt or uncle, and numerous grandparents of the elder generation were treated with veneration. Any adult could watch children, correct them, and keep them from harm. We have moved so far from this ideal that we now fear correcting other people's children. We need to have serious conversations within our communities about the importance of adults' watchful surveillance for children's safety and well-being.

Connection With School

For most children, school provides the closest community outside their families. Children spend nearly half their waking time in school, where they not only learn but also are socialized. Children who are well connected to their schools are more likely to thrive educationally, emotionally, and socially. If they view school as a safe place and understand that the adults at school care about their well-being, children are more likely to soak up knowledge and absorb the invaluable life lesson that learning is pleasurable and rewarding.

Parents also need to get involved and stay connected because children sometimes need advocates to negotiate their world at school. Parents who are connected with teachers will know what's going on in school and be better prepared to help their children navigate school successfully. Teachers are valuable allies because they may pick up on difficulties that parents might miss, especially social difficulties or learning differences. As child professionals, they can help parents evaluate certain concerns and sort out the difference between normal development and a more serious problem.

Connection With Nature

Our resilience is enhanced by our connection to nature. Many children today are increasingly *disconnected* from the natural world. They spend most of their time indoors. Even when they take a trip to a nature center, the experience is limited and usually structured by adults. Few kids have leisure opportunities to explore nature on their own. When was the last time your child walked in the woods, looked under a mossy rock, or poked a stick into a pond and discovered a tadpole?

What does nature have to do with resilience? Children need to understand that they are part of the natural world as well as the human community. Nature can nurture their sense of belonging. Children can learn that they are the future stewards of the planet. In observing nature, young people are exposed to countless examples of resilience—pinecone seeds, for instance, that survive forest fires to sprout new seedlings, or recurring seasons that bring birth, maturity, death, and rebirth. Mother Nature is a great teacher of resilience.

To learn about the full offering of* Building Resilience *videos, please turn to page 327.

Some Cautions About Connection

Is it possible to love our children too much? No, but it is possible to be too centered on our children. While they should be central to our lives, they cannot be our sole focus. Many parents are so committed to parenting that the lines become blurred between their lives and their child's. This is the "We are worried about the test on Thursday" phenomenon. Children need their own lives that are interdependent with, but clearly independent from, parents' lives.

When children perceive that they're the sun, moon, and stars in a parent's universe, it is too much pressure. They often feel the need to be perfect (see Chapter 8). Every shortcoming is magnified because they worry about letting parents down. Children who worry excessively about parents' emotions may not be willing to try new ventures. If they believe that their actions are the sole determinant of parents' well-being, they may try too hard to be trophy children and will become frustrated and ashamed when they don't excel. Their fear of failing their parents will prevent them from success—they'll lack confidence in their own resilience to take the very chances necessary to succeed.

We certainly want kids to experience security and connection, but at the same time we need to maintain our adult lives—to preserve our own time, personal relationships, and connections to our communities. If we maintain connections to spouses, friends, and coworkers, we will do a great deal for keeping our families happy and together, and at the same time we'll model for our children a good example of meaningful relationships.

As a child advocate who desperately wants parents to cherish their children, I strongly urge you to take care of yourself, savor your accomplishments, and nurture your adult relationships for the good of your children and yourself. If nothing else, you will find it easier to bounce back as your children inevitably grow up and lead the independent lives for which you've prepared them.

When Connection Verges on Control

When children are small, we naturally protect them. As they get older and more competent, we loosen the reins gradually. They're allowed to cross streets by themselves when they've demonstrated that they watch traffic and look both ways before stepping off the curb. Later, we let them go out with friends when they've shown us they can be responsible by calling us to check in and coming home on time.

Throughout this process, we try to balance their increasing independence and separation with our need to know they're safe. This is one of the greatest challenges of parenting—giving just enough freedom or rope. If we let the rope out too much, they may figuratively strangle themselves; if we give too little rope or hold it too tightly, the rope may snap.

We are mindful that children need to separate from us gradually. We know that the job of an adolescent is to find her own identity and ultimately separate from parents to become an adult. But we're often tempted to hold the rope too tightly or step in and fix something for the child.

Cell phones make that rope readily available and easy to clutch tightly. They provide a great way to stay in touch, but this electronic connection can be overused. If parents expect teens or college kids to call in throughout the day to report minor matters ("I just ate lunch."), perhaps the parent-child connection is too taut. We need to be aware that this sort of "connection" is really verging on *control.*

I grow concerned when parents tell me that they don't worry about what may be going on in their child's life "because she tells me everything—we're like best friends." Remember that an adolescent's job is to become an individual, separate and distinct from parents.

Until adolescence, most of children's values and perspectives are directly formed by observing their parents. Teenagers cannot become independent adults until they confront their parents' values, decide to reject some of them, and form their own values. When teens go through this normal process, they need parents to be a stable rock that they can keep referring to by saying, "That's not me. I'm not at all like Mom or Dad." Parents are like a yardstick—teens measure themselves against us.

If parents try to be their teenager's best friend by dressing alike, using teen lingo, or smoking and drinking with their child and her friends, how will this young adult figure out how far she has to go to come up with her own stands? I worry that well-intentioned parents may drive children over the behavioral cliff as they force them to move closer to outrageous choices just to differentiate themselves from their parents. Children need loving, connected, even fun and friendly parents, but they don't need parents to be their best friends. If your teen tells you that you're no fun, remind her that she has lots of friends but only one mother/father.

What Gets in the Way of Connection?

Let's look at connection from another perspective. What gets in the way of parents staying connected with children from infancy through adolescence? In our early discussion of resilience, I described how we snuggle with our precious babies and play with their tiny fingers. But what happens over the years that makes us feel so burdened as parents? What takes away so much of the joy and replaces it with seriousness and even anger? I don't have all the answers—no one does. But it is an essential question to examine if we are to figure out how to maintain an ideal connection with our children. We may not achieve that ideal, but it is our goal.

I become teary as I consider the prospect of my twins going off to college. My house will transform instantly. Suddenly my wife and I will be alone. How will my babies handle it? How will I handle it? Sage parents who have been through this have assured me, "Don't worry. You'll be ready." I think they sometimes mean, "You'll be glad to have them gone." I cannot imagine that now. Remember, you will not be sending your small child or young adolescent away. They will be different—taller, at least; wiser, I hope. And they will prove that they will be ready to go!

Perhaps it is biological. All animals grow up and leave the nest. They go through their playful phase, practice adulthood, and then are on their own. Our human children just play longer and we parents just worry more.

If our children didn't prove to us that they were ready to go, would we let them? It's not just about going to college or moving out to start working. Throughout childhood, children become increasingly independent. First their legs begin working and we don't have to carry them everywhere. We lose a lot of snuggle time because they are always scampering off on another exploration. This process goes on through adolescence, when it becomes painfully obvious that they do not believe we are needed, or so they tell us.

During this march toward independence, part of what happens is that they really don't need as many protective bonds with us. They also need to break these bonds to create the appearance of independence, if only to deal with the anxiety within themselves as they take those next steps.

Yes, children may be excited when they reach new developmental milestones, but they are also human. They may not be able to tell us clearly, but they worry about whether they will succeed. They worry about whether they will lose us, their parents. Remember the metaphor of leaping over a chasm? Think of every milestone (like learning to walk and talk, staying overnight at a friend's house for the first time, or going to college) as a huge, gaping chasm that needs to be crossed.

A child can't gingerly slide her feet across the ground or she will fall in. She must jump across if she has any chance of getting to the other side. Swinging her arms won't propel her across. She must go back several steps and take a running start. She has to stop thinking, suppress her fears, and leap!

Children seem to regress just before their milestones. Is it any wonder that a 10-year-old about to start a new middle school or a ninth grader about to enter high school sometimes seems cranky and irrational before these necessary leaps?

What about us, the loving parents? Why don't our children simply come to us and ask us to help them build that bridge across the chasm? There are 2 answers. First, they do. They constantly do, but they don't ask directly. They sometimes seek our attention in ways that anger or frustrate us, but they do get our attention. Don't be fooled into believing that they need us less during major transitions. They actually need us more. Second, if they told us how much they needed us or how confused or scared they are, they'd be unable to take those next important steps. They need those figurative blinders for a moment. It is very difficult for even the most emotionally intelligent adults to be so in touch with their feelings that they can articulate them clearly, especially in times of change or crisis when we suppress our emotions. Rather, we come up with rationalizations that help us move forward sometimes against our better judgment that yearns for comfort and familiarity.

Remember when your child was ready to take those first steps? Rocking on her legs, wiggling her bottom just before she pulled herself up to stand on those little legs? Did she cry or push your arm away when you approached her to offer help? She wanted to say, "Gosh, thanks, Dad. I sure do appreciate your effort, but I'm struggling here to assert this new step toward my independence."

When your child was learning to talk, she knew what she wanted to say but couldn't. She couldn't express, "Guess what? I'm on the cusp of a whole new world—suddenly able to use language! I will be less dependent on your doing everything for me because I will command attention." Instead, she cried in frustration, grunted, and pointed toward the objects whose names she could not yet pronounce.

And what about the first date? What a wonderful opportunity to have a conversation about sexuality, puberty, and morality—the talk that you looked forward to (with dread) since kindergarten. Here goes: "Darling, I think that you are a maturing young lady, and there are some things I think you are ready to learn." A noble try. Why did she respond, "You're such a dork, Dad. I don't need you to tell me anything!"? That was much easier for her to say than the truth: "I'm really scared, Dad. This emerging sexuality is really overwhelming."

When children are ready to go to college, parents want that last year at home to be so special. It's the last opportunity for family togetherness. It should be a perfect time. (Incidentally, it is absolutely *not* the final opportunity. Parent-child relationships last a lifetime.)

You want the last family vacation before your child leaves home to be ideal. Why, then, does your daughter say, "Mom, I hate you. I'd rather be with my friends. It's a good thing I'm leaving in August because I couldn't stand one more minute in this prison"? Why does she say this? Because it's so much easier than saying, "I love you so much that I can't even find the right words. You've done everything for me. I'm terrified. Do you think I'm ready to go off on my own? Do you think you'll miss me as much as I'm going to miss you?"

Kids challenge us because they need to loosen the connection that involves our assuming full responsibility for them. As they challenge us, we get hurt or even angry until we are ready for them to go. This is completely understandable, predictable, and perhaps even partially necessary. But if we understand what is happening and learn to celebrate our children's growing independence, we will all be healthier. Otherwise, every time they push us we will tighten control. This will only breed resentment. When you receive pushback, set appropriate rules and boundaries that ensure safety. Your child needs to understand that these boundaries will get looser as he demonstrates responsibility. Then remind yourself that your baby is becoming more independent, and that means you are doing your job well. If we can do that, we can celebrate and grow more comfortable with the changing nature of our connections.

It wouldn't be honest of me to say that every time children behave badly or speak meanly to us, it reflects their growing independence or inability to say something much kinder because of their conflicted emotions. Sometimes kids might just be acting meanly. They know our vulnerabilities. Whether they are justifiably or unfairly angry, they can be masters at saying hurtful things. Often it's a way of shouting, "Listen to me!"

Perhaps they're testing the waters to grab your attention before they can bring up something that's troubling them. If you respond with anger and shut them down, they may feel justified for not sharing their concerns: "Remember, I was going to tell you, but then..." Yes, even our angels can be manipulative. It's really OK to tell kids when they hurt your feelings—not in a way that makes them feel guilty, but just a clear statement of fact that their behaviors are inappropriate and hurt you. That is an important part of your job in building their character. You deserve empathy too.

Even during times when children challenge our connection to them, we must remain consistent about one thing—our love is unwavering and we will always be there for them. With this clear message, we say to them, "Go ahead—grow. I've got your back."

***Building Resilience* Videos (www.healthychildren.org/BuildingResilience)**

Video 21.1 Preparing to Cross the Chasm: Our Teens Hate Us Because of How Deeply They Love Us

To learn about the full offering of* Building Resilience *videos, please turn to page 327.

Supporting Resilience in Military Families

The next time you say, "Thank you for your service," to one of our men and women in uniform, please think about the family members who also serve our nation. Only a small portion of our populace chooses to serve, and their families deserve our gratitude for sharing the burden. This chapter is a tribute to the spouses and nearly 2 million children of service members. It is rooted in patriotism but is not political. Our service members do not create the policy of our country; they live it, as do their families. This chapter focuses on strategies parents and caregivers can use to maintain healthy connections and reinforce positive experiences even while facing the challenges that come with being connected to the military.

I invite you to read this chapter even if you have no direct military affiliation so that you are aware of the needs of military children, adolescents, and families. Odds are, though, that you know a military-connected child whose parent, brother, or sister is serving our all-volunteer forces or is a post-9/11 veteran. Ongoing conflicts have created a generation of military children whose parents have been repeatedly deployed (sent into action, usually overseas). These parents haven't been able to share important parts of their sons and daughters' childhood, missing developmental milestones and opportunities to offer guidance. Non-deployed spouses have needed to act largely as single parents. This is a resilient population that has by and large endured this with grace, but resilience does not mean invulnerability. The stresses on family life have been prolonged, and the families are tiring. We know they do better when communities and neighbors recognize their contribution, and your awareness will be an important step toward creating the supportive environment that contributes to their well-being. If you want to know how you can best help, the answer may be in supporting the families of those who serve.

You may benefit from gaining a better understanding of how these families are trying to remain connected whether or not you know a child directly affected. Many other children also deal with separations, including children of divorce and others who deal with frequent moves. We can use the experience of the military-connected family to learn about values, strength, sacrifice, courage, resilience, sense of service, purpose, pride, and even the frailties of the American family. These children and families are not alone in needing to worry about the well-being of one or both parents who sacrifice to serve. In your own communities and within your own lives, consider first responders and other professionals who are regularly called to serve, such as police officers and firefighters. We tend to take them for granted instead of honoring their commitment and thinking about their families' special needs. We need to acknowledge the real heroes in our midst, rather than those who get attention because of money or athletic talent. When we recognize that heroes are those who offer service to society and their communities in one way or another, we build children with stronger character and a desire to contribute.

If you are a service member or spouse, remember that how you model resilience is more important than what you say about it. Your kids will learn how to problem-solve and manage stress by watching how you cope. They will learn from you that strong, capable people sometimes reach out to others for support. In uncertain times, they need to know that you can protect them, and you will be more capable of offering security when you are emotionally, physically, and spiritually healthy.

Please go to www.healthychildren.org/BuildingResilience for a full chapter on supporting resilience in military families. We thought it was important enough to make freely available on the Web. The following outline offers a preview:

1. Why Many Military Families Are Models of Resilience
2. Connection: Core to the Well-being of Children and Adolescents
3. The Deployment Cycle as THE Challenge to Connections
4. Sibling Connections
5. Extended Family Connections
6. Friendships
7. School Connections
8. The Connections Between Parent and Child
    a. Concrete Reminders for the Youngest Children
    b. Maintaining Family Rituals
    c. Listening
    d. Talking
    e. Maintaining Communication With the Deployed Parent (as Best as Possible)

  f. Staying Connected to the Mission (the Whole Mission)
  g. Building Memories
  h. Avoiding Perfectionism
  i. Maintaining a Consistent Parenting Style and Appropriate Discipline
  j. A Word on Teens
  k. A Note for Single Parents
  l. A Note for Blended and Divorced Families
9. Pulling It Together

The educational materials listed below, written by Paula K. Rauch, MD, are included online (see www.healthychildren.org/BuildingResilience). Dr Rauch is a consultation child psychiatrist at Massachusetts General Hospital who directs programs for military-connected families (Home Base Program) and for families in which a parent has a serious illness (Marjorie E. Korff Parenting at a Challenging Time [PACT] Program).

A Dozen Lessons Learned From the Parenting at a Challenging Time Program

These lessons are from Dr Rauch and colleagues at the Marjorie E. Korff PACT Program (www.mghpact.org) and the Home Base Program (www.homebaseprogram.org) at Massachusetts General Hospital.

Talking With Children About Upsetting News Events

These thoughts are from Dr Rauch and colleagues at the MassGeneral Hospital for Children and the Home Base Program.

To learn about the full offering of **Building Resilience** *videos, please turn to page 327.*

Nurturant Connections Offer Meaningful Protection Against the Effects of Childhood Trauma

It is becoming increasingly clear that childhood trauma has lifelong implications for physical and emotional health and well-being. It is not surprising that traumatic childhood experiences influence a person's likelihood to go through a divorce in adulthood or to be a substance user. It may be surprising, however, to learn that childhood trauma affects one's likelihood of being obese, becoming a diabetic, or having heart disease and strokes. In fact, what happens to us as a child seems to even make a difference in our ability to fight infections into adulthood.

Childhood trauma, also referred to as adverse childhood experiences (ACEs), also influences the way our brain functions and, therefore, how we behave. Survivors of childhood trauma may remain hypervigilant throughout life, always surveying for danger and finding it more difficult to trust others. They also may be more reactive, responding intensely to environmental stimuli that another person would barely notice or assess briefly and then move on. For example, a person sitting in a quiet theater would notice a noise across the aisle when a man tripped on a seat, but after a quick assessment that the man was all right and posed no danger, this person would quickly return focus to the play. A traumatized individual, however, would take a longer time to settle and refocus. A person with ACEs might space out more frequently because in earlier times, separating from reality was a critically protective emotional tool. A person with a history of trauma might be more likely to unconsciously make up stories that seem not to be based on reality. This may be because earlier, she would have been hurt if she told the truth. Imagine an abusive father asking, "Who took the last hot dog?" If a child in an unsafe home responded, "Me," and then was beaten because of the admission, you can imagine her learning to coming up with an elaborate story.

There is important news about the effects of childhood trauma that we should be screaming from the rooftops. First, if we are to build a physically and emotionally healthier population (far into adulthood), we must do everything in our power to protect children from toxic stress. Second, it seems clear that *children who are exposed to trauma but who also have a loving, nurturing adult alongside them are much less likely to have lifelong emotional and physical effects.* The news here must be underscored: Love, nurturance, and caring are protective. Resilience in the face of trauma is promoted by the presence of adults who listen to children, believe them, and help them know they can get through situations with their support.

If you are reading this as a parent and your child has been through something beyond your control, you still remain the key to him getting through this. He can still thrive precisely because of your presence.

If you are reading this as a professional, being trauma-informed positions you to serve more effectively. When parents offer unconditional love and nurturance to children and adolescents, we are additive, but when parents are unable to give children what they need, we are critical. When we are trauma-informed, we are able to shift our lens from "What's wrong with you?" to "What happened to you?" This increases our empathy and, therefore, the effectiveness of our relationships. Being trauma-informed also prevents our own burnout. It allows us to learn to hold people's pain without owning their pain. It allows us to understand others' behavior in context, rather than taking their behaviors (eg, their wariness of trusting us) personally. We know what is and what is not about us. Knowing when not to personalize protects our boundaries and stems our frustration and, therefore, may increase our professional longevity.

Professionals can refer to the chapter "Trauma-Informed Practice: Working With Youth Who Have Suffered Adverse Childhood (or Adolescent) Experiences" from *Reaching Teens: Strength-Based Communication Strategies to Build Resilience and Support Healthy Adolescent Development* for additional information (see www.aap.org/reachingteens).

There is a wide body of research now about ACEs. We are all grateful to the original study.

Felitti VJ, Anda RF, Nordenberg D, et al. Relationship of childhood abuse and household dysfunction to many of the leading causes of death in adults. The Adverse Childhood Experiences (ACE) Study. *Am J Prev Med.* 1998;14(4):245–258

To learn about the full offering of* Building Resilience *videos, please turn to page 327.

Character

A child can be very competent, confident, and deeply connected but still not be prepared to thrive. Renee is a good example. She is intelligent and highly competent. She has great problem-solving skills. She knows how to stand up for herself. She is not intimidated by peer pressure. Her confidence has often helped her get out of a jam.

Renee has strong connections—she is a member of a girl gang to whom she is extremely loyal and which serves as a surrogate family. She may be able to survive in a world that is too tough for most to comprehend. But despite all her competence, confidence, and connection, Renee will not rise above all the challenges in her life to be a positive, contributing member of society without another vital ingredient of resilience.

Character is the component that's missing for Renee. Her family members have been a passive influence in her life, perhaps because of their own struggles. Her parents didn't instill values such as responsibility to the broader community or the value of each and every life. Perhaps her school failed her and didn't allow her to grasp that she had other competencies that were far more valuable to society than those she learned on the streets. Her community failed her by not ensuring that she grew up in a safe enough environment, so survival alone had to become her core value.

Renee's connections were formed with a dangerous peer group that offered the allure of family. But these connections have been negative for the most part. Renee has not been supported by relationships with positive role models or caring relatives and community. It is these positive role models and loving relatives who would have instilled that basic sense of right and wrong—character.

Every family has its own recipe for what constitutes good character. We may prioritize these traits differently. Some families may value humility, while others more avidly nurture the ability to present oneself aggressively. Some parents' highest priority is that their children are respectful of others. Other families most highly value generosity, while others value individuality.

We can probably agree about traits that we *don't* want in our children: hatred, bigotry, self-righteousness, and insensitivity. I believe we would agree that we want children to be moral, responsible, decent, and kind. I have no right to tell you which character traits to instill in your child. Only you know what is best for your child, family, and community, but I will tell you that all parents need to be active about developing character. Children hear so many messages about what kind of people they should be. The media tell them what they should look like. Peers tell them how to behave. Teachers have one set of expectations, clergy another, coaches still another. It isn't surprising that young people are confused by all these mixed messages.

My point is that character development responds to feedback and direction. Parents want to make very certain that direction comes from them and people who they believe will help their children build strong character. In short, we cannot leave character development to chance. In Chapter 5, I addressed getting out of the way so that parents don't stifle a child's natural resilience or inhibit competency by interfering too quickly. When it comes to character development, however, parents must be active.

There is nothing purer and with greater potential than a small child, but children are also inherently selfish. They have needs and will do what it takes to get their needs met. When they resort to tantrums or pull out every play in the book to get what they want, we adults have to modify their behavior. We have to take action. We need to make them understand that cooperation is a greater value than fighting, waiting your turn is better than shoving, and talking gets better results than tossing tantrums. It's up to us to ensure that those lovable but self-centered youngsters become fine human beings capable of loving the next generation.

Challenges to Character

In our fast-paced society, we face many challenges as we try to raise young people with character. Our culture values personal success, so how do we make sure that our children are hard workers but still value kindness, cooperation, sharing, and compassion for other people? In a society that fosters winning the prize, how do we reinforce that it is how we play the game that defines us as humans? In a world in which independence is a hallmark of success, how do we convey that the finest people are those who can admit they need others to achieve contentment?

These rhetorical questions pose some of the heftiest challenges of our times. I invite you to struggle along with me here. I do know this—character development does not come in a bottle, nor will it come through a lecture. Telling kids how to act ("Be nice to your sister."), how to care ("You should be kinder to the new kid in your class."), and what to value ("Honesty is important.") is simply not enough and usually doesn't work.

Children learn character by the values you teach, your words of praise, or the way you correct them. They learn character by observing your values and behavior in daily interactions outside your home and watching how adults treat each other in your home.

While I don't have all the answers, I can offer some suggestions designed to spark conversations. They are not intended as a definitive list of everything you have to do to build character, but I hope you will use this section to trigger a conversation with other adults who care about your child's developing character. I'm taking the liberty here of listing 15 categories that my wife Celia and I have discussed in terms of raising our daughters. Please use this as a tool to make a list that works for you.

1. **Notice children's acts of kindness.** How often do we praise children for accomplishing a new task or achieving a good grade? Probably a lot. They get the most adult recognition when they produce. We also need to catch them when they are kind, generous, and thoughtful and tell them how pleased we are.
2. **Notice acts of kindness and decent behavior in others.** Think about what makes news. What do we choose to talk about around the office water cooler? What do we gossip about with our neighbors? Isn't it usually the appalling behaviors that get our attention? Children are watching and listening too, but they don't know that we edit out the normal behaviors and most of the decent deeds that people do. If we aren't careful, we expose them to a world much worse than reality. Let's begin talking to each other about the positive things our friends and neighbors do that go unnoticed—the coworker who visits her mother every day, the grandson who takes meals to his grandmother, and the block captain who makes sure there are activities for children in the neighborhood. Let's redefine our heroes and minimize our scandals, and let's do it in front of the kids.
3. **Treat each other well.** Children pay close attention to how adults treat each other. Whether their parents are married, separated, divorced, or never married, they notice how the adults around them relate to each other. The best marriages include disagreements, sometimes about parenting

styles. Divorces, of course, are likely to produce even more conflicts. While younger children may become frightened by disagreements, adolescents worry less about them and more about how they are resolved. When partners treat each other with respect, young people observe and remember. When problems are discussed and resolved honestly and openly, without hostility, children learn it's safe to voice opinions.

4. **Treat strangers well.** Children learn to value qualities like compassion when they see their parents acting compassionately toward others. No words we say to children will ever be as influential as our own demonstrated behavior and acts of kindness and understanding. For example, my wife's father, Eli Pretter, was a *mensch* (a real man) if there ever was one. At his eulogy, I retold the story that Celia says defined her childhood. On a bitingly cold winter day, a shabbily dressed man was walking along a nearly deserted road. Celia, then 6 or 7 years old, and her father were driving toward him. Celia asked her father to give the man a ride, but Eli explained that it was not safe to pick up strangers and drove past. Celia wept. Eli then turned the car around and drove the stranger to his destination. Eli later told Celia, "Sometimes, a grown man has to learn from a little girl. Thank you for being so kind." It may not have been wise to pick up that man, but I know it had a lasting effect on my wife.
5. **Reinforce the importance of including all children.** Childhood seems innocent enough, but it sometimes centers on *in*-groups and *out*-groups. Those cliques shift so frequently that they are difficult to define. Often the best way to ensure that a child is welcome in the in-group is to reject the "outs." Help your child realize the importance of other children's feelings while still maintaining his best friendships. This means knowing who is invited to parties and who is not. It also means reinforcing his acts of kindness when he befriends a less popular child. It means asking what's going on when your daughter suddenly bursts out, "Julia is weird. I don't like her anymore." It means going out of your way to enable your child to play with others who may have a physical disability and not travel as easily as others in the group. The friendships your child makes with others who have differences are likely to expose him to peers with strong character traits. Children who are physically disadvantaged are often greatly advantaged spiritually and emotionally. Having a wide variety of friends is a great asset, but it's even better when children choose friends for themselves rather than based on what others say or think. That is a priceless quality that your child will carry over into the adult world. Don't be surprised when peers your child has befriended and supported during tough times will support him when they are needed.

6. **Promote responsibility.** A key trait of resilient people is taking responsibility for their behaviors, including failures, and taking action to improve them. This important character trait will make a large difference in how a young person performs later in his work and personal life. Parents can do a great deal to teach children to accept responsibility. (This will be addressed further in Part 5.)
7. **Don't spoil your children.** How we'd love to give our children everything they want—they're so darned cute! But adults who expect everything instantly and on their terms, who feel that they're entitled to anything they desire, are not so cute. Here are some thoughts to consider.
   - Don't worry about spoiling infants when you meet their every need.
   - If children realize that some people are less fortunate, they are less likely to be demanding. It's important for children to know that they aren't the center of the world. If they are taught to take responsibility for their actions, they will understand the causes and effects of good behavior and good works. They will not feel entitled to what they have not earned.
   - Parents who listen to their children carefully and give them undivided attention are less likely to feel the compulsion to shower children with material objects or grant all their wishes.
   - Help children learn patience. If they want something, they may have to wait. This is the reason we have birthdays only once a year!
   - It is perfectly OK to explain that something costs too much money to buy.
   - Offer your child a safe home, adequate clothing, nutritious food, and lots of love. Sure, he needs some toys, but he doesn't need every toy-of-the-week. Help him develop his imagination by using old toys for new purposes or making playthings out of natural or found objects. Make your child work for special objects. Teach him that things cost money. Let him earn certain items he craves. By doing extra jobs around the house, children as young as 4 or 5 years can earn something special. Older children can do jobs that you would pay someone else to do (like painting a fence or mowing the lawn) so they grasp the clear connection that money buys things.
   - When children learn to win at parents' expense, they absorb a dangerous lesson that their needs are more important than others' needs. This is why giving in to a tantrum does children a great disservice.
   - Don't ever worry about spoiling your child with love. Love doesn't spoil children, it only makes them sweeter.

8. **Watch television and listen to music; be there when they receive unfiltered messages.** Because most children spend about as much time with media as they do in school, they may be heavily influenced by what they see and hear. They may come to believe what they see on television is normal and acceptable. Music has wonderful potential to stir or soothe emotions, but some lyrics contains violent or hateful messages. Whenever you can, try to screen the material before your child is exposed. It's not uncommon for sexist, homophobic, antireligious, or intolerant words to be inserted into songs. Adults who don't pay attention to the lyrics will not be aware of the words creeping into their children's perceptions of the world. Don't allow children to buy material you think is inappropriate. When your child gets older, he will probably reject your screening of what he listens to and watches, so be specific. If you say, "Turn that awful music down. That stuff is trash!" you are only widening the generational divide. Instead, voice your precise concerns. "Are you listening to the words? Do you hear how hateful they are toward women?" Enjoy entertainment with your children. Watch programs along with them; use fictional characters' choices and behaviors as starting points to have family discussions.
9. **Work toward a better world.** The next chapter is framed around children's contributions to the world, but what about yours? You may or may not have time to volunteer for a good cause, but certainly you have a moment to pick up trash instead of walking by it. You can give your seat to an elderly person on a bus. You can make time to call your relatives. Your children are watching and learning from you. Talk to them about the injustices in the world. You cannot fix all the problems, but you needn't remain silent either.
10. **Give charity in the name of justice.** If your child is to count his blessings, he must know that many people are less fortunate. In a world driven by accomplishment and individual success, do you want your child to be aware that he has a responsibility to others? If so, make charity a central theme of your household. The amount is not important. Younger children don't even understand the difference between a $10 and $1,000 donation. When you talk with your child about giving to charity, let him know you aren't doing it out of the goodness of your heart but because it is the right thing to do. For example, we have a tzedakah (justice) box in our house as a centerpiece in the living room. Our children have no idea what amount we give, but they know we do give. When they are feeling fortunate, they put something in the box so others might have better fortunes. As they grew older, we allowed them to help decide where our contributions were made. We narrowed our choices down, they researched the charities, and we donated to their selection.

11. **Honor plurality.** We are a nation that draws strength from our differences. Within our pluralistic society, we may feel connected to certain familiar groups—ethnic, political, or religious. We may want our children to be tightly connected to these groups because they share our values. This desire for connection should *never* be an excuse for not teaching children tolerance or for allowing prejudice. It is highly destructive to turn people who do not belong to our group into "the other." Honoring plurality means that we respect the fact that others also have strong value systems, and we remain open to rich discussions. Character develops when ideas grow and thoughts are honored, and nations are built by individuals with this strength of character.
12. **Avoid prejudice.** An unfortunate, sometimes deadly human trait is the tendency to divide into *us* and *them.* We may feel safer among those we call "us," and that's not necessarily a bad thing. It becomes worrisome, though, when people define themselves by saying they are glad they are "not them." It becomes dangerous when they need or want others to fail so that they can succeed.

    Prejudice is not always intentionally malicious and is often unconscious. Prejudgments we make based on limited information, however, come in many flavors and have some very troublesome consequences, including justification for discrimination. In the least, prejudice prevents us from getting to know each other better.

    On a summer day several years ago when I was working on the first edition of this book, my 10-year-old daughters were with me at a swimming pool. My eyes were burning from chlorine as I tried to review a book that could inform this section. Talia offered to read it to me. After a few pages, I wasn't sure she understood the meaning, so I asked her to explain it. "It's about racism," she said. I asked her what the word meant (though we have discussed it in the past). "It's when people don't like other people just because of their color." I asked her what that meant to her. "It means if I was a racist, I wouldn't be able to have some of my very good friends. That would be really sad."

    The United States is becoming more diverse by the day, and the world is becoming more connected by the hour. Children need to be raised free of prejudice if they are to thrive in this world. Prejudice rears its head in many places, often very subtly. No matter how subtle, even preschoolers pick up on the building blocks of intolerance and racism.

    Children are like sponges, absorbing ideas and attitudes from everyone around them. They notice parents' words and unspoken language. Assuming we parents do everything perfectly, we can't overlook other influences like the media, music, children's books, and our children's friends. Overtly prejudiced statements may be rare and screened by parents, but subtle messages are everywhere. If we don't want our children to be socialized by these worrisome stereotypes, we must closely examine the messages they receive and look for materials that do not contain harmful hidden stereotypes. The Anti-Defamation League book, *Hate Hurts: How Children Learn and Unlearn Prejudice,* by Caryl Stern-LaRosa and Ellen Hofheimer Bettmann, proposes an exercise to alert parents to biased messages. I draw on this exercise and add some thoughts of my own to summarize it here.

When looking at children's books, listening to their music, or considering whether they should see a movie, for example, examine how many characters are of different races and consider who are heroes and heroines and who are villains. Who's smart and capable? Who solves problems? On the other hand, who creates problems and who is unable to solve them without the help of others? Are minority characters only able to perform heroic acts because they've been helped by a white hero? Who is brave? Who is weak or scared? Who fights? Who resolves conflict? Who is successful or rich? Who are passive and unable to help themselves? Who is poor? Who are the criminals? Who leads? Who follows?

We wouldn't be honest with ourselves if we didn't acknowledge that certain minorities are portrayed more often in an unflattering, unrealistic manner. Here's my mantra again: Children live up or down to our expectations of them. Imagine you are an African American or Latino child—what would it feel like to see yourself, or an image you relate to, portrayed in this manner repeatedly? If you are raising children who are in a racial minority, point out the distorted message. Tell them with pride about what it really means to be an African American, Native American, or Latino member of this society. If you are raising a white child, point out that these messages are unfair and untrue. Talk about the fact that some groups, like Native Americans and Asian Americans, rarely appear in the media, but when they do, they are frequently cast as stereotypes. In the post-9/11 world, we need to prevent children from developing distorted images of Muslims. It's very easy for them to watch the news and pick up misconceptions of Islam. We can explain that there is a great difference between a minority of fanatical terrorists and the vast majority of Muslims who make our country stronger and richer.

Don't simply tell children that prejudiced messages are untrue; show them by exposing them to positive images of diverse groups. Multicultural books, media, dolls, and museum visits can help children understand the history and culture of other people, including the history of their painful oppression. Equally important is the opportunity to make friends with other children of diverse backgrounds.

Talk about why members of minority groups may be poor. Don't be afraid to talk about economic disparities, racism, and failing schools. If our children don't know about them, who is going to invest in fixing them? Point out that poverty and wealth come in every color and that what matters most is that we strive for a world in which everyone has enough. Mention all the wonderful contributions made to this world by people of every ethnic group and color. Make certain that children understand that we're stronger and wiser because we are diverse. Help them realize that people with different experiences, perspectives, and backgrounds challenge us to think outside of our own boxes and make us richer.

It is not just the media that molds biased images. Children hear our words and pick up our subtle body language when we become angry or apprehensive. The words we say hold great weight with them. What may seem like a casual ethnic or sexist joke to a parent can mistakenly become a child's image of that ethnicity or gender. If we travel in unsafe neighborhoods and automatically lock the car doors or become apprehensive if a shady-looking character walks into the mini-market, children will notice our unspoken biases. In certain circumstances, it may be wise and justified to become protective. Be aware that children who are not exposed to a wide variety of people may make quick judgments that sear into their subconscious and last a lifetime. I am not advising you against trusting your instincts, but I am suggesting that you discuss your anxiety with your child and make clear how targeted your action was. For example, "That man made me nervous because [for whatever specific reasons] and that's why we left the store." This will help your child understand that you did not react because of the man's race.

Prejudice and racism are not just a black-white or Latino–non-Latino issue. Harmful prejudgments are made about gender, sexual orientation, religion, ethnic groups, and every race. A group of Asian American youth shared with me how they continually deal with many people's assumptions that they are "foreign." Native Americans still face assumptions that they are "uncivilized." Girls sometimes receive messages that they are less capable at sports or math and science. Gay youth find themselves amid a culture war. The list goes on for every group. Each shares a common experience of having other people make quick, hurtful, untrue assumptions about them. All share the desire to be seen as individuals who are enriched by being members of a group that gives them strength and identity.

Many parents are deeply committed to raising children who see no difference between groups, essentially to be color-blind. When children ask about race, these parents tell them, "There's no difference; all people are the same." This is a well-intentioned answer, but it is not true. It may be correct to teach that on a spiritual level, people are the same, but here on Earth, a wide variety of differences exist between groups and individuals. That is what makes us strong. That is what makes us interesting. This is why it is so important to broaden our horizons by knowing others. Rather than raising children to be color-blind, we can raise them to respect and appreciate differences.

Not being color-blind unfortunately means becoming aware of prejudice and unfair treatment of ourselves and others. No matter how we want to make life fair in our children's world, life is not fair for everyone. Regardless of children's backgrounds, at some point in their lives, they will be treated unfairly. This will happen to some more than others. Denying this truth robs children of the tools to advocate for themselves and others. Don't wait for your child's school to teach lessons about discrimination. We need to talk about issues such as the tragedies inflicted on our indigenous nations, slavery, the Holocaust, present-day human trafficking, and other injustices. If we choose silence, our children will have to navigate this road independently, which can be harrowing and hurtful.

Remember, our children hear our silence loudly and clearly.

The struggle for every parent is how to expose children to these painful issues in a developmentally appropriate way. Too much, too soon can be harmful. Thankfully, many books are designed for children of different ages (see Resources at www.healthychildren.org/BuildingResilience).

I admit discomfort in attempting to take on as complex, volatile, and urgent a subject as prejudice and simplifying it in a few brief pages. I feel committed, however, to at least acknowledging the importance of tolerance as a crucial character trait children need to thrive in this world.

13. **Care about nature.** What child doesn't love to climb a tree or wade into a stream? Children relate easily to efforts to save the environment. They can get almost immediate satisfaction by planting tree saplings or clearing trash from a creek. Because most children love animals, they relate to saving endangered species. Getting involved with environmental efforts carries great social good. Let children know how much you care about nature and that there is only one planet where we all live, so we must preserve it.

14. **Believe in something bigger.** I wouldn't venture to tell you what to believe in, but people who believe in a higher power or the interrelatedness of humanity have something greater than themselves to turn to on a daily basis and especially in times of crisis. Your connection with a group of people with similar beliefs can ensure that your children can draw character-building lessons from many people in addition to you.
15. **Be human.** Enough already with kindness, decency, and altruism—let's get real. Every human has a full range of emotions and traits, including selfishness, impatience, anger, and greed. Our challenge is to ensure that our better selves prevail and control our unattractive, even destructive impulses. Children have the same struggles. Anyone who has ever spent time with 2- to 4-year-olds has witnessed the mighty battle between wanting things ("Mine!") and the desire to please adults who extol sharing and cooperation. We do children an injustice by pretending to be perfect. Let them know that we adults also struggle to be good people. We can give them permission to struggle themselves; this will help alleviate guilt and the catastrophic fears that they sometimes have when their all-too-human emotions surface. When we talk aloud and share how we strive to make sure our better sides prevail, even after an outburst, we model how to do the same. We remind children that the world does not come to an end when we have uncontrollable feelings.

When people have strong character, they have the ability to return to a set of core values during times of crisis, which makes them more resilient in the most trying of times. But it's about more than adaptability and recovery; children need to develop character so that we can build a society with greater attention to the planet's needs and a firmer resolve to treat each other with integrity, honesty, and fairness. We need the next generation to tell us old folks what we're doing wrong, question our decisions, and poke at our hypocrisies. Youth are our resource, and they need strong characters to make the greatest contribution.

To learn about the full offering of* Building Resilience *videos, please turn to page 327.

Grit: The Character Trait That Drives Performance

We hope that our children have a full range of character traits. Certainly, we want those moral traits described in the previous chapter so they will be the kind of people poised to lift others up and repair our world. But we also want them to have the kind of traits that will lead them to personal success—that "secret sauce" that will allow them to perform to their potential.

It had long been assumed that intelligence was the most important predictor of success. That was convenient because intelligence was something easy to measure (albeit with known biases against some marginalized groups!) and we presumably knew how to build on it with knowledge. It has become increasingly clear, thanks largely to the work of Angela Duckworth, PhD, at the University of Pennsylvania, that while intelligence is important, it may not be the primary driver of performance. Perseverance, diligence, and a commitment to hard work and practice may better predict real-world success. Dr Duckworth calls this *grit.* She describes young people with grit as those who view life as a marathon rather than a sprint. They exhibit tenacity and a passionate desire to reach a goal. They are willing to work hard in the moment and plan ahead to reach an intangible target, even at the expense of immediate gratification.

Runners can look ahead and see the finish line when they are running a sprint. They might run their heart out, but they still know precisely where they are going—the end point is clear and finite. Marathon runners can only visualize the finish line in their mind's eye as they go around curves and up and down hills. They run knowing the reward cannot be seen but exists nonetheless. Perseverance itself is the accomplishment; improvement is the reward.

Let's take this metaphor a step further. People who are going to succeed in life are those who learn to recover when they stumble. When a sprinter trips, it is disastrous. A marathoner can stumble and have plenty of time to make a full recovery.

I know that you are sitting with baited breath now waiting for the answer. If grit is such a great predictor of success, how do I get some of this for my kid? Sadly, I don't have an answer yet. I do believe, however, that the work being done by Dr Duckworth and others promises to offer answers in the not-too-distant future. Currently, they are solidifying how to measure grit and considering how it predicts success while various schools and programs are developing and testing different models of how best to reinforce and develop this essential character trait.

Because you want to raise a child poised for optimal performance now, I am going to share with you what I *think* might be effective based on existing research in other areas on what we know works to build success. Before we venture into these as-of-yet unproven suggestions, I want to offer caution. Some kids just might be naturally more gritty. The last thing in the world I want to suggest is that you can make your child gritty because it might become another thing we pressure our kids to become or add to our list to feel disappointed about. Therefore, I am going to stick to those suggestions I *know* will make your child more resilient and that *may* also increase her tenacity, diligence, and love of learning. Let me be even more direct: I believe that this movement toward developing the character of performance holds the potential to backfire if we hover over our kids and constantly repeat, "Concentrate, focus, why do you give up so easily?"

Each of the following suggestions is developed fully in other sections of this book:

- Children with the ability to delay gratification (see Chapter 34) will certainly be better able to focus on mundane tasks like studying. However, because this may be tightly linked to temperament, your influence may be minimal. Nevertheless, you can reinforce patience by helping your child learn that "better things come to those who wait." Help children learn how to save money or cook with them. Every chef learns that meals well tended to and seasoned by patience taste better than food right out of a can. Raw cookie dough might taste good, but it is not as satisfying as a warm cookie. As with almost all areas of parenting, children learn this best through modeling. Talk out loud occasionally when you choose to forgo something that would give you immediate pleasure to invest your time in something that will reap a greater reward.
- Children who love learning are undoubtedly destined for greater lifelong growth. Children grow to love learning when it is stimulating, fun, and associated with something they care about. Children have natural curiosity

and are programmed to be excited about new surroundings and adventures. Don't be annoyed when I reiterate the importance of your being a model; your curiosity and fascination will be observed. If you want your child to grow up loving reading, have her associate it at a very young age with her greatest joy, being with you and relishing your undivided attention. If you want a child fascinated by the mysteries of the universe (ie, a lover of science), take walks in the park and notice all of the layers of life in the environment. Digging for worms with your child or laying in a field and seeing animals in the clouds and then going home and learning about the science behind cloud formation makes for a child who loves learning about the mysteries of life.

- A child with resolve will long for constructive criticism, whereas other children will be defeated by it. People who can harness the energy of constructive criticism will improve their work, learn on the job, and grow to be successful. The best body of work that describes how to raise children better prepared to benefit from constructive criticism comes from Carol Dweck, PhD. In a nutshell, kids raised with unearned praise and whose parents focus on results (eg, grades, scores, goals) rather than effort or the process of learning are more likely to feel as though constructive criticism is an attack. For more details, read Chapter 7 or Dr Dweck's book, *Mindset: The New Psychology of Success*.
- Above all, children learn tenacity by learning how to recover after failure. They learn that second and third (or 17th) attempts often produce vast improvements over the first. We simply have to allow our children to learn to fail gracefully (and sometimes not so gracefully) so they also learn to recover. They need to be clear on their limitations so that they can develop their work-arounds. Many of our kids are being raised with the belief that the stakes are too high to fail. I counter that the stakes are too high for young people *not* to learn to fail in childhood and adolescence. If young people do not learn their own unevenness and the compensations that minimize that unevenness, they will be making mistakes in adulthood when the stakes sometimes really are too high.
- A little bit of adversity is good for our kids. Remember that we are raising 35-, 40-, and 50-year-olds who will not have someone to protect them later. People who learn to overcome adversity have the lifelong gift of resilience. Childhood and adolescence is the time to learn how to walk through life's puddles. So don't get out of the way entirely. You should protect your child from adversities that could compromise their safety or long-term well-being. But when a challenge will teach the lesson of failure and recovery and not have lifelong scars, we should get out of the way. Your child usually

has the capability to right himself; your trust in his ability to do so will send an immeasurable message of confidence in his own abilities. That, in turn, will give him the confidence to trust that setbacks are temporary when effort is applied and trust is given to one's own ability to recover.

Building Resilience Videos (www.healthychildren.org/BuildingResilience)

Video 5.2	The Toughest of Balancing Acts: How Do We Protect Our Children AND Let Them Learn Life's Lessons?
Video 7.1	Using Praise Appropriately: The Key to Raising Children With a Growth Mind-set
Video 25.1	Grit: A Character Trait Linked to Success

To learn about the full offering of* Building Resilience *videos, please turn to page 327.

Contribution

Confident young people who recognize their competencies, feel connected to people, and have strongly rooted character are poised to contribute to the world. Contribution may flow from the other Cs, but those who take active steps to contribute will gain experiences that prepare them to thrive. Parents and communities who ensure ample opportunities for children to contribute will build the next generation of leaders.

When young people work to improve their communities, they develop a meaningful sense of purpose. They receive positive feedback that protects them from negative messages about youth. They hear from numerous people besides their parents, "I think you are wonderful," and absorb the important belief, "I have high expectations for you." They are surrounded by thank-yous rather than condemnation. Because kids live up or down to expectations set for them, these thank-yous can be highly protective.

My wife and I wanted to teach our daughters from a very early age that contributing to others is an important value. We wanted them to know that the world could be a better place because they are in it, so our girls began contributing as pass-around babies at a nursing home when they were 3 months old. They don't remember how their smiles brightened the days of elderly residents, but that experience was the beginning of many volunteer efforts.

When they saw famished children on the front page of a newspaper and asked about it, I gave them an explanation tailored to 4-year-olds: "They don't have enough food." My girls asked, "Can we send food?" I told them how difficult that was, but we could send money. At their prompting, I then spent $40 and an entire day building a lemonade stand (and building is not one of my competencies!) so they could earn $3.75. Of course it was worth it! The girls felt their efforts mattered and they could make a difference for a hungry child on the other side of the globe.

Throughout childhood, they continued to explore ways to repair the world. Sure, they knew it pleased me, but it seemed to bubble up from within them and was continuously reinforced by feedback from neighbors who viewed them as idealists. When times are difficult for them, I trust they'll be soothed by knowing they can immerse themselves in a project that demonstrates how important and valued they are.

They still care deeply about the world, but their contribution has changed now that they are teens. They are role models to many of our neighborhood's younger children. They are the athletic girls whose attention is valued and whose values are noticed. They are sought-after babysitters. They consistently receive messages that the children are watching them and parents are pleased with the model of teens they portray. I also know that neighborhood parents noticing my daughters adds an extra layer of protection for them. Perhaps most importantly, because they have been held as good examples, they are less likely to adopt behaviors not befitting role models.

Seeing Beyond Themselves

Contemporary culture is so focused on material things like electronic equipment, expensive shoes and clothes, cosmetics, and cars that children can naturally get swept up in this tide. To counter this influence or put it in perspective, parents can support opportunities for children to give rather than receive. Children will learn that the universe doesn't revolve around them or owe them everything they desire. When they raise money for earthquake relief, collect recyclables, or tutor younger children, they gain a more realistic perspective of the world and their places in it. They begin to see beyond their isolated, self-oriented circles. They recognize themselves as part of larger communities in which they can make a difference.

Children can contribute to society in a multitude of ways—collecting coins to feed the hungry, cleaning up the environment, volunteering with children who have disabilities, and even simple, spontaneous acts of kindness such as holding open heavy doors for a parent pushing a baby stroller.

Contribution directly fosters resilience because it helps children gain a sense of purpose, something positive to strive toward and achieve. When I met with young people at Barrington High School in Illinois, I learned that Ray Piagentini, a guidance counselor, had been taking students on a service project for the last 25 years to the Crow Creek Reservation, very near the Cheyenne River Reservation in South Dakota that had so powerfully influenced my perspective on the inherent strength of people. The students and I spent 2 hours after school talking about the meaning of serving others and the lessons they absorbed about the resilience of the human spirit. They learned that although they went to serve, they received so much more than they ever gave. They understood that experience was the greatest teacher and that they could learn life's most valued lessons by listening to those who shared their stories. They learned that even challenged communities with a strong connection to their culture could find most solutions from within their own timeless wisdom. And they gained a deep respect for people from a different culture and knew that this lesson in diversity would serve them throughout their lives. These young people, who were not even sure why they were drawn to this service project, felt that it would flavor their perspectives forever. They wanted to be active participants in efforts to repair the world.

I came to Barrington to inspire youth and left the one inspired.

Contribution is interwoven with competence, confidence, connection, and character as an integral thread in the web of resilience. Let's take a quick look at how contribution ties into the other components of resilience.

Competence. Children who actively participate in volunteer activities develop new competencies. They discover new interests and talents they may not know they have. If a project involves raising money for a good cause, for example, kids learn that they are capable of knocking on doors, talking to adults in a polite and convincing way, counting up their collection, and sending it in. They learn individual skills such as organization and responsibility, as well as the bigger lesson—they have accomplished something meaningful. They gain a solid sense of their own abilities and worth.

Confidence. When children carry out these efforts, they become more confident because they have demonstrated their abilities. They can see actual results: a collection of dollars or canned goods, applause from grateful nursing home residents, stacks of sandwiches made for a homeless shelter, or bags of garbage cleaned up from a polluted creek. When young people contribute and make a difference in the world or others' lives, they usually get positive feedback for their efforts, which further adds to their confidence and resilience.

Children who contribute to worthy causes not only gain confidence, but they also avoid problems. The Minneapolis, MN–based Search Institute, a nonprofit organization whose aim is to promote healthy children, youth, and communities, has reported that children and teens who volunteer just 1 hour a week are 50% less likely to abuse drugs and alcohol, smoke cigarettes, or engage in harmful behaviors. Of course, this may mean that the type of children who volunteer are not as likely to do drugs in the first place, but who cares? Don't we want our children to be that type of person?

Connection. Contribution also helps young people forge connections with their neighborhoods, schools, and world. From participating in service projects, children can see beyond their near horizons and recognize their place in the human family and on our common planet. The more strongly they feel connected, the more resilient they become. They come to appreciate their blessings and learn to give something back. They will also learn that giving and receiving, sharing during times of plenty, and asking for help during difficult times are normal, healthy things for humans to do. We want our children to know that just as they give, they will receive if misfortune hits. This is a vital lesson if they are to be resilient in the face of an unforeseen tragedy.

When looking for volunteer opportunities, talk with children about their interests and try to match them with appropriate resources. Don't do all this for them, but guide them along. Encourage them to ask at school or a local library where they can find volunteer openings. If children are interested in animals, for example, they might look for local animal or bird sanctuaries.

When children become involved in volunteer activities, they will likely work with adults who are good role models. As they work alongside adults who contribute to worthwhile causes, children not only learn specific skills but also connect with adults who are working to make a difference, and that will have a lasting positive influence on your children.

Character. Contribution strengthens character because it develops desirable traits such as responsibility, generosity, and caring. Youth learn responsibility when they know others are depending on them; they have to show up on time and do their part. The positive feedback they receive for their efforts and their own sense of accomplishment also enhance character. The more their generosity and caring are acknowledged, the more generous and caring they are likely to become.

Contribution is a 2-way street. When kids raise funds for cancer research or collect books for disadvantaged children, they not only give something, but they also get something. They realize that they have purpose and value, and the world is better because they are in it. We need to remember, too, that we adults *need* young people to contribute. They are our greatest resource for the future; our survival is tied to their contributions.

Words of Caution

Parents, scout leaders, teachers, and other adults sometimes take over youngsters' volunteer projects. We adults can be supportive from the sidelines, but children should choose and carry out these activities as independently as possible. Nothing discourages their efforts more than an adult who steps in and says, "Let me do that for you," when children can do it themselves. Even if they don't run the project as efficiently as they might with adult help, let them do it and learn from their experiences.

Contribution builds children's life résumés. It should not be encouraged primarily to have another asset on their college applications or impress scholarship committees. It should feel like a wonderful thing to do that also happens to build a résumé.

Some organizations offer cash prizes or scholarships to children who have made outstanding contributions to their communities or have demonstrated selfless acts of kindness. Those are wonderful rewards, but children shouldn't be encouraged to volunteer predominantly in the hope of winning a scholarship or prize. They should be encouraged and supported because it is a worthy thing to do.

Beyond Charitable Deeds

Contribution isn't only about good deeds and noble actions. Young people also need to know that they can contribute ideas that will be taken seriously and respected. When adults invite children and teens' opinions, especially about matters that concern them, we increase their sense of control, which in turn enhances their resilience. For example, when planning a neighborhood playground, who knows better what type of equipment to install than the children who will use it? Who knows better what it would take to keep youth away from drugs than the kids living in that community? As adults are designing programs, they'll find that the best ideas usually come from the young consumers themselves. As a qualitative researcher, I have found adolescents consistently arrive at wise answers that adults never would have considered.

In terms of our individual families, we can include children in family meetings and really listen to their ideas about how to resolve conflict and what kinds of specific supports or actions they need from us to help them reach their goals. When their ideas are heard and respected, kids learn skills, gain confidence, and come to understand that they can contribute to the well-being of themselves and their families—all immeasurable gifts.

Speaking of family contribution, children can also contribute to families by doing their fair share of chores. The word *chores* may have an unpleasant ring from your own childhood. You may remember your parents nagging you to take out the garbage or mow the lawn. Today's families don't delegate many chores to children because we have so many labor-saving devices or because some parents believe kids should spend their limited time on homework. Chores do have a place in developing several ingredients of resilience. They teach children that they are an integral part of the family and are expected to contribute to it. Chores also develop skills and responsibility that translate into new competencies.

Very young children can be given simple chores, such as collecting their toys and putting them in baskets when they finish playing. Preschoolers can learn to put dirty clothes in a hamper and carry their dishes to the sink. As children grow, chores should reflect more responsibility around the house. To make chores more tolerable, make sure that your child understands the steps required. Rather than saying, "It's your job to take care of the cat," give clear, specific instructions: "Pour out the dry food, empty the litter box." If your child is old enough to read, written descriptions of chores and a schedule to check off when she completes them will help avoid excuses. ("I didn't know that was my job. I thought it was Kayla's turn.") Many children love to check sheets or stick stars on charts because they show visible proof of all they've accomplished.

Be flexible and don't expect perfection. So your child missed some fingerprints when she sponged off the door frames—don't grab the sponge from her hands and do the job over again. This only deflates her confidence and doesn't enable her to become increasingly competent as she improves her skills.

Don't delegate chores that are too daunting. Try to make them fit each child's age, ability, and time. If it's exam week, for example, be flexible enough to say, "I know you're really studying hard this week, so I'll do that one for you today." Statements and generous gestures like this will model cooperation. The next time you're extremely busy, she may offer to help you!

Doing chores along with your child also promotes connection. Washing the car together can be a fun family activity, as can watering the garden, raking leaves, or shoveling snow. Even daily duties like walking the dog can be opportunities for togetherness. Rather than handing your daughter the dog's leash and sending her out the door, go along with her. It's a chance for both of you to get some exercise as well as talk and listen to each other.

A special note about chores: Don't take your child's efforts for granted. When she completes her chores, acknowledge that fact and express your appreciation. Gratitude is a powerful connection and confidence booster.

Resilience in Times of Great Need

The ultimate act of resilience is to turn to another human being in times of extreme need and say, "Brother (or sister), I need a hand." This is never easy, but it may be necessary. We want children to become adults who can seek help without shame. If they have the experience of service, they will have learned a vital life lesson: It feels good to give; it is deeply rewarding to help other human beings. People who contribute to others' well-being don't feel burdened or put upon; they feel honored, even blessed, to have been in the right place at the right time, perhaps with the right training. They often get more than they give. People with this experience can turn to others more freely because they're equipped with the understanding that the person guiding them through troubled times is there because she wants to be there, not out of pity. Kids deserve to learn this lesson through the opportunity of making a real contribution to another person's life. They will learn there is no shame in reaching out, only a moment of genuine humanity.

To learn about the full offering of* **Building Resilience** *videos, please turn to page 327.

PART 4

Coping

Getting a Grip on Stress

Resilience requires a wide repertoire of skills to cope with stress and challenge. Here's the bottom line: Life is stressful, so we need to prepare children to handle it effectively. They need to become competent at *coping* if they are to be resilient.

While we'd like to think that childhood is idyllic, children are not shielded from stress. They worry about school, their peers, the future, their identity, and their appearance. They want to please us, and sometimes they worry about us. They sense parents' stress even when they're very young. When we seem unnerved, they feel anxious. Older children worry about things beyond their immediate circles that we may presume they don't notice—war, violence, even the economy. They don't have the benefit of having lived through cycles of such events and haven't adopted the "this too shall pass" protective beliefs that adults use to move on.

How Do I Know if My Child Is Too Stressed, and What Do I Do?

Stress makes us terribly uncomfortable. We feel nervous, unsafe, insecure, and ungrounded. We can't think clearly. We become restless, lose sleep, become tired, and maybe get headaches. Our muscles ache, our bellies feel bloated, and our hearts throb. We grow irritable, less patient, and much less understanding of others.

Kids experience many of the same feelings but usually don't understand the connections between how underlying stress drives their moodiness or irritability. That's why parents need to consider whether their child's moods, isolation, tantrums, hostility, or even rage may be signs of stress or even depression. This can be difficult because it's normal for children to have occasional tantrums and for teenagers to be moody.

Children's bodies can accumulate stress just as adult bodies do. Frequent patterns of headache, belly pain, and fatigue tend to point to the possibility that stress is driving those uncomfortable feelings. This is especially true when there is no medical explanation. Tell your pediatrician if you've noticed that physical symptoms seem to be tied to stressful events. The health professional will still consider medical concerns but will be better able to get to the bottom of stress-related symptoms. (See Chapter 39.)

Many stress-reduction strategies offered in this book can be useful in helping children and teens manage existing stress. These strategies are also designed to be preventive. We hope that children who are well equipped to deal with stress will experience less of it in the first place. If you're worried about your child's ability to cope or just know that she has been under recent stress, please use your child's teacher, counselor, pediatrician, or clergy to help you decide the level of support your child needs.

Dealing With Stress

We all hate discomfort, whether it's emotional or physical. To avoid it, we figure out some way to make ourselves feel comfortable again. Anything that will banish those disquieting feelings will make us feel more settled, at least for the moment.

We have positive and negative ways of coping. It's not that positive ways always work and negative ones always fail. On the contrary, some negative ways offer immediate relief. The difference is that positive coping strategies enhance well-being and ultimately lead to at least partial relief. Negative strategies might offer quick relief, but they end up causing harm to the individual or community and ultimately perpetuate and intensify the cycle of stress.

Virtually all the behaviors we fear in children and teenagers are misguided attempts to diminish their stress. Procrastination, feigned laziness, and boredom are methods of dealing with school-related stress. They temporarily push stress out of sight and mind for a while. Bullying, smoking, drugs, gangs, sex, disordered eating, and self-mutilation are also efforts to deal with stress. Our challenge is to raise children who have a variety of positive coping strategies that will enhance their strengths (see diagram on page 196). We may have our greatest effect in helping children and teens avoid dangerous behaviors by equipping them with a wide range of alternative, effective, and safe coping strategies.

Unfortunately, I can't guarantee that your child will never try a worrisome behavior, even if he is emotionally intelligent and equipped with good coping strategies, because some of those feared behaviors are fun or feel good. A young teen may try drugs to test his limits, rebel, or have fun with friends. We hope he will move beyond this phase quickly. But a young person who seeks solace through drugs, who uses an altered state of consciousness to mask his feelings, may be destined for addiction. Children with safer, healthier means of coping with stress don't need to blur their consciousness with drugs.

Coping Styles

Everyone has an individual style in response to challenge. Research has looked at what styles help different people cope most effectively. Some people cope by tackling a problem head-on and trying to fix it. Others focus more on the emotions those problems create; they tend to do what makes them feel better to decrease their discomfort. Both styles, *problem-focused* and *emotion-focused,* are active styles that attempt to engage the problem. Some people choose to avoid the problem through *denial* or *withdrawal.*

People who choose to engage a problem actively tend to choose 1 of 2 approaches—they try to change the stressor itself to make themselves feel more comfortable, or they change themselves just enough to adapt to the stressor.

Children have the same styles, though they may not be aware of them. Ruby feels overwhelmed by homework. She uses a problem-focused strategy when she breaks her assignments into segments she can handle one at a time. When Amit's friends challenge him to smoke cigarettes and he talks with his best friend about why he doesn't want to smoke, he attacks the problem.

Some children who use emotion-focused strategies want to escape stressful feelings and may choose to deny the problem exists. What works for them? Drinking beer to cloud their awareness of the problem or bullying others to feel in control may make them feel better in the short term. But not all emotion-focused styles are negative. Many can be positive if they help deal with feelings in ways that are healthy, like exercise or meditation, or release pent-up stress, like journaling, crying, or laughing (see Chapter 30).

Stress and Coping Styles

As we think about dealing with challenges, a fundamental decision must be made: How much am I willing to change? Sometimes we try to change the environment. For example, if Amit's conversation with his friend Kyle ended with Kyle's decision not to smoke, Amit would have created a more problem-free environment. It would be less stressful because he could hang out with at least one friend who also doesn't smoke. He has changed his environment without compromising. But suppose Kyle convinced Amit to "just try one"

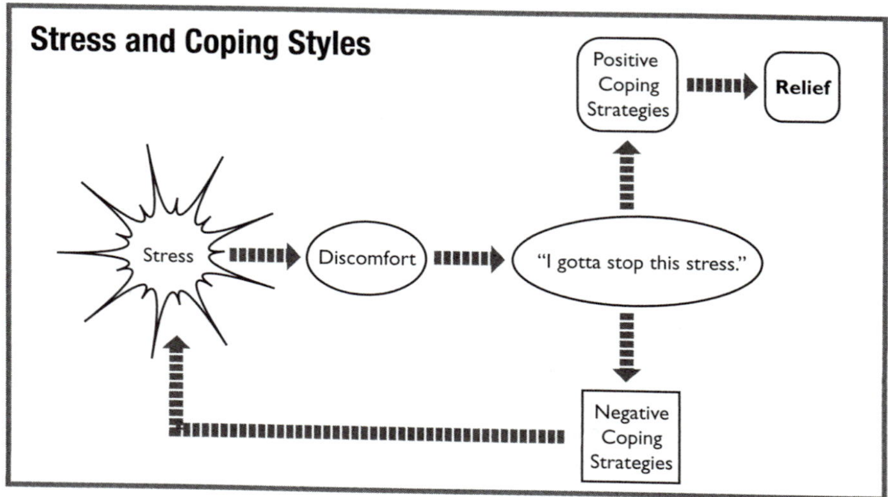

cigarette. He may decide that the best way of managing his stress is to smoke just a little, just to get Kyle off his back. As parents, we fear where this is leading, but it's worth recognizing that some compromise may be the wisest decision in certain situations.

The strategies discussed so far engage the problem or the child's reaction to the problem. Other coping strategies do not engage at all. Younger children often use denial or avoidance. They don't notice the problem because their cognitive abilities are limited or they find it safest to enter a fantasy world. Fantasy is fun, but when it's used as a response to a stressful problem, it may be a route to denial. Older children and adults also use denial to convince themselves and others that no problem exists. (How many times do we hear, "No problem"?) Sometimes we're aware of a problem and aren't truly in denial, but we choose to play down its significance or withdraw from the people who cause our discomfort. In the worst-case scenario, withdrawal can lead to isolation or depression. Substance use can also be included among avoidance or disengagement strategies because users withdraw from reality.

A word about denial and withdrawal: It would be a mistake to believe that we *should* rise to every challenge and face it head-on. Certainly, long-term avoidance of a situation will never overcome the obstacle. But sometimes a problem is so overwhelming or frightening that it is temporarily wise to say, "I really don't care; it doesn't bother me." I have learned time and again from patients who have every reason to be furious at their circumstances that they take the position of not caring because it is all they can handle. Don't push kids to show they care just because we know they ought to care. Give them time and space and allow for the skills to be developed that will enable them to react appropriately.

Although it's a mistake to state with certainty how anyone *should* cope, it is generally agreed that people who engage a problem do better than those who deny or withdraw from it. Those who use problem-focused coping strategies to address stressors, rather than the uncomfortable emotions they produce, usually fare better because the problem's intensity is reduced. When only emotions are dealt with, the problem remains to strike again. But positively oriented emotion-focused strategies are also useful because they help us feel better in the short term and may foster interpersonal connections as we seek support.

Resilient children are able to address problems competently *and* manage the physical and emotional discomfort that stress creates. They also need to feel comfortable withdrawing from or avoiding problems so they can conserve energy to address those problems they are prepared to change or solve. The challenge is to raise a child with effective problem-focused coping strategies, healthy emotion-focused strategies, and safe, thoughtful avoidance strategies.

Changing Coping Skills as Your Child Grows

A growing body of research explores which coping strategies work best in varied situations for children at different developmental levels. The findings are beyond the scope of this chapter, but I want to emphasize that coping skills change over time. It would be a mistake to think that a 3-year-old requires the same approach as an older child or adolescent.

Even infants experience stress and have their own strategies to address it. They cry to get an adult to meet their needs. Then they calm as they suckle. An adult's presence is enough to return them to a lulled calm. This is also true for small children who can calm themselves with a snuggle and draw their sense of security and normalcy from parents. Other children carry a security blanket or toy everywhere to comfort them with something familiar in a world full of unfamiliar objects and strangers. Preschool children begin to develop fantasies to soothe upsetting emotions and reassure themselves. Think about how many fables and fairy tales involve vulnerable children being rescued by a superhero or fantasy figure.

Another common coping strategy for young children is avoidance—don't see it, run away from it, and the problem ceases to exist. As children reach school age, they begin to grasp how stress affects their emotions and become better able to begin calming those emotions. They start to problem-solve and take active steps to address their concerns as they get older. They learn to relax without thinking about a fantasy figure to solve their problems. They may reassure themselves that parents will become available if they are not present at the moment. They learn to reframe situations and soothe their emotions by reassuring themselves with positive self-talk. As children approach adolescence, their coping strategies become increasingly sophisticated.

My point here is not to make you obsess about which strategies your child uses at different ages but help you realize that your child's repertoire evolves over time. If you deliberately or actively focus on coping with a younger child, you may only add to his worries by making him wonder whether he is doing a good-enough job in dealing with his fears. Focus your energies instead on modeling appropriate coping strategies. Help preschool-aged and older children know that most of their worries represent a problem, and they can take steps to address that problem. Expose them to the kind of things they'll be able to draw from later as they widen their repertoire. Adolescents, in particular, need to see you make wise coping decisions. They will reject your words if they feel hypocritical.

To learn about the full offering of* Building Resilience *videos, please turn to page 327.

Taking Action

Getting Into the Right Mind-set

Before we discuss specific coping strategies, it's important to first think about how much weight we give to a stressor. Sometimes stress comes from a real and present danger, in which case we should mount a full response. But in most cases, how stressed we are has a lot to do with our perception. There is no better coping strategy than using our thinking skills (see Chapter 9) to accurately assess a stressor and, when appropriate, to downplay its meaning in our lives.

Whenever a challenge arises, we can learn to ask ourselves 3 questions to help us use the appropriate lens.

1. **Is this a real tiger or a paper tiger?**
   Recall that we are designed to be able to flee ferocious carnivores. Our stress responses instantly transform our bodies into fight-or-flight mode. In this survival mode, there is little room for rational discourse or focused study. You are not supposed to say to the tiger, "You seem rather upset, but is there any way we can work this out? I really have to focus on my trigonometry homework right now." This means that people cannot solve problems in crisis mode. Because so few adversities really represent imminent danger, it's an imperative first step to calm your thinking by reminding yourself, "I am not under attack."
2. **How will I feel about this thing that is bothering me so much right now next week? Or tomorrow? Or next year?**
   My grandmother, Belle Moore, prepared me to reassure myself with the inwardly spoken words, "This too shall pass." She said that no matter how much something was hurting in the moment, it was always going to feel better with the passage of time. Martin E.P. Seligman, PhD, in *The Optimistic Child,* mirrors this point when he writes about the adaptive benefit of viewing problems as temporary and surmountable.

3. **Is this good situation permanent?**
   Sometimes we become anxious or worried even when, or especially when, good things happen to us. Will we lose this opportunity? Did we never deserve it in the first place? Does this luck seem out of the ordinary? Will it be fleeting? Stop! This is a perfect time to catch those self-defeating thoughts and just appreciate the good fortune. Perhaps you earned it.

A 10-Part Stress Reduction Plan

I have met remarkable young people who've thrived despite enormous stresses. I've asked how they have managed to survive and succeed. By synthesizing their wisdom with the scientific literature on effective coping, I have developed a 10-part stress-reduction plan. It is not a 10-step plan; there is no designated order. It offers a repertoire to draw from at appropriate times. For example, some strategies involve thinking, but during times of extreme stress, it makes more sense to work out the stress through exercise before even attempting to resolve an issue with thought.

These 10 parts will be addressed in chapters 28, 29, and 30. Here's a preview.

1. Identify and then address the problem.
2. Avoid stress when possible.
3. Let some things go.
4. Contribute to the world.
5. The power of exercise.
6. Active relaxation.
7. Eat well.
8. Sleep well.
9. Take instant vacations.
10. Release emotional tension.

Each of the points includes a variety of activities and actions to handle stress. The goal is to offer as wide a range of useful coping strategies as possible. While this plan is quite comprehensive, no one should expect to use all the techniques. Pick an item or two from each category to see which ones fit best. For example, the creative arts offer vital outlets for expression, but not everyone needs to excel at art, music, dance, and photography. As you tailor a stress-reduction plan, keep in mind that approaches can change over time. I'm trying to say gently, "Don't stress about the stress plan." It has too many ideas for anyone to do them all. It has to be individualized and fluid, changing with a child's development and circumstances.

You'll notice that nothing in this plan specifically addresses childhood. The plan can help adults and children cope with a stressful world, which brings up an essential point: Parents who use and actively model this approach not only help themselves reduce stress, but they also influence their children far more effectively than any words they say.

Even the youngest children pick up ambivalent messages. They know the difference between what parents say and what they actually do. Adolescents pounce on hypocrisy, point it out mercilessly, and use it to explain why parents shouldn't have the authority to set rules of behavior. So if we don't want our children to use negative strategies to cope with stress, such as fighting, smoking, or using drugs, we have to use healthy strategies ourselves. We can't model problem-solving if we take a nap to avoid our discomfort each time we get stressed. We can't tell kids it's good to talk about their feelings if we bottle up our own emotions. We can't teach the danger of drugs while using alcohol to treat those emotions.

I want to give you a prescription to take care of yourself. Don't think it's selfish to have a hobby, take time to relax, or have creative outlets. When you take care of yourself, you show your children how to be emotionally healthier. You are the model they will follow as they learn to manage stress. Role modeling is most effective when you talk aloud about what you're doing. Some of the following self-talk suggestions give you a glimpse of ideas in the stress-reduction plan:

"This is a gigantic work assignment to finish in just a week. I'm going to break it down into smaller parts that I can handle." Then later say, "I feel so much better. I really got a lot done."

"I'm so stressed out. I'm going for a run. That always makes me feel better."

"I really need to clear my head. I'm going to take some deep breaths and imagine I'm on that beautiful beach we visited last summer."

"I really need a few minutes to myself after the day I've had. I'm going to soak in the bathtub for a half hour."

"I'm so angry I can't think straight. If I make a decision now about how to deal with your behavior, you won't like it. Right now I need some time to cool off. I'm going for a long walk to relax. Then we'll deal with this problem."

"I had such a hard time today. Come and give me hugs. I always feel better when I'm with people I love."

"I need to figure out how to handle this situation with the neighbors. I'm going to call Aunt Mattie. Just talking makes me calmer, and sometimes she helps me find a totally different way of looking at things."

"I'm not even going near that casino. Just being near it makes me want to spend money. If I'm not there, I don't miss it at all."

"You know, I feel awful today. I ate junk food instead of lunch, and I always feel like I have no energy after that."

"I'm exhausted. I sleep so much better whenever I relax before bed or at least make a list of things I have to do the next day so they don't keep spinning in my head."

Before we plunge into the details of the stress-management plan, I want to make some suggestions about how to use it. At first it may seem that this set of strategies is a résumé for life. In fact, if children learn some of these techniques, they will build a balanced résumé that prepares them for college and adulthood. As you guide children in developing these approaches, here are the basic points to remember.

- When you choose strategies from this plan, select those you think will work for your child, not those that will impress someone else. For example, if you focus on the musical expression part of the plan because your child loves playing the guitar, just let her play the guitar; don't make her take bassoon lessons because you think that will impress a college admissions committee.
- The plan cannot be imposed on a child; it has to be welcomed to be effective. If your child doesn't take to one strategy, try another.
- Don't feel that your child must be exposed to everything in the plan to cope with stress successfully.

As children learn to manage stress, they need to find that fine balance between living in the moment and working for the future. One strategy is to enjoy the little pleasures surrounding us, but it's difficult to do if we are always thinking about it. So as you guide your child through these wide choices of coping strategies, take it casually. Let your child's individualized plan develop over time, and don't worry about every detail. Enjoy your child and your life right now. By your actions and attitudes, you'll be modeling a far more effective approach than any written plan. Keep in mind that children at different developmental levels naturally need different coping strategies. Don't expect a 3-year-old to problem-solve. At that age, escaping through fantasy (perhaps by acting out a situation with action figures, dolls, or puppets) is normal and healthy.

Chapter 42 is designed for tweens and teens to build their own coping strategy. Children younger than 10 years will need more direct guidance from adults. I encourage you to share this plan with as many young people as you can reach. You can also find it at www.fosteringresilience.com and on this book's Web site at www.healthychildren.org/BuildingResilience. The plans in Chapter 42 and on the Web, however, do not offer the detailed explanation that this chapter does. The remainder of this chapter and the following 2 chapters are intended for parents or child professionals as a guide for helping children learn to manage stress. Many of the techniques are explained so that you will be able to follow them yourself, so you can be a role model, and because you too deserve to be healthy.

Connection: Critical to Coping

Before we start with the 10-part plan, it is essential to underscore that perhaps the most important element of coping has already been discussed thoroughly: connection. In the worst of times, those who survive are those who reach out to others. In routine times, those who thrive are those with rich relationships. Connections are discussed a bit in the emotion-focused elements of the plan but must be placed front and center here. As in all other aspects of coping, you do your child or teen tremendous lifelong service by modeling how your connections to others are central to your ability to manage stress and, generally, to a meaningful existence.

1. Identify and Then Address the Problem.

Problem-solving is the most effective way to begin coping with stress. Any effective approach to managing stress begins by identifying the concern and determining what can be done to solve it. Without this attack-the-problem-first strategy, we chase our tail.

Two important steps are necessary to problem-solving. The first is to make a realistic assessment of the magnitude of the problem; the second is to break it into manageable steps.

It's inefficient to tackle problems until we first remove the barriers of anxiety, fear, and frustration that get in the way of solving them. As a starting point, learn to assess a situation realistically. We may be able to teach children to be problem-solvers, but those lessons are useless if kids cannot manage the emotions and discomfort caused by stress. Clear thought and steady nerves are required to assess and solve most problems. The aforementioned 3 questions can be a starting point to clear our minds. Sometimes exercise or relaxation techniques can help to regain our rational thought and allow us to downgrade situations from crises to manageable events.

A problem sometimes feels so overwhelming that until a young person thinks differently about it, she can't possibly begin to deal with it. She is paralyzed by anxiety or catastrophic thoughts and can't imagine any strategy will work. The thinking clearly skills discussed in Chapter 9, drawn from the work of Karen Reivich, PhD, and Dr Seligman, help manage emotional responses by reframing catastrophic thoughts into more realistic appraisals. These cognitive strategies help young people calm themselves and use their intellectual abilities to solve problems. Some children may experience so much anxiety that professional guidance is needed to help them clearly differentiate real tragedies from those manageable bumps in the road. Even if you determine your child's starting point should be to seek professional guidance to teach her to rethink how she interprets stressful events, the other coping strategies offered in this plan will likely still be helpful.

Once someone has a realistic appraisal of the problem and whether it poses a real immediate danger or one that just needs to be addressed, the next step is to break it into manageable pieces. As long as we visualize a problem as huge, it will overwhelm us. If we view it as a mountain, we cannot imagine navigating around it and certainly cannot imagine scaling it. On the other hand, if we understand that a mountain is really just a series of hills piled on top of each other, it feels less foreboding. If we imagine climbing the hills one at a time, the top of the mountain feels reachable.

The way we transform figurative mountains into manageable hills is by breaking problems into their component parts. This includes creating lists and timelines to make work manageable. It also includes looking at an overwhelming social problem and considering which inroads will solve it. For example, when a 13-year-old girl has been rejected by her friends, she may become emotionally overwhelmed and never imagine having another friend again, let alone reconnecting with this group. If she can get past her catastrophic thoughts, she might be able to think the problem through and realize that one of the friends may be able to create an avenue for her to reconnect with the others. As we tackle each step, it becomes easier to take on the next.

It becomes easier to move the hills when we have the figurative shovels (or skills) to move the dirt. If the problem feels catastrophic, turn first to the skills taught in Chapter 9 on thinking clearly. If the problem is homework, the shovels are confidence, knowledge, academic preparation, and an organizational plan. If the problem is social, the shovels are emotional and social intelligence coupled with some of the peer navigation strategies discussed in Chapter 13. If the problem creates emotional pain, even to the point that one feels incapable of feeling the pain for fear of opening Pandora's box, the shovels are strategies to safely release emotions (as will be discussed in Chapter 30).

2. Avoid Stress When Possible.

We can avoid negative situations to reduce stress. This technique involves a little analysis. What brings you down? What makes you tense or upset? What always gets to you?

I teach my patients to think about which situations have gotten them in trouble in the past, then pay attention to the subtle signals their bodies send out to warn of a similar potential problem. If they learn to pay attention to those sensations (like butterflies, anxiety, and heart racing), they can recognize what might get them into trouble before they actually find themselves in a crisis.

The answer to "What brings you down or always gets to you?" can usually be found in 3 categories: people, places, and things. If we teach kids to identify the people who frustrate or bother them, places where stress usually rises, and things that provoke or intensify stress, they can learn when and how to avoid those stressors. They cannot always avoid them, of course. If a child must sit next to an annoying classmate and the teacher refuses to change the seating arrangement, the child can't completely avoid the people (in this case, the classmate) or place (the classroom). But the simple act of identifying the situation helps children recognize potential stress so they can try to ignore the pesky classmate. In other cases, they can avoid negativity by going to the mall at a different time than the friends who dumped them last week. If scary stories or movies make children nervous, they can learn to choose more upbeat books or movies.

For teenagers, the key to staying out of trouble is recognizing which people, places, and things have brought them down in the past and are likely to pull them down again. People, places, and things are a central theme in many recovery programs. The concept is used to prepare people with addictions to return home. To succeed, they must learn to stay as far away as possible from the triggers of their old behavior and the forces that pressure them to relive old habits. It's particularly important to avoid friends with whom kids have shared bad habits. Those friends have a great deal invested in making sure that others don't rise above them.

Marc, for example, used to get high with friends Andrew, Jorge, and Jacob. Marc found his life seriously affected by drugs. His grades plunged and he had a near-death experience. He realized that he had no choice but to quit drugs. Jorge, his pal since kindergarten, also wanted to stop clouding his own mind and supported Marc's decision. But Andrew and Jacob weren't ready to quit. Every time they thought about quitting, they pushed the thought away. Facing their own stress was too overwhelming. "Everybody does it," they told themselves. "This is just what you gotta do to survive." When Marc found the motivation to quit, their fallacy of "everybody does it" fell apart. They became motivated to find ways to ensure Marc's recovery failed—to pull him back down again—which allowed them to avoid guilt and their own demons. People, places, and things—kids who understand the negative influences in their lives are prepared to avoid sources of stress and move beyond negative behaviors. Marc and Jorge learned they had to stop hanging out with Andrew and Jacob.

Why wait for a problem? The old adage, "The strongest person is the one who does not need to fight," applies here. It is much easier to avoid problems from a distance than up close. Teach your child that many problems do not have to be confronted—they are best managed by avoiding them in the first place.

3. Let Some Things Go.

Not every problem is worth attacking. Some problems may upset us but are of no real consequence. Problems (like bad weather) may bother us, but we are powerless to change them—that game we were looking forward to is simply rained out. To conserve our energy for the things we can change, we need to learn to let go of problems we can't fix. It's important for parents to model for children that we sometimes advocate strongly for change but at other times, we just need to move on.

Not every problem can be tackled. Even though we want to raise children with that "I can handle it" attitude, it's important to have the ability to realistically assess a situation to see whether it should be handled or if the better way to go is to conserve your energy for an issue you can handle. This idea is best summarized with the well-known Serenity Prayer.

God grant me the serenity
to accept the things I cannot change;
the courage to change the things I can;
and the wisdom to know the difference.

4. Contribute to the World.

Chapter 26 is devoted to the importance of contribution as one of the critical 7 Cs of resilience. It merits a recap to earn its place in the stress-reduction plan. Contribution helps people cope for 2 major reasons.

First, when we contribute to our communities or attempt to repair the world in any small way, we put aside our own troubles. When we contribute to an effort bigger than ourselves, we gain perspective on our own stressful situations. The thank-yous we receive remind us of our own value even if we are not feeling good about ourselves.

People who have faced major misfortunes often turn to activities that allow them to give something back or heal their own traumas. At the adult level, for example, mothers of children killed by drunk drivers are committed to Mothers Against Drunk Driving (MADD). Teenagers who have lost relatives or friends are active in Students Against Destructive Decisions (SADD). Even young children benefit by contributing to causes like Alex's Lemonade Stand Foundation, the nationwide effort to raise funds for cancer research that was started by Alex Scott of suburban Philadelphia before she died at the age of 8 years. She used this mission to give back even while bravely fighting cancer.

Second, remember the ultimate act of resilience is to turn to another and request assistance without humiliation or shame. When your child makes a contribution to another person's life, he will learn that it feels good to give. And at a time of unimagined stress, he will more easily seek help from another person because he will not feel like a burden. He will not feel as if he is pitied. He may feel instead as if he has given, and it is now his turn to receive.

Building Resilience Videos (www.healthychildren.org/BuildingResilience)

Video 2.3.a	Stress Management and Coping/Section 1/Tackling the Problem/Point 1: Identify and Then Address the Problem
Video 9.1	The First Step of Managing Stress: 3 Critical Questions

To learn about the full offering of **Building Resilience** *videos, please turn to page 327.*

Taking Care of Your Body

The following 4 parts of the plan can help children and adults manage stress more effectively by nurturing minds that are better prepared to overcome emotional challenges by being calm and focused and bodies that are prepared to remain healthy and responsive to physical challenges. This chapter discusses exercise, relaxation, nutrition, and sleep. Each benefits the body and the mind. The lessons learned here will contribute to a child's resilience now and—as importantly—will promote healthy habits for a lifetime.

5. The Power of Exercise.

Exercise can change the body and make it better able to withstand all kinds of challenges. In moments, it can transform moods like nervousness, frustration, and anger, and it can have an ongoing effect on anxiety, attention-deficit/hyperactivity disorder (ADHD), and even depression. Appropriate exercise can help alertness, focus, and concentration and can even contribute to a good night's sleep, which has its own stress-management benefits. Finally, people who exercise may be more likely to choose healthful foods.

Stress is not our enemy. When well managed, it is quite useful. Some experts have compared well-managed stress to the strings of a guitar. If there is no tension, the strings will not make a sound. Yet when there is too much tension, the sound is harsh and unpredictable, and the strings may even break. An appropriate amount of stress is the key to making music. Likewise, our bodies contain many different hormones that sometimes help us respond rapidly to danger and other times calm us. Fear causes the release of adrenaline, but exercise and relaxation release endorphins and other calming brain chemicals. Being aware of this dynamic is one of the secrets to finding the right balance.

A rush of adrenaline is harmless in certain situations, like taking a scary amusement park ride. It puts us on alert at other times, such as when we're walking along a dark, deserted road. Or it prepares us to run from tigers or modern dangers. When I tell young people about our ancestor Sam, I explain a few choice details, depending on the child's age. Even a 6- or 7-year-old can understand that blood had to rush to Sam's legs so he could sprint from a tiger. I then explain that the reason kids feel butterflies when they're anxious or afraid is because blood leaves their gut to rush to their legs to prepare them for running. Kids also understand that their hearts beat faster and their breathing is more rapid to help them run. They particularly like learning about how their pupils dilate to let in more light so they can see well while running.

Few kids today have to run from wild tigers, but they certainly have other tigers in their lives that provoke the same physical responses. When young people learn to listen to their bodies and read their stress responses, they become better able to cope. This is especially true when those stress responses are so strong they get in the way of meeting a challenge. If a bully starts to chase them, the shift from a calm to an aroused state makes kids ready to run and is an appropriate response. But it's counterproductive when the "tiger" is a history examination. They can't focus on studying if they're only focused on fleeing. Remember that you're not supposed to turn to a charging animal and request a time-out. "Excuse me a moment, I'm quite busy. Could you attack me later?"

Move It!

The most direct way to listen to your body when you're stressed is to exercise. Your body is shouting, "A tiger is gaining on me fast; I don't want to get eaten! Hey, legs, get moving!" If you don't move, the stress hormones circulate, unused and confused about why you aren't paying attention. In fact, these recirculating hormones explain much of chronic disease. The hormone that replenishes our bodies after bursts of adrenaline is cortisol. Excess cortisol leads to weight gain, high blood pressure, and heart disease.

This body confusion occurs because our stress hormones are saying "run" and we are sitting still. The solution to stress, therefore, lies largely in listening to our bodies. It makes biological sense for exercise to be the starting point of stress management. Unfortunately, it's often the first thing to go when people think about time management because they fail to realize that most tasks are performed more efficiently *after* they exercise.

When one of my patients is cramming for a test and feeling tense or nervous, I tell him to go outside and run, jump rope, or play ball. This physical activity simulates running from the tiger and relieves stress by using up that surging adrenaline. Once the body thinks it has survived the challenge, it can kick back, chill, and prepare for the next adventure—in this case, to study better. When kids tell me, "I can't exercise. I have no time because I've got to study," I tell them, "You have no time *not* to exercise. You'll think better, be more alert, and be able to remember what you study."

How Much Exercise and What Kind?

Exercise reduces stress even when no figurative tigers are chasing us. We should exercise regularly when all is going well because it keeps our bodies healthy. Healthy people manage stress better. Active kids will enjoy lifelong physical and emotional health benefits. We now know that people who exercise regularly protect their brains and keep them developing well into advanced age. John J. Ratey, MD, summarizes evidence behind the power of exercise to help people think more clearly and manage behavioral concerns, including ADHD, anxiety, and depression, in *Spark: The Revolutionary New Science of Exercise and the Brain.*

Exercise is key to successful stress management. It should not be the source of stress. As with all things, we seek balance, not compulsive but healthy exercise. It doesn't have to include competition; movement itself offers benefits.

Some children are pushed too hard to become little superstars, which simply is not healthy if they focus on one sport intently and year-round. Traditionally, youth sports seasons lasted 3 to 5 months. Kids trained, played hard, and then played a different sport the following season. Each sport used different sets of muscles, bones, joints, and parts of the mind, so the body had an opportunity to alternate movement and thought patterns. Recently, a trend has appeared to breed young athletes to focus on the same sport year-round. This causes more repetitive wear and tear on the developing muscles, bones, and joints, which leads to an increase in sports-related injuries and, potentially, single-patterned thinking.

Athletic pursuits offer children a chance to be at their most competent and confident, but they should be well managed by coaches who understand young bodies. If children love a sport and enjoy playing, that's terrific. But if they are pushed to excel for the primary purpose of getting into college or winning an athletic scholarship, that is not always healthy and can produce unnecessary stress. A better solution is to encourage them to participate in a variety of athletic activities.

Parents shouldn't select sports for children or make them sign up for certain leagues if they aren't really interested. Encourage them to play sports, but let them choose activities based on what they enjoy with their friends around the neighborhood or at school. Some children shy away from competitive team sports. That's OK as long as they remain active through play or individual sports. Whether or not they enjoy team sports, all kids should be exposed to individual sports like track, swimming, bicycling, or skating and some 2-player sports like tennis, golf, or racquetball because they'll be able to do these activities and reap the health benefits throughout adulthood. By the time many kids reach high school, it is harder to gather a whole team together, but they can usually find one other person to play with.

Most importantly, exercise should be fun. When children are young, just let them play without worrying about scores and rigid rules. As they get older, let them select their athletic activities. If they feel that participating in sports is a chore or another kind of pressure, they may give up on exercise as soon as they're old enough to make their own decisions. Walking, riding bikes, hiking, and swimming are lifelong activities that make a difference in adult health and are great for family togetherness. You don't have to push any of these on your children, but if you offer them as healthful, fun ways for the family to connect with each other, your children may enjoy the same activities with their children. In this way, healthy living is a multigenerational investment in your family. Paul R. Stricker, MD, FAAP, speaks about all these issues and more in *Sports Success* R_x*! Your Child's Prescription for the Best Experience: How to Maximize Potential AND Minimize Pressure.*

Releasing Stress and Conquering Anger

Stress hormones generate a fight-or-flight response. Fear or nervousness makes us want to flee. So it makes sense that any exercise that involves running (including most sports) or moving your legs (like swimming, dancing, or jumping rope) will help relieve that anxiety. On the other hand, raw anger drives us toward fighting, a behavior we certainly want to discourage. When children and teens are angry, I urge them to recognize what that rage is doing to their bodies and to release it by screaming, ripping up papers, or hitting pillows or punching bags. When they're irate and "want to get something off my chest," I tell them, "Lie down on your back and lift weights to get it off your chest, or do push-ups." Anaerobic exercise, such as weight lifting, can give young people a sense of control and power. Just as they think they can't do one more rep, they somehow find the strength from within themselves to push it out. This also engages the mind, allowing whatever made them angry to seem less important, even lost, in the full-on focus required for such activities. (Note that weight lifting should be guided by adults who understand young developing bodies.)

6. Active Relaxation.

Relaxation is often thought of as the absence of activity. Certainly, to relax you need some downtime just to be. But by *active* relaxation, I mean you can take active steps to transform your body into a relaxed state. If you are really busy, you might even have to schedule time to achieve a relaxed state, but the health benefits and efficiency you will gain in other areas of your life are well worth the investment. With a little practice, we can train the body to have a relaxation response that will help us be more efficient and feel better and contribute to our health. *Guided meditation, mindfulness, visualization,* and *progressive relaxation* are useful techniques. While each sounds different or even exotic, they are actually quite simple and similar; each has particular strengths that might be tailored to appeal to the uniqueness of your child's strengths.

By exercising or being physically active, kids use up all those stress hormones that tell their bodies to flee the tiger. After they use them up, or if they are unable to exercise them away, they can still learn to fool their bodies into thinking they aren't stressed. To see how this is possible, it's necessary to understand the power of the mind over the body.

For starters, we have 2 nervous systems. The *voluntary* nervous system makes our muscles do what we want, like stand up, lift a heavy box, or climb stairs. The *involuntary* nervous system controls the functions that happen automatically without thought, like heart beating, swallowing, breathing, and digestion. Interestingly, it actually has 2 contrasting components. One fine-tunes our body for relaxation, thinking, and digestion. The other rapidly adjusts to prepare us for a sprint or battle. Here's the really cool part that science is only beginning to understand: We can take control of our involuntary nervous system if we use our brains to trick the system. By definition, stress is tense and relaxation is supple. Our bodies cannot be calm and in crisis simultaneously. That simple fact is the key to our mind's ability to relax the body. If we learn to fool our bodies into sending out signals to our relaxed, involuntary nervous system, we can flip a figurative switch and our stress hormones stop firing. Our relaxation response then takes over. This is one of the key secrets to many ancient methods of healing.

Because the 2 components of the involuntary nervous system cannot work together at once, we can fool our bodies by making them do the opposite of what they'd do under stress. This isn't always easy. We can't reroute our blood back to our bellies after it has shifted to our legs in preparation for running away. We can't reverse our sweating or stop our faces from flushing. It's extremely difficult to calm our thinking and slow our heart rates. Breathing, however, can be consciously influenced and therefore is the most direct way to flip that switch. The next few pages offer a brief overview of techniques to calm the body so you can consider which may be worth pursuing further.

Breathe to Relax

Controlled breathing is at the core of almost every relaxation technique. Slow, deep breathing is a highly effective way to fool a stressed body, and breathing exercises can be done at any time—while lying down, sitting, standing, walking, or even engaged in activities. Here's one simple method to get you started: Just sit comfortably with your back upright but not rigid. Put your feet flat on the floor if you're sitting in a chair or sit cross-legged on the floor. Let your hands rest halfway between your knees and hips and gently close your eyes. Begin by inhaling slowly and concentrating on your breath as it flows deep into your abdomen. Let your belly expand with air. As you inhale, notice whatever comes to mind, perhaps that the air is cool. Don't hold your breath; allow your lungs to empty slowly and naturally, and allow your mind to empty along with your lungs. You might notice that the outflowing air is warm. The key is to take it easy and fully engage your awareness in the repetition. Continue to breathe in and out in a relaxed, steady rhythm. Fill your lungs fully and exhale slowly, with no force or strain. When your attention wanders, as it likely will, focus on your breathing again. Remember, this is a technique to relieve stress, and being overly strict and performance-oriented can defeat the purpose. Congratulate yourself for noticing when your mind may have strayed some, and then gently return to the practice.

Interestingly, this mind-body thing is a 2-way street, and sometimes how your body feels will affect your mind's ability to focus. Luckily, the solution is the same. The breathing exercise you just learned is one of the most basic yet profound meditations—constantly returning your attention to the breath, truly marrying mind and body. For our purposes, we can define *meditation* as any method that helps free you of your thoughts' tendency to snowball and gain power over your body. With practice, many people discover greater levels of self-control.

Later, with a little practice, you can add in a slight pause at the end of each inhalation and exhalation. This opens the door to a deeper practice. Here's the breakdown. The in-breath is the opportunity to notice. Anything that comes up is fair game; it may be a thought, a feeling, or maybe just the sounds around you. Just notice it as you inhale. Then there is a slight, comfortable pause to simply recognize whatever may have come up. Hold no judgment and know that at least for now, you don't have to do anything with it. Just "be" with it. Finally, allow your body's natural elasticity to release the breath and with it, everything you just noticed, felt, heard, or thought about, allowing your mind to become as empty as your lungs and aware, prepared, open to the next breath, the next moment. Allow for a slight, comfortable pause, and then your body will naturally begin the process again.

This is my favorite method because it mirrors what the body's wisdom does when surprised in a healthy state (which is what our stress system is for). First, there's a stimulus (like a "tiger," a fancy car, or surprising news) that "takes your breath away" or causes you to "wait with baited breath." Often this is accompanied by common expressions, such as, "Whoa." Then there is a brief pause for evaluation. As you get better at paying attention in moments like this, you will find that all your breathing muscles are briefly inactive while your mind is deciding what to do with the new information. This is a moment of evaluation, where in a split second you figure out what to do, usually by asking questions like, "Am I in trouble?" "Did you see that?" or "How am I going to deal with this?" Finally, there is a "breath of fresh air" that readies you for action. "Whew, that sure got my attention! Next moment, please." To recap, breathing in, you notice; pausing for a moment, you "be with"; and letting the out-breath go naturally, you make yourself available to the next thing (in the case of meditation, the breath).

You might decide that a more proactive approach is better for you; in this case, visualization can help a lot. You can get really creative here. In your mind, picture your breath flowing in and out of your lungs and through your body. Imagine breathing in colors that make you feel peaceful and breathing out colors that remind you of the stress you wish to release. For example, breathing in "sky blue" and letting it flow through your body, then washing away all the "icky green" that is then exhaled might work for some. For others, the opposite may be true—breathing in "spring green" and breathing out "sad blue." Getting creative in this way not only personalizes your relaxation time but helps to make it more engaging.

Deep, slow breathing is the simplest way to begin calming your racing mind. Outside thoughts will probably intrude, but keep refocusing on your breath. Meditate. Visualize. Breathing exercises can be used whenever you feel tension rising. But for the same reason an athlete prepares before an event, it's beneficial to make breathing exercises a regular routine even when you're not stressed. Five or 10 deep breaths when sitting down at the desk helps to relax and focus on the task at hand, but try to breathe this way for about 15 minutes a day and make it as much a daily habit as brushing your teeth.

Even young children can learn controlled breathing. When teaching them this technique, sit with them quietly and talk them through the process. ("Breathe in slowly. Puff out your tummy with air. Slooooowly let your breath out through your nose.") Do the breathing with them and leave long, silent pauses between instructions. When I work with older teens and young children alike, everyone has a relatively easy time imagining breathing like a balloon. Generally, I'll have them sit or lie down and say, "Imagine that you are a balloon, just the same shape and size as you are. What color is it?" The color question is a trick from hypnosis and basically serves to engage the imagination more fully through visualization. Let's say the child picks red. I then say, "You know how a balloon blows up, right? When you breathe in, imagine this big red balloon that is you getting blown up. How would that feel? Imagine your whole body making room for the air. Let's try this a few times."

The goal is to relax every abdominal muscle so that the real workhorse of breathing, the diaphragm muscle, can move more freely. Once I see the belly moving freely with the breath, I continue, "Now, while balloons don't blow themselves up, they do empty themselves, right? So just let yourself become empty. Now let's put them together. Blow yourself up…hold for just a second and whew…let it all out." After several practice sessions, kids will be able to do it on their own.

Blowing bubbles is another simple, effective way to show young children how to relax through breath control. When they are tense, pull out a jar of bubbles. The focus isn't on blowing the biggest bubble or chasing after a stream of bubbles. Instead, have your child sit quietly and guide him along this relaxation route. "Take in a slow, deep breath. Pull the air way in to your belly." (Demonstrate it as your child follows your example.) "Now blow out slowly, slowly through your lips. Watch the bubbles float away. Let's do it again. Pull the air into your belly sloooooowly, pucker your lips, and blow out through a little hole between your lips." Keep doing it as long as it takes for your child to become calmer.

Swimming laps is another great way for children, teens, and adults to use breathing as a stress reliever. It is not just good exercise; swimming laps also requires rhythmic breathing that helps people relax and even meditate.

If teenagers struggle with the idea of deep, meditative breathing, I make the analogy to smoking. If they are smokers or have tried cigarettes or marijuana, they catch on right away. "Just try this," I say. "Pull a breath, pull it deep, hold it, and…aah…." If they are regular smokers, this is a way to help them quit. I teach them that part of the relaxation they get from smoking comes from choosing to take a break and then, once outside, from the pull. If they try deep breathing as a regular stress-reduction strategy, they can enjoy the drag without the poison and it won't cost them $6 or $7 a pack, risk a drug bust, make them smell, or pollute their lungs. And taking a break is always a great idea as well. For many, it may be the most important aspect.

Body Position

Some simple physical postures can fool a tense body and reduce stress. If someone confronts you in an aggressive way and moves in close ("gets in your face," as kids say), don't stand chest-to-chest. That's a hostile posture and makes you want to fight back. Instead, turn slightly to one side and drop your shoulders into a more relaxed position. This simple postural shift can be compared to the 3-second rule in defensive driving, which says that there should be enough room between cars that it takes 3 to 5 seconds for your car to pass the same inanimate object as the car in front of you. Being aware in this way buys you time to evaluate, brake, and evade hazards, and so it is with the non-confrontational posture. Martial artists know that this is not just a superior position for diffusing a potentially hostile situation. It is also a better position should things get ugly, as they sometimes do, because it narrows the aggressor's selection of potential targets and offers more angles for blocking, countering, and escape. Such analogies appeal to the young people who find themselves in these situations, as it is empowering and appeals to their aggressive side without encouraging violence. It also ties in somewhat with the fast-rising sport of mixed martial arts. As parents and educators, it is important to realize that if this is the stuff television uses to reach our kids, it is our responsibility to capitalize on it as well. Tense situations can be neutralized by sitting down, angling your body, and taking deep breaths to control your thoughts, then problem-solving through negotiation. It is likely that a skillful navigation of adversities and other stressors will yield better results than non-skillful means, and that is exactly the toolbox we are trying to build and encourage.

The study posture is a common position that makes the body tense. How often have you seen kids hunch over a desk? They're compressing their breathing apparatus with tight, rounded shoulders, bent heads, and curved spines. Their legs and hips are bent in a position as if they're preparing to leap up and sprint. Often their legs are shaking to work out their nervous energy. Their entire posture seems to say, "Why am I doing homework when I should be running from this tiger that's chasing my butt?"

If they want to be calmer while doing homework or taking a test, suggest that this posture and leg shaking make them even more tense. Instead, they can take control of what their bodies are feeling by sitting up straighter, with shoulders back and relaxed, and legs stretched out comfortably, without shaking. They can take deep breaths to remind themselves that they can be calm. Now they are physically prepared to problem-solve while taking an exam or finishing homework. Simply knowing these easy tricks makes kids feel more in control of their situations and thus, less anxious.

Yoga

Yoga is sometimes described as meditation through movement. While there are many variations, the core intention of yoga is to become healthy and free of anxieties and worry. Often this is done by combining breathing, movement, or posture. Concentrating on slow, deep breathing, people who practice yoga relax while moving through poses that strengthen bones and stretch muscles. There is an intimate relationship between how the body and mind feel, so it makes sense that broadening the range of motion in the body can help to broaden the mind's range.

For children and teens, yoga offers a counterweight to the stressful world of school demands, competitive sports, and peer pressure. Yoga develops concentration and stillness that promote relaxation of body and mind. It fosters physical competencies because children master balance, breath control, and flexibility. They gain confidence, strength, and body awareness in a noncompetitive, cooperative setting.

Children learn yoga postures in familiar terms—they pose like trees and flowers, sit twisted like a pretzel, stretch like a cat, and take a warrior's stance. They balance like a flamingo and breathe like a bunny. Few young children like to remain silent for long, and yoga allows them to make noise. They can meow while in the cat pose, hiss like a cobra as they stretch their spines, and bark during the downward dog pose. Some yoga instructors encourage kids to count or recite their ABCs while holding different poses.

Learning to do yoga is probably best accomplished in a class where a qualified instructor makes certain that poses and breathing are done correctly. Once learned, you and your child can continue them at home with a DVD, an online resource, or an illustrated book for guidance. Also teach your child that whenever he feels tense or upset, he can cope better if he does some yoga breathing and poses during stressful times. In practice, yoga is a way of discovering and releasing tension in its many forms. At the least, it will help him feel better. At the most, it will offer access to a feeling of calm, helping him navigate an often confusing world.

Meditation

Meditation comes in many forms and has been practiced all over the world for thousands of years. The core of meditation is breathing awareness, often combined with movement and visualization. The goal of meditation is to turn off mental activity, to calm the thoughts racing wildly through your mind. While meditating, you turn off your thinking process but remain in a clear state of awareness. This gives your mind a rest and lets your body relax.

People who have learned to meditate often discover that meditation helps them focus better when doing daily tasks in times of high stress. If you're multitasking under a lot of pressure, you can use meditation to concentrate on getting through the tasks step-by-step without letting them overwhelm you with anxiety.

Meditation techniques take the power from those thoughts that run away with you and put it back in your hands. Rather than thinking, "I am angry," which makes us feel as if this were so, meditation gives us the power to realize, "I am *experiencing* anger." The difference seems small but gives us the freedom to experience other things at the same time. When we *are* angry, we do things we might later regret. When we *experience* anger, we retain full self-control. The same goes for any "I am" statement. We are so much more than any one thing, like depressed, mad, or sad, and meditation helps us realize that.

Imagine that your thoughts are clouds. Scary thoughts become big, dark, scary clouds, and happy thoughts become bright, airy, poofy clouds. Just imagine that each thought, as it crosses your mind, is a cloud crossing the sky. Simply recognize and watch. Imagine your breath is the wind blowing the clouds across the sky. Do this for 10 minutes and notice how you feel.

Another method is to simply notice whatever comes to mind as you inhale. It could be a noise, feeling, or thought, but be with whatever you notice as you hold your breath momentarily. As you release your breath, let it all go—the breath, the thing you noticed, everything. Make yourself available to the next breath, the next moment. Repeat.

Even young children can meditate if we show them how to do so in age-appropriate ways. The following example is not technically meditation, but it suggests a way to teach a relaxation method to very young children. An experienced Montessori teacher in a Philadelphia suburb, Ellen Sheehan, has used a book called *Play With Me* by Marie Hall Ets to introduce the concept of silence to 2- to 5-year-olds. In the story, a little girl meets a frog, turtle, grasshopper, bird, rabbit, and snake. She runs after each one and says, "Play with me." But they all hop, slither, swim, or fly away. The unhappy girl sits on a log and sadly contemplates why no one will play with her. As she sits motionless and quiet, all the creatures return and sit with her. A little fawn comes close to lick her face.

When the story ends, teacher and children talk about what it means to be silent like the girl sitting on the log. They close their eyes and listen. Gradually, voices from the hallway, the sound of an airplane, and the chirp of birds outside all drift into the quietness. The group listens silently for a full minute. Then Ms Sheehan tells them in a gentle voice, "You made beautiful silence," and asks them if they have anything to share. One by one, they open their eyes and respond. "Silence is viewed as a positive act," Ms Sheehan explains. "It is something the child makes, and the child feels a sense of accomplishment, satisfaction, and peace."

Mindfulness

Mindfulness is a type of meditative practice but is much more. It is about being in the moment, with an open heart and without judgment. Much of our stress and suffering comes from being pulled away from the present moment. We spend much of our time in "autopilot" mode, going through life's motions without being fully present in the here and now. Our body may be in one place, and our mind may be somewhere else entirely. Our minds may be caught in regrets about the past, worries about the future, or judgments about the present. In this ruminative or "mindless" state, we are vulnerable to "reacting" to stressful and painful situations from a state of fear, with our higher brain functions overwhelmed by our stress response. We can get caught in negative moods or reactive behaviors that can make the situation worse. Mindfulness returns us to the present where calm can exist and situations addressed. Videos of Dzung X. Vo, MD, author of *The Mindful Teen: Powerful Skills to Help You Handle Stress One Moment at a Time*, demonstrating mindful strategies are offered here.

Progressive Relaxation

This simple and effective method of active relaxation systematically moves awareness through the body. Where your awareness goes, relaxation follows. For many, practicing progressive relaxation from scalp to toe is very sedating, as the awareness gradually moves away from the head, where a lot of tension starts. Moving from feet to head is also relaxing but often has a more energizing effect because the awareness that is relaxing the body ends its journey in the body's control tower, the head.

There are a number of simple ways to do this. First, become fully aware of your scalp, then allow it to relax completely, including your mind's effort to notice. Next, become aware of all the little muscles around your ears, then allow them to relax completely as well. Next, work with your eyes and forehead, then your neck, then your throat, and so on. Continue in this way, working through your body, bit by bit, all the way to your fingertips and toes, being sure to address every area of your body.

A useful variation is to tense and release each body part as you go, using muscle energy to encourage results. Muscle energy also helps to maintain focus, as does visualization. You can even combine all 3—progressive tense and release while visualizing, imagining, for example, that your muscles are "milking" the tension right out of your body. You can also work from feet to scalp; once you're well practiced, you can even work part-specific. If your shoulders are tense, you can just focus on them, but be sure to take care of all your parts regularly to maximize your results.

Aromatherapy

Place a drop of fragrant oil on a cotton ball and breathe it in as you practice deep breathing. To ensure you get good quality oils, be sure the bottle says "organic" or "therapeutic grade." If it is difficult to obtain pure essential oils, you can use the ones nature provides—flowers, citrus peels, and pine needles are all rich in therapeutic fragrance. If nothing else, it makes the experience of deep meditative breathing varied and more pleasant.

A Note on Very Young Children

When working with very young children, visualization is usually the way to go. Use familiar terms that they understand and will enjoy. As you give them direction, asking them to describe their imaginings helps to solidify their experience and creates an opportunity for you to join them in their land of make-believe. Visualization is further described in the next chapter as a way of taking an "instant vacation."

Here are some scripts you might use to get young children started.

For progressive relaxation

- "Imagine your whole body is loose and wiggly like spaghetti, wiggling from head to toe."
- "Imagine the ocean is inside you, and the waves are washing from head to toe, cleaning you on the inside, making you feel better and better."
- "Imagine all your good feelings are your favorite color and all your bad feelings are your least favorite color. Imagine all that favorite color filling you up from the top and washing the other color right out through your feet."
- "Imagine bunches of little garbage collectors going through your head, back, belly, arms, and legs, taking away all the garbage and leaving you squeaky clean inside."

For visualization

- "Imagine that you are in the most beautiful place you have ever been. What is it like?" (After this opener, you can discuss the place, the details, and how it makes the child feel.)
- "Imagine you're in a beautiful field of flowers, relaxing in the sunlight. Do you see any animals? Do they have a name?" (Discussing what comes naturally might be a clue to the child's overall well-being. Perhaps frogs and

birds are happy signs, but scary animals like bears deserve a conversation to find out what is wrong and how to make it better.)

- "Imagine you are at the zoo. What animals do you want to see?" (While discussing the animals, imitate their qualities. Cats know how to relax, elephants are strong, monkeys know how to play nice with each other.)

Maximizing the Effects of Exercise and Relaxation Strategies

To maximize the stress-reduction benefits of exercise and relaxation, it is important to know how to coordinate these tools. Here are some key points.

- Morning exercise can increase alertness and have a powerful effect on mood for the rest of the day. This may be particularly true for people with concentration difficulties.
- Exercise is a good first strategy to use when stress feels overwhelming. In fact, you may not be ready to use the other strategies, especially those that involve calm thought and planning, until you've worked out those overwhelming feelings by exercising.
- When exercise isn't possible—like the moment your boss delivers bad news—the best first step can be to control your thinking pattern. Divert it away from moving toward catastrophic thoughts (see Chapter 9) by sitting in a comfortable position that tells your body there's no emergency worth running from. Then draw in slow, deep breaths to flip the switch that turns on your calm nervous system.
- The ideal combination is first working out your stress physically and then taking active steps toward relaxation.

Let's use a child's tantrum to illustrate an appropriate sequence of exercise and relaxation through breathing. When a 4-year-old has a tantrum in preschool, the teacher could send him into the corner and tell him to calm down. The problem is that his frustration or anger is so intense that he simply can't calm himself. He shakes, cries, and feels he's even more of a failure because he can't follow the teacher's instructions. All of this will be worse if done in front of classmates because he will also be ashamed, and embarrassed people feel as if they are being attacked and may lash out preemptively.

Alternately, the teacher could remove him from the peer audience and then tell him that she understands he's feeling angry and frustrated, but until he can explain his feelings, she can't help him as much as she wants to. She could tell him to run in place for a minute or two and really work out his feelings. After the energy is released, she could have him blow bubbles with slow, controlled breathing. In this way, his tantrum can serve as a valuable life lesson about how the choices he makes can control his uncomfortable feelings instead of reinforcing his feelings that he is out of control.

7. Eat Well.

Nutrition is vitally important to children's physical growth and development, but it must also be seen as part of an overall stress-reduction plan because a healthy body helps us manage stress.

A particularly valuable resource is ChooseMyPlate.gov. But before you look for external sources, remember, your modeling is more important than any words you say or resources you guide children to use. Keep in mind, we buy the food and model eating habits.

Some General Guidelines

- Treat soda and other sugary drinks for what they are—candy water. Sodas should be highly restricted or drunk only occasionally. Soda can be harmful to tooth enamel. When children drink a lot of soda, they tend to drink fewer nutritious beverages like milk. Even many juice drinks are packed with high-fructose corn syrup, so they are not as nutritious as the term *fruit drink* might imply.
- Make sure children drink lots of water. Water gives the body exactly what it needs without all those empty calories. If kids find water boring, give it to them in a cool sports bottle. Show them how to give it a twist (with a squirt of lemon juice, for example) but without added calories.
- Offer lots of milk and dairy products, or high-calcium beverages like soy milk if your children are intolerant of milk. Some brands of almond and rice milks are also enriched with calcium. Generally, children younger than 2 years should drink whole milk from the time they stop breastfeeding or using formula. American Academy of Pediatrics recommendations, however, state that children at risk of being overweight or with a family history of heart disease, obesity, or high cholesterol can switch to low-fat (1%) or reduced-fat (2%) milk between 12 months and 2 years of age. (Check with your child's doctor before switching from whole to reduced-fat milk.) After 2 years of age, all children should drink low-fat or nonfat (skim) milk.
- Make plenty of fresh fruits and vegetables available. Put out bowls of fruit or cut-up vegetables as snacks. Recommended amounts of fruits and vegetables—8 or 9 servings a day—may seem nearly impossible, but numerous studies extol their nutritional benefits. Many kids reject certain fruits and vegetables; try to experiment until you find some they like. Just because they reject steamed broccoli one day doesn't mean they won't like munching on raw broccoli dipped in yogurt next week.
- Avoid linking food to punishments and don't use snacks and desserts as bribes or rewards.

- If you want to be certain that children get adequate vitamins and minerals, be sure they eat lots of different-colored fruits and vegetables that supply a healthy variety of nutrients.
- If you want kids to maintain an even-keeled temperament and therefore be better prepared to manage stress, teach them how to have a *steady* supply of energy. This means avoiding foods that cause quick peaks and crashes of energy to the brain. A little background: Glucose is the source of energy to the brain. It is found in simple and complex sugars *(carbohydrates)*. Simple sugars are those that taste sweet and are found in candy and soft drinks. They get quickly absorbed and deliver a burst of energy but then are followed by a crash. Complex carbohydrates don't taste as sweet and deliver a slower, more steady supply of energy to the brain. Complex carbohydrates are found in fruits, vegetables, and whole grains.
- Help your children distinguish between healthy and non-healthy snacks. I simplify this idea by asking kids to imagine 2 kinds of snacks, *soap* and *no-soap*, that they eat only with their hands. After eating those snacks, do they need soap to wash their hands or just water? This is an easy way for kids to recognize greasy foods that are less healthy than most alternatives.
- Children are growing and burn a lot of energy. Don't eliminate snacking. Instead, provide a variety of healthy snacks. Everyone knows that fruits and vegetables are the healthiest snacks, but many people don't realize that there are large differences among all the salty, crunchy snack foods available today. The greasier they are, the less healthy they are. Some examples are included in the following Table:

Snacking Can Be Healthy!

Unhealthy Soap Snacks	Healthier No-soap Snacks	Healthy Snacks
Potato chips Corn chips Cheese puffs Buttered popcorn	Pretzels Salted unbuttered popcorn Baked crackers	Fruits Vegetables Low-fat yogurt Unbuttered popcorn with fat-free spices

Why Do You Eat?

A major difference between people who eat healthily and those who don't is found in their answers to the question, "Why do you eat?" Healthy eaters tend to eat when they are hungry. Unhealthy eaters often eat when they are hungry *and* when they are sad, excited, or bored. Sometimes they eat without thinking, just to give themselves something to do while they are watching television.

Try to make mealtime an event that your family enjoys together in the kitchen or dining room and not in the family or recreation room. As difficult as it seems, I suggest that you ban junk-food snacks from the room where you watch television, but fruits and vegetables or air-popped popcorn are OK.

How Much?

We live in a super-size-me nation. Portion size matters to weight control. Most people eat what is in front of them. If the all-you-can-eat buffet table overflows with tempting foods, we load our plates and go back for more—not because we're still hungry, but because the food is within view. The more we see, the more we eat.

Parents can dish out reasonably sized portions on each child's plate or place platters on the table for family members to serve themselves. Don't offer second helpings unless children say they're still hungry. It takes about 20 minutes for the body to register whether it is satisfied, so encourage eating slowly. Having a relaxed conversation during meals will slow the pace.

No Fighting Over Food

Don't make food a battleground. Model good nutrition yourself, and make sure your child has healthy foods to select, but don't take away the pleasure of eating. Mealtime is a great opportunity to enhance family connection and check in with your child. The atmosphere should be relaxed. But if you turn "Eat all your rice" into a battleground command, tensions rise and your child may refuse to eat.

When we talk with children about good nutrition and healthy bodies, we should be careful not to send the wrong messages. This isn't about how kids *look*. So many destructive media messages exist about what we should look like. Men are supposed to have 6-pack abs and women should be skinny. Please be careful not to encourage those images. Never tell children that they don't look right. If they eat well and get regular exercise through play or sports, they will be fine. Be cautious, too, of the overuse of body mass index (BMI). It is a useful tool that is more accurate than simple weight and height, but never forget to look at your child and consider her body type. For example, a girl may have a high BMI even though she is in excellent shape because her muscles weigh more than fat. Use BMI as a screening tool, not a label.

If you think your child is overweight or obese, yet you're modeling healthy eating habits and providing good food choices at home, let a health professional counsel your child. When food becomes a battleground within families, not only does it add extra stress, but serious consequences may result during adolescence if teens choose to control their anxieties—or you—by limiting what they eat or by overeating.

Meals as a Bonding Time

Research demonstrates that family meals are highly protective for young people. It's not about food on the plate; it's about the connection that occurs when families spend time together. An added benefit of these meals is that family time becomes associated with nutritious, leisurely meals. When people take time to eat and associate it with pleasant times, they may be more likely to develop lifelong healthy eating habits.

8. Sleep Well.

Sleep affects everything. Stressful situations that could be easily managed when you're well rested can put young people (or you) over the edge when you're tired. Inadequate sleep can have a profoundly negative effect on health, the ability to think, and mood. Adequate sleep is necessary to solidify newly gained memories or skills, so it isn't surprising that school performance declines with lack of sleep. Sleeplessness has also been associated with other serious consequences such as an increased incidence of car crashes and even depression.

Getting children to bed on time and up at 6:00 am can be nearly impossible. Sleep research data indicate that adolescents require 9 to 10 hours of sleep each night. But the majority of them aren't getting nearly that much, which is why excessive daytime sleepiness has become a widespread problem among teenagers.

What's Interfering With Sleep?

Most cases of sleepiness result from insufficient time in bed, often caused by external pressures (like studying) to go to bed later and wake up earlier. Worrying in bed can also keep us from falling asleep and wake us throughout the night. Stimulants like caffeine can impair sleep quality. Finally, the sleep/wake cycle changes dramatically during adolescence, making a teen's clock quite different than an adult's.

Although medical conditions are not the most likely cause of sleepiness, it's important to consider them as a possible cause of a child's lack of sleep. If your child often has trouble sleeping or is unusually sleepy during the day, talk with your pediatrician, who can help determine whether your child may be suffering from chronic sleep deprivation or an underlying sleep disorder. A health professional may ask your child the following questions:

- Do you have trouble falling asleep at bedtime?
- Do you feel sleepy a lot during the day? In school? While driving?
- Do you wake up a lot at night?
- What time do you usually go to bed on school nights? Weekends?
- How much sleep do you usually get?
- Has anyone ever told you that you snore loudly at night?
- Do you have disturbing dreams?

In addition, your child should be asked about mood and stress to consider the possibility of depression. The next thing to consider, and possibly the easiest to address, is the use of stimulants. It takes 6 to 8 hours for caffeine to get out of our systems. Caffeine is found in coffee, tea, colas and other soft drinks, and chocolate, and at very high levels in energy and power drinks. Research finds that teens who drink caffeine in the afternoon and evening have more difficulty sleeping and are more tired during the day. Although caffeine does keep us awake for a short time, it won't overcome excessive sleepiness and does not overcome a sleep debt. In other words, it works in the short term but really adds to the bigger problem of sleepiness. Caffeine is a real drug and should be used sparingly.

Most of us can relate to another major cause of sleeplessness: using the bed to do some of our best and often toughest thinking. Sometimes we're so busy that there is no downtime in our lives, no time for processing our thoughts and feelings or even for planning for tomorrow. The first chance to be alone with your thoughts is when your head hits the pillow. Although it can be a relief to finally have some alone time, when the bed becomes the place to deal with important issues, it becomes a friend, even a counselor. No wonder it becomes difficult to fall asleep. And then we wake up in the middle of the night for another opportunity to think through our problems. We all deserve a space to work through our feelings and develop solutions; it just shouldn't be the place where we sleep.

It is not just worrying that prevents the bed from becoming the place our bodies naturally associate with sleep. Anything that creates too much stimulation keeps our minds revved up and prevents us from falling smoothly into sleep. If young people move from activity to activity, they sometimes lack time to wind down; they're still spinning from the day's activities.

Any activity done in bed increases the possibility of sleep problems. When homework is done in bed, the bed can become associated with anxiety about grades and tests. And nighttime awaking may increase in frequency because teens wake up to get the work done. When kids sprawl in bed while texting or talking to friends, the bed can become associated with excitement and social pressures. The brain doesn't turn off when we fall asleep. It's just dialed down, like when your computer goes into sleep mode, and it's easily revved up when subconscious concerns come close to the surface. When the bed is used for purposes other than sleep, the brain is more likely to do its low-level thinking when you're asleep. As sleep naturally cycles from deep to light sleep throughout the night, we wake up in light sleep when our brains suggest we can finish our "work" if only we wake up. (Work can be emotional work, schoolwork, or a progress report.) We are much more likely to awake if the bed is our work space. I don't tell kids not to communicate with their friends or to skip homework. I just want them to learn to do those things somewhere other than in bed.

If you think that your teen has become a night owl, you may be right. Adolescents' biological clocks actually shift during puberty. They naturally want to stay up later because as puberty progresses, the brain's sleep-timing system switches on later at night. This sleep-timing system is controlled by *melatonin,* a naturally occurring chemical that regulates biological rhythms; one of those is the circadian rhythm of wakefulness and sleep. Because high schools have generally not shifted away from early morning start times, most teenagers lack adequate sleep. Some school districts are moving toward later start times for teens, but that is not yet a widespread practice.

Sleep 101

Before we put together a plan for adequate sleep, it's important to review some basics of sleep.

- We fall asleep when we allow our minds to turn off. We stay asleep when we believe that the bed is just for sleeping. We have a natural circadian rhythm that regulates our patterns of wakefulness and sleep. We are naturally diurnal, meaning that we are designed to be awake during the day and asleep at night. Anything that interferes with allowing our bodies to stick to that rhythm may interfere with sleep.
- As diurnal creatures, we tend to become awakened with light and sleepy in the dark. This is critical to understand because artificial light has affected this natural design, and we can partially restore it by using light and darkness appropriately.
- As diurnal beings, we awake when our bodies become heated, as they do in the sunlight of day, and become tired as they cool down. Our bodies become heated with exercise and bathing. It takes 5 to 6 hours after exercise and 1 hour after a bath or shower to cool down.
- Digestion takes work. Large meals before bedtime can cause indigestion. A lot of liquid before bed can necessitate nighttime bathroom visits.

- When we wake in the middle of the night, we sometimes worry about getting back to sleep. As our anxiety builds, the chance of getting back to sleep lessens. It is better to get out of bed, sit in a chair, and return to bed when really drowsy.

Dos and Don'ts

If we combine everything we know about sleep patterns with what we know about actions that interfere with sleep, we can make a list of dos and don'ts. Remember, the reason to follow these rules is not to take away late-night fun; it is to help manage the stressors of daily life while remaining alert and healthy.

Dos	Don'ts
Drink soothing beverages like herbal teas or warm milk before bed.	Consume caffeine after 6 to 8 hours before bed.
Keep the cell phone recharging dock in the kitchen or living room, and insist all electronic devices get recharged there overnight.	Have televisions, computers, or cell phones in the bedroom. (If they're already in the bedroom, they must be turned off at bedtime.)
Have a place to release emotions and express feelings, not in bed.	Worry in bed.
Complete homework before bedtime and feel satisfied that it is done.	Do homework in bed.
Make lists before going to bed and feel secure that the next day is strategically planned.	Plan tomorrow in bed.
If you awake at night and can't fall back asleep easily, get up, stay in a dark room, and return to bed when drowsy.	Stay in bed worrying about getting to sleep.
Maintain a regular (but not rigid) sleep pattern.	Take long naps. (They interfere with developing a steady sleep pattern.)
Take power naps, limited to 20 minutes and not remotely close to bedtime.	Stay in bed very late on weekend mornings. (This also prevents a sleep pattern from developing.)

Dos	Don'ts
Eat healthy.	Eat heavy meals or large drinks before bed.
Exercise 5 to 6 hours before bedtime.	Do a heavy workout before bed.
Take a relaxing bath or shower an hour before bed.	Go to bed overheated.
Dim the lights an hour or so before bed; open the shades or turn on the lights in the morning.	Stay in bright lights late at night.
Create a dark, quiet, comfortable sleep environment.	

A Plan for Young People Who Are Struggling With Sleep

The bed should be a special, almost sacred place. It should only be used for sleeping, *not* to eat, read, listen to music, play games, veg out, talk on the phone, watch television, or play videos. Kids who treat their beds as sacred will more easily relax and fall asleep.

A leisurely bath an hour or so before bed helps relax the body and prepare it for sleep. I urge young people, as they are falling asleep, to unwind from the day and put aside worrisome thoughts. It's easier to do this if they have followed one of the strategies for releasing emotions (more in the next chapter and the ninth point of this stress-reduction plan). They must release their emotions somewhere other than in bed—perhaps sitting at a table or in a comfortable chair. We need a pattern to teach our bodies to sleep. This lesson starts with determining a reasonable bedtime. My intention isn't to create a rigid bedtime or for them to feel that it's a punishment; rather, their bodies need a healthy sleep/wake pattern. They set a time that will allow them to complete homework and still get at least 8 hours of sleep. We then call this *time zero* (T0) and work backward like this.

- **T0-6 hours:** Work out. Exercise will help them manage stress and get their brains ready to be productive for homework. No more caffeine.
- **T0-5 hours:** Do homework until it's finished. When homework is done, relax, play, or hang out. This is well-deserved downtime.
- **T0-1 hour:** Take a warm relaxing shower or bath in dim lights.
- **T0-30 minutes:** Release emotions through prayer or written, artistic, or verbal expression. (See stress-reduction point 10.) Plan for tomorrow by

keeping a list or creating a timeline. The point is that all this work should be *done* before bedtime. It should be completed in dim light and, if desired, while sipping a calming drink. A note of warning: For young people who are particularly stressed, this wind-down emotional work may bring up anxieties too close to bedtime. If this is the case, the time for expression can be moved earlier and this time can just be used for emotional vacations (see stress-reduction point 9), like listening to music, meditating, or reading a book.

Some young people still struggle to wind down even after following this routine. At Covenant House Pennsylvania, we work with young people who have endured very difficult lives. Many have great difficulty falling asleep and ask me for medication. Instead, I've had them work with Jed Michael, our stress-reduction specialist, who has been trained in Eastern Medicine healing practices. As I have learned from him, a person needs to have the opportunity to slip away into sleep and can do this best when they're distracted from their thinking. The old technique of counting sheep is designed to distract people from their thoughts. But that technique does not take full advantage of the relaxing tonic of controlled breathing. Jed teaches our patients the 4–8 breathing technique. First, he teaches that full breaths are belly/balloon breaths. They learn to lie on their backs and place their hands on their bellies with their fingers loosely interlocking. Normal breathing does not distend the abdomen and therefore does not cause the hands to rise or fingers to separate. Deep, cleansing breaths first fill the belly, then the chest, then the mouth; the breath expands the belly and the hands pull gently apart. Our patients are taught to take a full breath while counting to 4. Then they hold that breath for about twice as long, or an 8 count. Finally, they slowly exhale to the count of 8 or even longer, if that's comfortable. This meditative breathing relaxes the body after a few cycles, but just as importantly, it requires full concentration. The mind is too preoccupied on the cycle of breathing to also focus on worries. We have found that with dedicated practice, even young people with a long history of insomnia slip away into a peaceful sleep. In many cases, results are obtained the first night.

Expect Resistance

I get more resistance on the topic of sleep than any other guidance I offer. Everyone knows sleep is important, but they just don't feel it is practical to get even close to the recommended amount of sleep. Adolescents worry they won't have time for homework or with friends. They cherish sleeping into the afternoon on Sundays, so they especially reject sticking to the same number of sleep hours on weekends as weeknights. Parents worry most about homework;

they just don't think there will be enough time for exercise, relaxation, and emotional releases as well. Many teens and parents think that life will become cloudy without that late-afternoon jolt of caffeine.

I challenge them to endure a trial period with a healthy amount of exercise, good nutrition, and adequate sleep. Their increased efficiency, lighter mood, and newfound ability to concentrate will more than make up for all that time they "wasted" taking care of themselves.

To learn about the full offering of* Building Resilience *videos, please turn to page 327.

Taking Care of Your Emotions

The next 2 parts of the stress-reduction plan suggest ways to cope with the effect stress has on our emotions and well-being. These strategies include some that calm emotional reactions (to be used with exercise that fools our bodies into thinking we've dealt with the stress) and others that engage us in healing activities or use the power of distraction.

9. Take Instant Vacations.

We don't always have to travel for miles or spend a lot of money to take a vacation. There are several ways to reap the benefits of a vacation and de-stress wherever we find ourselves. Remember, some people cope by avoidance, withdrawal, disengagement, or running away. Most of these techniques are counterproductive and some, like drugs, are dangerous. But there are healthy ways to disengage too. One of the best ways to conserve energy, especially when your subconscious mind needs time to mull over solutions, is to healthfully and temporarily disengage. Many of the techniques listed in Chapter 29 as relaxation strategies also could be described as healthy disengagement strategies, although they should also be seen as ways that enable deeper engagement in the present.

Here are other techniques that help us escape stress for a while, find a safe refuge, and reenergize ourselves.

Visualization

When my daughters were 5 years old, we found an out-of-the-way beach with black sands, crashing turquoise waves, and salt spray in the air—one of the most beautiful places I have ever visited. I wanted my daughters to be able to "return" there if they ever needed to get away from anything, a place of extreme calm whose memory would be bathed in love. To imprint the spot into deep memory, we used each of our senses one by one. I asked the girls to close their eyes and pay attention to everything else.

"What do you feel? The warmth of the sun on one side of your body and a cool breeze on the other; the wetness of the ocean spray against your skin. What do you hear? The sound of crashing waves, the softer sounds of birds singing. What do you smell? The salt in the air. Now open your eyes, look around you, and tell me everything you see. Now close your eyes and describe it to me again."

Finally, I told them how much I loved them and why, and my wife did the same. I told them this would be our special place and anytime they needed to be calm and quiet, they could take an instant vacation by closing their eyes and recalling this place, which we named our family spot. Over the years, they found this to be an effective way to de-stress. I went through the same process on another beach when they were 9. This time, they led us through the sensory imaging.

There are many simple ways to show your children how to visualize. Visit a serene, beautiful place, or go outside on a quiet, clear night and gaze at the stars and moon. Ask your child to imagine her own special place and make it a memorable mental snapshot that she can pull out whenever it is needed. It doesn't have to be a visually astounding place; it could also be a place of profound warmth and safety, such as a grandmother's kitchen. The key is to take the step beyond the visual or sensory memory and bathe the place in the security of your love.

Think of your instant vacation spot as a screen saver on your computer. You can click on this tranquil picture in your mind's eye whenever you need to escape the stress of the moment. Simply close your eyes and be in the moment. Do nothing else, be still, and think of nothing else.

Hobbies

Hobbies provide another way to escape for a little while. A hobby may be something you choose for your child as a birthday gift, or it may start with casual play and become such an interesting activity that it takes on a focus, even a fervor, for your child.

A real passion for a hobby can be more than a good way to spend a rainy day; it can become something to turn to for an instant vacation when feeling stressed or upset.

Reading

Instant vacations can come in many forms—listening to music, watching television, or going to a movie can provide relaxing escapes. But there's nothing quite like reading. It is a full-immersion experience and offers a true escape. A reader visualizes the panorama, hears the dialogue, smells the aromas, and feels the feelings. Unlike television, which hands the sound and visuals to you, reading requires several senses to kick in actively for a fuller, more engaging escape. There is no room for anything else.

There's no question that reading is one of the most important things parents can do with children. Read aloud to them when they're babies and preschoolers and have them read to you when they're in school or take turns reading chapters aloud. Reading together is a wonderful way of fully engaging with children. They will associate it with your time and attention and develop a lifelong love of reading. While this has beneficial implications for their schooling, it will also provide a useful escape, a full immersion in another world or time.

Baths

Soaking in a warm bath is a great way to relax. A bath is also like a mini-vacation—a private time and a safe space. You deserve 30 minutes a day to decompress with no disturbances allowed. You may want to light candles or play soothing music.

"Is he crazy?" you're thinking. "He doesn't know my family. Thirty minutes without interruptions? Must be a fantasy." Protect this time for yourself. Think of it as a selfless act because you'll be modeling for your child the importance of a daily, private relaxation zone.

Young children won't use the bath in this leisurely way. You'll be lucky if they bathe long enough to scrub the mud off their knees. In the early years, a bath is usually a time of play and connection with parents as you splash, rinse, and perhaps sing to them. As they get older, preteens and teens crave a private space of their own. If you've modeled the soothing bath routine, they may find it's a useful tool for them too. Even if they don't use a bath, they will understand that their parents have private time to replenish themselves at the end of a long day—an important lesson that they can use to give themselves permission to refuel throughout their lives.

A bath an hour before bedtime is a particularly good way for adolescents and adults to cleanse away the day's stress and get a better night's sleep. Baths can have a certain meditative quality. As you take deep breaths, your lungs act like balloons, and your body gently rises and falls in the water if you allow your upper body to float. If you submerge your ears under water, leaving only your face above the surface, you can draw those deep cleansing breaths and listen to your rhythmic breathing. If you take your pulse, you will notice it slow. The bath becomes an effective biofeedback machine to help achieve relaxation. Visualize your problems and concerns disappearing as the water drains; they are swirling away and, whoosh, they're gone.

Vacation From Conflict and Worries

When the bills are piling up and work is overwhelming, we get caught in a cycle of worry, stress, and conflict. We may act out our stress at home on the people we love the most. It feels safer to do this at home than outside the home, so we find ourselves in fights over money or other matters. The arguments feed on themselves, and everything seems to spin like a tornado—the cycle has to be stopped, but how? A brief vacation from worries can interrupt the cycle. It may not solve the underlying problems, but it can keep the spiral from spinning out of control.

We can't hop on a plane to a tropical island, but we can make our homes peaceful, safe islands. We can structure an hour every day—or once a week—to take time off. We can put aside the home improvement projects; we can let the grass grow—we can forbid outside worries from encroaching on family life. Ongoing conflict is suspended because our love for our family remains solid. Then we can enjoy the love and safety within our homes that sometimes gets dwarfed by worries or conflicts.

This kind of break helps everyone. Children don't have to pay bills and they don't go to work (though school is certainly work), but they have their own tensions and, if there's more than one child in the family, some conflicts on the home front. Children can thoroughly enjoy a break, too, when conflicts are suspended and none of the touchy subjects are broached, when family members just enjoy each other. This can be a time for reading, hobbies, or laughter.

I'm not suggesting you say to your family, "I declare a brief holiday from conflict." This technique isn't one that you explain to children or teach them. Rather, simply do it. Your child will learn that just as we have the ability to escalate tension, we also have the ability to turn to the people we most cherish, in the place where we feel most secure, and say, "Time-out. Let's enjoy each other." If you do this, you will help your family thrive even during stressful times, and you will expose your child to a lifelong stress-reduction tool.

Smelling Local Flowers

Children benefit if they learn from us (forgive a twist on the cliché) to take time to smell the local flowers. When we take time to be refreshed by the beauty in our yard, trees in the park, or a baby gurgling in delight when adults make silly faces, children notice that it takes little to enjoy life.

Even when they are very young, take them on walks, watch the birds, help them see all the mini-vacations that surround them. This is another reason to encourage unstructured play. Children who are rushed from activity to activity never learn to explore their immediate environment, so they don't learn to discover pleasure and fun exactly where they are.

10. Release Emotional Tension.

So many young people tell me that their biggest problem is anger, and they don't know where it comes from. Others tell me that they cannot sleep because their heads spin with the day's worries or excitement and their anticipation of the next day. I worry most, though, when they tell me that they feel numb and have nothing worthwhile at all in their thoughts. What they have in common are disorganized, overwhelming thoughts. In some cases, they have been exposed to emotional, even physical, traumas that overwhelm their capacity to deal with or even feel their emotions.

Many of my teenaged patients lead what would seem to be charmed lives—a wealth of material goods, good schools, and intact families—but they feel pressures coming at them from every direction. They can't figure out how to diffuse those pressures. (Of course, kids with charmed lives are also exposed to the world's complexities and the struggles that exist even in well-functioning homes.) While these teenagers might not have anger, they do have frustrations and are overwhelmed by the expectations placed on them.

I visualize these overwhelming feelings as a chaotic maelstrom of emotion. Each thought, concern, or painful memory seems to be shooting from a different direction. To maintain our sanity, we build a container to enclose and control what would otherwise be chaos.

Those of us with healthy outlets have release valves attached to our containers that prevent the pressure from blowing in a dangerous way. Many of us, however, become afraid of opening our containers because the emotions within feel too painful, scary, or totally unmanageable to face. Instead, we keep squeezing our day-to-day troubles into the container for safekeeping so we can avoid dealing with them—we fantasize that we will deal with the contents later. Over time, the walls of the container have to become thicker and thicker to keep all our stresses inside. It becomes a figurative leaden box—too heavy to lift, impossible to see through, and indeed toxic.

What happens when we have so many important, though painful, thoughts and emotions trapped inside our self-created leaden box? Occasionally, someone will push our buttons and cause the lid to pop open. Inexplicable, uncontrollable rage pours out.

I visualize the anger described by many of the teens I see as the lid cracking open from a crammed leaden box. The adults in their lives see only the anger and problem behaviors without understanding the emotions and experiences beneath the rage.

Some kids describe the sensation of having overwhelming, boxed-in emotions as their head spinning. One young man said it feels like a tornado.

Another visualizes his head squeezed like a tennis ball by a powerful man intent on making it explode.

Many say drugs do a great job of stopping the spinning and releasing some of the pressure. They may be correct for the moment, but we know that drugs create bigger problems that will accelerate the spinning out of control. Hence the cycle of abuse—more spinning, more drugs, more spinning, and so on.

The leaden box can create something worse than anger. It can make us numb. It can stop us from caring, losing what we value most—our humanity. When we expend so much energy squeezing those painful, passionate, but real experiences inside our box, it becomes too difficult to care about the things that make life worthwhile.

When a 7-year-old worries about being bullied and doesn't feel safe at school, how can he experience the thrill of reading a story that takes him to fantasy worlds? When a 14-year-old is struggling over her burgeoning sexuality, her parents' divorce, pressure to earn high grades, and peer pressure from cruel classmates, how can she possibly savor the smell of spring flowers or recognize the unconditional love of her parents? How can she engage in polite conversation when she is working so hard to suppress intense emotions? She may cut to create a feeling she can control.

Numbness is a lost opportunity for cherishing every moment. When the present isn't cherished and small things aren't appreciated, it is hard to be resilient. We don't want this for our children. Although they will be exposed to challenges and pressures, we desperately want them to thrive and have the resilience to survive no matter what curveballs are thrown at them. We have to raise children who can be exposed to stressors without locking their thoughts into emotionally toxic leaden containers.

Our children need to be secure about accessing their emotions rather than fearing them. To do this, they need a strategy for feeling and dealing with their experiences and concerns in manageable doses.

Containment is a good thing. People who feel everything fully in the moment can become dysfunctional. You probably know people who share every thought, feel every experience intensely, and send group e-mails in response to every perceived slight. While these people do not have a leaden box, they are rarely happy and find it difficult to maintain relationships because they exhaust themselves and others.

Building a Better Box

I propose a different kind of container: a Tupperware-type box. In contrast to a leaden box, it is made of light, flexible, nontoxic material. The container may be transparent so the contents can be seen and are safely stored in neat portions, but the contents don't stink. More importantly, you can lift the lid, remove one portion at a time, burp the box, and tightly reseal it.

People who know the contents of their boxes are emotionally intelligent and aware of issues that challenge them and experiences and memories that haunt them. Rather than letting tornados swirl in their heads, they can choose to release a bit of pressure by selecting one issue to deal with at a time.

When I work with troubled young people who tell me that they have uncontrollable anger, I help them build a Tupperware box. This type of container allows them to name the issues in their lives that overpower them. Once they name those troubling issues, they can begin the healing process by choosing one at a time to process while safely storing the others for a while.

The parallel process of naming their *strengths* is vitally important. It might be dangerously frustrating to categorize problems before one trusts in the capacity to deal with them. Before going through what might be a painful process of identifying stressors, it's important to be aware of one's strengths to feel confident about having strategies to prevent feeling overwhelmed.

You don't need to discuss leaden or Tupperware boxes with young children. Instead, as a preventive strategy, help them learn to identify and name their problems. Help them understand that when they feel overwhelmed or confused, they can identify a few manageable problems and work on them one at a time. If they are equipped with some of the following techniques, they can manage the swirling emotions that are paralyzing them from taking action. I'd like to return to the mountain metaphor for a moment. Remember that when our problems feel like overwhelming mountains, we become frustrated and feel powerless to address them. This technique breaks these mountains into smaller hills. Through the process of emotional intelligence, we decide which hill to climb first. The following techniques are the figurative release valves for the Tupperware box—the shovels to move the dirt from the hills:

Using Our Creative Energy

Creativity enables us to develop the perspective and flexibility needed to be more resilient. As I have watched my children grow, I've seen how creative expression can give kids a voice to articulate their emotions, as well as lose themselves in the act of creation. I am grateful for 2 teachers in particular, Maryanne Yoshida and Debbie Pollak, who have fostered creativity in my children. I wanted to learn more from them about how to engage children in art and nurture their creative sides. I thank them for their thoughtful contributions to this section, which I've added to the wisdom that my patients have shown me over the years.

People with creative energies have a built-in antidote to perfectionism. It may take years to develop the skill to paint a perfect picture or sculpt a flawless statue, but the process itself is rejuvenating. Learning a new process and making many messy attempts can be more exciting than the end product. The best results usually come after many attempts, much practice, and hard work. Artists enjoy the process of creating and, despite frustrating fits and starts, keep trying.

Creative expression also draws on our ability to look at situations from different angles and approach a problem from various perspectives. It's like a photographer who changes vantage point, lenses, and lighting many times to capture totally different images, while most people would have just snapped a shot. People with only one perspective, who see life through a single lens, are limited in their approach to problems. People who shift perspectives understand how to focus on a problem and attack it from different angles, as well as see other people's vantage points.

The Joy of Artistic Expression

The processes of singing, acting, drawing, painting, sculpting, writing, dancing, composing, or playing music can be joyful releases. For some, artistic expression is a solitary event that allows time for reflection, introspection, or simply quiet private time. For others, participating in a group effort, such as a class performance, offers an opportunity for expression while connecting with other people.

Ms Yoshida and Ms Pollak have taught children and adults for years. They told me that in their early years of teaching, they were disappointed whenever students left their work behind, seemingly forgotten. They later learned that the students' joy lay more in learning to be creative and practicing their new skills than in their completed masterpieces.

We want to educate children by fostering their creativity and expanding their minds. By the middle of elementary school, many kids' success is defined by how well they can recall those facts and figures. Art as a steady presence in children's lives allows them to continue having open-ended opportunities to express themselves with less emphasis on the final product.

Creativity as a Release

I have seen many young people tap into their creativity as a means of coping with their problems. They use music, art, dance, poetry, or prose to express their feelings vividly and intensely. These outlets allow a degree of privacy; whether to show them is the artist's choice. Each creative work is subject to interpretation, but only the artist or creator fully understands the meaning.

Rather than containing emotions to fester within, artists are able to say to themselves, "I know how I feel, there it is!" Rather than bottling up their emotions, creative people express them and literally place them outside their bodies.

I am amazed by how many poets and artists I find among the youth I serve who have lived the toughest lives. Their creative expression has helped them survive. When words don't come easily, it isn't uncommon for them to rap, sing, write poetry, or draw to express themselves. These are powerful survival tools that soothe their souls. In my work with homeless youth, I sometimes create a simple book for them, a place for them to place their creative work. Some look at their picture and can describe what it means, using their verbal skills to magnify their emotional release. Others could never describe out loud what the picture means, but their subconscious pent-up emotions may still be released. Don't assume because young people can't always put into words what their art means to them that we should help them tell the story. The art does the work itself.

Can We Foster Creativity?

Every child is creative. Each is not a Rembrandt or Mozart, but all children express themselves through some form of art. When they are young, we encourage this creative outlet in a few kids and stifle it in many, who then decide they have no talent. All children need to be able to draw on their creative side as an avenue to release their tensions, fears, hopes, and dreams. It gives them an opportunity to experience the joy of creating, and it trains them to see other perspectives. It gives them another way to cope.

Parents can do any number of things to nurture children's creative expression. You don't have to enroll them in classes or buy expensive equipment. The following ideas apply primarily to the visual arts, but if your child is more inclined toward the musical or dramatic arts, you can adapt the same principles:

1. Make a wide variety of art supplies available. Some of the least expensive creations are made from sticks, stones, and scraps of cloth. Socks and mittens can become hand puppets by decorating them with buttons, yarn, and colorful laundry pens.
2. Expose children to tactile stimulation so they can discover the joy of working with their hands. Nothing fancy is needed—try clay, wood, sandpaper, or various textured fabrics.
3. Have some turn-off-the-screen time. Many kids turn to television, handheld devices, or the computer when they have "nothing to do." Without pushing art per se, simply make art supplies available and limit time wasted in front of a screen.

4. As they produce their artistic masterpieces, make open-ended comments like, "Tell me about that," or "It's beautiful! Explain it to me, please." This will avoid the embarrassing and belittling exchange we have all heard ("What a darling little elf you've drawn." "No, that's you, Grandma."). Exchanges like that embarrass children and convince them that they have no talent, so they stop creating. More importantly, open-ended comments give children an opportunity to explain the content of their pictures or meaning of their poems or songs, and that is good practice for self-expression. Occasionally, you might add, "What were you feeling when you created this?" If a child doesn't choose to answer, just drop the subject.
5. Look for beauty in their creations. Not all their works will be gorgeous, but all have something special. Be genuine when you point out something noteworthy. A boat floating on an ocean might not look at all seaworthy, but the ocean may be inviting. "Look how well you used the blue paint. I want to dive in and go swimming."
6. Display their art, listen to their poetry, watch their dances, and applaud their music to show them that you're paying attention. You are genuinely interested in them, proud of them, and appreciate their creative efforts.
7. Look for art everywhere. You can go to a museum or concert, but you can also notice designs in cloud formations or point out how junk can be turned into beautiful or whimsical objects. It's simply a matter of keeping our eyes open. Public art and unintentional art are all around us. Give a child a camera and let her see how many perspectives exist in each picture.

Here are some steps to avoid when thinking about children's creative expression.

- Don't supervise or direct their creative endeavors. It's about their expression, not yours.
- Don't rave so much and so often that they think you expect them to create masterpieces every time. This only adds stress. But do show appreciation for their creations.
- Don't sign children up for lessons in an effort to make them the best in the field. That produces stress and may take away their joy of the creative process.
- Don't automatically display their creative works without their permission. Some works may be deeply personal items, as they should be. Encourage children to keep it personal and only display it at their discretion.

Spirituality

People with strong faith or a deep sense of spirituality find comfort in prayer or meditation. While parents certainly can expose their children to religious practices and beliefs, ultimately each child will decide what role religion has in her life. She may see it as a community institution, cherished family tradition, or personal means of managing her life, or she may reject it entirely.

In the context of resilience, I am interested in how young people can use spirituality as a moral compass, as a means to reduce daily stress, as solace in times of crisis, and as a means to solidify a sense of purpose in their lives. Spirituality is a way for young people to grasp the interrelatedness of life on Earth and strengthen their sense of connection and responsibility to others. Speak to your spiritual leaders about how to encourage children to use their beliefs as a personal, portable tool to manage life's stresses and disappointments and draw inspiration.

Journaling

Journaling, or keeping a diary, can be a powerful tool for releasing emotions. It's another technique that says, "You want to know how I feel? Here it is, tucked away securely. My emotions are in a safe place where I can access them when I want to. I am in control of them. They aren't swirling around inside and taking control of me."

Encourage younger children to begin journaling by buying them a simple diary or having them make one for themselves. Tell them that this is a private special book to draw or write anything they want, and no one will ever look at it.

It can be tempting to gain insight into a child's innermost thoughts whether they are 6 or 16 years old, but I strongly urge parents against looking at a diary. That would be a deeply felt violation that takes away this important tool from children and teens—"If it's no longer private, why keep it?" they would conclude. Violating this trust can harm relationships. Although parents may explain that they looked at the journal out of love and concern, kids never accept this argument. The journal is a place to write absolutely everything, true or untrue, real or imagined. If it's to be effective as a way to release emotional baggage, it must be a place where young people can play out their fantasies, darkest thoughts, or most romantic dreams. If parents read a journal, they might get an unnecessary scare. In other words, their yield will be low and they'll have taken away their child's release valve.

If parents become so worried about a child's behavior or emotions that they feel the need to check the journal, it is far better to open up communication instead of the journal. If the child shuts her parents out, get professional help.

As much as privacy should be respected, parents should be aware of the Web log or *blog.* Many young people who may not take to a journal, perhaps because pen and paper are so old-fashioned, prefer blogging. These online journals can become very public. Anyone can check in on a child's most private thoughts or at least those she chooses to make known through the blog. Some blogs can be made more private if children give passwords to friends they want to keep in the loop. If your child does blog, talk to her (perhaps through a choreographed conversation) about the possibility that some of the things she reveals online may find their way to people who don't respect her privacy even if they do use passwords. Perhaps an old-fashioned paper journal would be more secure for her innermost thoughts and feelings. (Visit the National Center for Missing & Exploited Children Web site, www.missingkids.com, for advice on Internet safety.)

Young people who don't blog may use social networking sites where they much more casually express their feelings. Once the "send" button is pushed, those feelings spread like wildfire among "friends" and can't be taken back. Rapidly developing technology has had many benefits, but it also allows alarming, even dangerous situations for young people. Talk with your children about *cyberbullying* and *sexting* (sex + texting), which have become all too common. National surveys report that 1 in 5 teenagers has sent or received sexual images electronically. Sending risqué or nude photos or videos over the Internet and harassing classmates electronically with cruel notes or pictures have serious consequences.

Talking With People Who Have Earned Trust

The greatest release of emotion for many people occurs when they share their thoughts, fears, and frustrations with others. It is a way of letting it go while getting needed attention. Sometimes, talking is also a way to problem-solve because it helps the talker focus ideas and develop strategies to deal with the problem or because the listener has a different perspective or experience with a similar challenge. Someone else's viewpoint can throw new light on a problem and shed wisdom on another set of choices.

Talking to another person also provides a chance to decompress, to let it all go. Sometimes we feel better when someone else knows all the things we're trying to handle. Talking can be more effective in 2 phases. First, get it off your chest. Use the opportunity to talk about what's bothering you as an escape valve to prevent all your emotions from swirling inside your leaden box. Then focus. Pick one issue to make it manageable. Just talking about it may be all that's needed for you to begin bringing it under control. Talking about that issue may be the catalyst for solving the problem. Either way, the Tupperware box is burped and less chaos spins inside.

Young people need to be exposed to different perspectives, so it's important that they can talk to a variety of people. Parents often become frustrated when children are so eager to talk with their friends (in person, on the phone, through incessant texting), yet they're so monosyllabic at home. When we ask them, "How was your day?" they're likely to reply, "OK." We make another attempt: "What did you do?" The answer is, "You know, stuff."

We acknowledge that they talk more with friends who, after all, do share more of their time and experiences. We hope those friends care enough about our children and have the good sense to steer them in the right direction. Friends can be ideal sounding boards, or they can be poor influences.

Other people can also offer children varying perspectives—older, mature adolescents; teachers; relatives; clergy; and coaches. Some parents feel guilty or insecure when children confide in another adult, but they should know it's more beneficial for their child to talk with someone than to talk to nobody at all. During mid-adolescence in particular, when teenagers' struggle for independent thinking is at its height, it's vital for them to know people other than parents who will listen.

Most parents naturally want to be their child's favorite listener. When I first meet families, parents often tell me, "Oh, yes, we can talk about anything. My kids tell me everything." Sadly, teenagers tell me a different story. Many say that they stop talking to their parents because their parents "just don't listen." This is partly developmental, a distorted perception that's a side effect of kids' need to trust their own decision-making skills. They reject out of hand their parents' potential for good advice. But the statement is often the truth. When parents don't listen, kids stop talking. Volumes have been written on this subject, and we discussed the importance of listening in Chapter 18. The good news is that parents who learn to listen better find that their children talk to them more readily. Parents earn their children's trust when they make themselves worthy of talking to by responding less and listening more carefully.

Some kids' stress levels can become so high that they need to talk to a professional. It's an act of great strength and resilience to seek help when burdened. Never feel as if you have failed because your child needs someone more objective and trained to help her through critical times. Sometimes a parent's job is just to love the child unconditionally while another trusted adult helps her resolve an important struggle. As parents let this other adult do much of the talking, they should remember that the security of their love remains the bedrock of any solution. Seeking professional help is discussed in Chapter 39.

Laughter—It's No Joke

Laughter is such a silly-looking thing. We snort, grunt, and make ridiculous sounds. There must be a biological reason that we're given this gift. Did you know that laughing has been proven scientifically to release stress? Every once in a while, science proves what our grandmothers told us. My grandmother used to say, "With a sense of humor, you can get through anything."

I see laughter as a refresh button. Let's say you're listening to a boring presentation at work. You can't pay attention for another minute—and then a well-timed joke wakes you up. Or you're feeling down and someone tells a story that evokes a belly laugh. Afterward, your mood is completely changed. You can start over.

So whenever you feel tense or worried, laughter can be a quick release. Make a point of reading funny stories, telling jokes, or even making yourself laugh for no particular reason. Just start laughing as an exercise. Do you know the ha-ha game? Someone begins by saying, "Ha"; the next person says, "Ha-ha"; the next says, "Ha-ha-ha"; and so on until someone breaks down and laughs. Yes, you'll sound silly, but laughter cascades. You'll relieve tension and feel lighter.

Most kids are born comics. They make us laugh at their antics. We may get tired of their making silly faces or telling poop and knock-knock jokes after a while, but encouraging children to have a sense of humor is certainly worthwhile. If we are always too serious, kids may stifle their natural ability to make us laugh. Trust me—trust my grandmother—laughter can help us rebound during difficult times.

Crying

Crying is another of those biological oddballs. People look so vulnerable and unattractive when they cry. It simply must have a purpose. Perhaps vulnerability is the point. Perhaps our need to get others to pay attention to our grief is the reason that crying is so entrenched in our social repertoire. Perhaps we need the attention to gain the sense of security that reminds us we remain connected to others.

Certainly, crying is a powerful tool for releasing pent-up emotions. The old saying, "Have a good cry," is on target when we're sorrowful or consumed with stress. Think of how we comfort someone who's in tears: "That's OK, let it out." Letting it out is the goal. People feel lighter after they've released those pent-up feelings. Crying doesn't solve the basic problem, but it cleanses the emotions and prepares us to move toward a solution.

When little children fall down or feel frustrated and cry, why do we instinctively say, "Don't cry. It's OK. You're all right," or worse, "Big boys don't cry"? How can we deny half our population such an important inborn tool to release emotions?

Of course it's OK to cry. Tears are a normal reaction to sadness and pain. Saying, "Don't cry," is not the way to comfort children or build resilience. It forces them to create a disconnection between their feelings and their ability to express them. It makes children ashamed of their real emotions and may prevent them from seeking the support they need.

When children are genuinely hurt or upset, it's more empathetic to say something like, "I see you're sad. Would you like to tell me what's bothering you?" and then listen and encourage them to talk about it. Oftentimes, no words are necessary. A hug and a shoulder to cry on silently communicate, "I'm here for you; this is your secure base. Lean on me."

Making Lists

Getting organized is a key problem-focused strategy that can also help release emotional frustration. When you are being pulled in a hundred different directions, you can't enjoy anything because your head is spinning with thoughts about everything you must accomplish. You can't focus, you're inefficient, you can't fall asleep because you're making tomorrow's plans. You need an escape valve.

This isn't an adults-only phenomenon. Children's heads also spin with worries about homework, after-school activities, friends, and chores. Like adults when they feel snowed under, kids make excuses and procrastinate. Sometimes it seems so impossible that they freeze and do nothing.

It's helpful to understand that getting organized can remove a lot of their stress. They don't have to accomplish everything at once; they simply can begin by breaking a big job into smaller, manageable steps.

With young children, a task like "clean up your room" seems gargantuan because toys, books, and clothes are scattered all over the place. They may think the job will take a week. Parents can help them organize by suggesting, "Just start in this corner. First, put all the clothes in the hamper, or begin by putting the books on the shelf." Older kids and teenagers can break down jobs and to-do schedules by making lists on paper or computer. "What I need to do today. What I need to do tomorrow. What has to be finished by Friday." When their lists are written down, there's a strategy in sight. They begin to feel they've taken some measure of control over the chaos by organizing it, and the pressure is diminished. Their mental and emotional energy can then be directed toward tackling problems one by one.

Two tricks make list making more effective. First, make sure something on the list is pleasurable. Breaking homework down into manageable pieces is important, but there should be some balance too. It is important to teach our children to schedule breaks—a half hour to play outside, work on a favorite hobby, or play a game. Second, it's also important for daily lists to be constructed to ensure forward movement each day. For example, a child may be worried that his group science project can't be finished by the deadline 3 weeks from today. So several items on his list can be broken down into doable segments like, "Look up Saturn's rings," "Sketch my model of the solar system on big paper," and "Make sure Owen gets the wire to connect the planets." As each segment is completed, he can check off that item on his list, see that he's making progress, and diminish his anxiety about completing the entire project.

Once again, parents can show the effectiveness of list making as a stress reducer by modeling the technique. When your child sees you making your own to-do lists, she'll pick up the lesson more easily than if you simply say, "Get organized." Talk aloud about the fact that you make lists not just to organize all your responsibilities but because it helps you reduce stress, preserve your energy, and enjoy the rest of your time.

One caution: List making can be overdone. If you become compulsive about it or notice that your child is doing it to excess, pull back. This is meant to reduce stress, not add to it. You might say, "I have so many things on my mind and this list is getting too long. I'm going to put my list on the table and take a well-deserved break," or "Right now, I'm going to work on just one thing and not look at the other things on my list until tomorrow."

Now that you have read through this comprehensive stress-reduction plan, I want to remind you again that these points are suggestions; no one is expected to use all of them all the time. You're probably familiar with many of these techniques but may not have tried them, or you may have other techniques that I've omitted.

I hope you expose your children to a wide selection of stress-management techniques so they're better prepared to deal with stress when they feel challenged. When I say *deal with,* I have a specific point: Children can be helped to cope with stress and somehow get past it, but nothing in this plan can make them immune to stress or make stressors disappear entirely. Everyone has times when they feel they simply cannot take any more stress. I believe that the tools in this plan can equip children to bounce back faster and stronger. I don't want to leave you with the false sense that this plan is an answer to every problem or that you (or your child) should be able to handle everything just because you have a plan. It's OK to go through periods of absolute rage or profound sadness. Don't deny your own emotions. Give your child the comfort zone to acknowledge her own feelings. We're all human; if we deny emotion, we deny the most complex, perhaps most valuable part of being human.

Above all, take care of yourself first. Model for children that there are healthy ways to manage life's bumps and bruises. It is the best lesson you can offer.

To learn about the full offering of* Building Resilience *videos, please turn to page 327.

PART 5

Control

Styles of Discipline

By *control,* I do *not* mean inflexible parental control, the "Do as I say because I'm the parent" style. We cannot and should not attempt rigid control of our children's actions, emotions, thoughts, or choices if we want them to become more resilient. When I discuss control in the context of building children's resilience, I mean *their* controlling their actions and therefore the outcomes.

Children who learn inner control by making decisions and facing the consequences gradually become more independent and ultimately more resilient. Children who understand that they have control over their lives take responsibility rather than blame others for problems and failures. Look at it from the opposite side—children who routinely blame someone or something else for adversity ("Why does that always happen to me? It's never my fault.") will see themselves as victims and will be passive in the face of difficulty because they do not believe an action they may take will make a difference. Resilient children understand that things don't just happen to them. They can be decision-makers and problem-solvers who control outcomes. They learn that delaying immediate gratification often leads to success at a long-term goal.

The development of resilience depends on parents' relinquishing tight control in favor of guidance, attention, and support so that children have opportunities to test their inner control. That is not to say that parents take a completely hands-off approach, of course. Parents can enhance children's growing sense of self-control by observing, offering a steadying hand, and guiding children rather than controlling their every action.

This discussion about ways parents can contribute to a child's having control will be divided into the following 4 basic categories:

- Considering how controlling we should be as parents
- Disciplining in a manner that teaches self-control and delayed gratification
- Helping children trust their own decision-making skills
- Knowing when to take control and when to conserve our energy

How Controlling Should We Be?

Before I suggest various ways to help your child develop control, I ask you to consider your own parenting style. Of the following 4 general styles of parenting, which best describes you?

Authoritarian. This parent's attitude is, "Do as I say. Why? Because I said so. Don't question my authority. Until you're 18, I'm the boss in this house!"

Permissive. This parent may teach values and give support and love but ultimately says, "I trust you," instead of setting appropriate boundaries. Permissive parents often treat a child like a pal and fear the child won't love them if they clash. They hope that their children will do the right thing because they do not want to disappoint their parents.

Disengaged. This parent is too busy or otherwise occupied to monitor a child's activities closely or set limits unless the child is in trouble or imminent danger. This parent says nothing or says, "Do what you want." This parenting philosophy is "kids will be kids." Disengaged parents don't believe that they have much influence anyway. But when major problems erupt, they may come down hard, leading to inconsistency and mixed messages.

Authoritative. This parent sets reasonable limits, expects good behavior, offers a lot of love, and encourages kids to make choices and be independent, but when it comes to the big issues, it's, "Do as I say." Authoritative parents balance warmth and support with control when necessary.

Children raised with authoritarian parents heed the line to a certain point, but then may rebel fiercely. Even if they remain obedient, they may become unwilling or unable to make their own decisions and instead seek authority figures to control them, even into adulthood.

Children raised with permissive parents know how loved they are, but they sometimes crave boundaries because it may be their conscience (guilt) that sets boundaries. They are terrified of the D word. The thought of *disappointing* their parents can paralyze them or force them to weave a web of lies. Those with disengaged parents fare the worst because there is nothing more painful to children than being ignored by people who are supposed to care for them. They sometimes need to push their behavior to the extreme to get the attention they crave.

If you find your parenting style leans toward the authoritarian, permissive, or disengaged models, I would suggest you consider how to become more authoritative. Ample evidence suggests that children raised with authoritative parents are less likely to engage in worrisome behaviors and more likely to be resilient. The balanced, authoritative model requires lots of love and attention and opportunities to gain increasing independence, with close supervision and clear boundaries. This parenting style has been shown to delay sexual initiation, lower drug use, improve school performance, and decrease delinquency. Our own research at the Center for Injury Research and Prevention has demonstrated that teens who describe their parents as caring and supportive individuals, who also monitor them and have clear rules and boundaries, are half as likely to crash cars, twice as likely to wear a seat belt, and 70% less likely to drink and drive.

Before you convince yourself that this will be easy, reflect on which of the 4 styles best describes your own parents. Did both parents have the same style? If not, how did their conflicting styles confuse you? How did you manipulate them if their parenting styles didn't match? Most importantly, how did you respond to their styles? Chances are that you have copied their styles or moved in a clearly opposite direction. Parents who give no thought to this may be destined to react according to their own childhood experiences rather than arrive at a parenting style that's best for their children. Even with reflective thought and the best of intentions, don't be surprised when your child misbehaves and your father or mother's words leap from your mouth.

Overcoming Your Authoritarian Side

Many of us were raised with authoritarian parents and even if we rebelled, we turned out OK. On some level, our fond memories of our parents urge us to honor them by raising our children the same way. Much anecdotal evidence tells us that children are becoming more spoiled, self-centered, or out of control, which leads some people to believe that we should return to stricter styles of discipline. Some people even advocate a return to physical punishment, though ample evidence indicates this is harmful. If nothing else, physical punishment makes children feel like victims and interferes with their learning a lesson. While they have been punished, they have not been truly disciplined or taught anything.

I could not say it better than Thomas Gordon, PhD, who wrote in his classic book, *Parent Effectiveness Training,* "Each and every time they [parents] force a child to do something by using their power or authority, they deny that child a chance to learn self-discipline and self-responsibility." Precisely because self-discipline and self-responsibility are such important ingredients of resilience, I will discuss discipline in detail here.

Giving Yourself Permission *Not* to Be Permissive

In any given moment, kids seem most appreciative of permissive parents. They get more. They have fewer rules to follow. What's not to love from any child's perspective? Let's be honest: Sometimes we do things simply because they differ from the way our parents did them. Many parents today who were raised in authoritarian homes vow to be very different—looser, more laid-back...permissive.

This style feels good in the short run but may raise more neurotic children because they are forced to self-monitor through guilt. When parents don't set boundaries, children have to set their own, without the wisdom or life experience that says where those boundaries should be drawn.

Even though it doesn't feel as comfortable, parents do children a great service by setting appropriate limits. We don't have to swing in the opposite direction, either; we can be different from our authoritarian parents. With an authoritative approach, we can shower children with affection and still explain and monitor the rules. This is vital because kids will only acquire a sense of control if they understand that their actions lead to consequences.

When you feel conflicted about not always giving in to your child's impulsive requests, remember 2 things. First, clear boundaries create a sense of safety; kids want to know where they stand. Second, sometimes saying "no" is the best way of showing your love.

Making Boundaries Acceptable

Children crave boundaries so they can know if they're pleasing you and because they're eager to prove they are good. Adolescents need boundaries so they can better learn to define themselves. Boundaries allow teens to experience and test their limits while knowing deep down that they will be protected. Still, don't count on being thanked for setting boundaries, at least until your children have children of their own.

The challenge is to give clearly defined rules and boundaries in a way that is acceptable to children. The book, *Adolescents, Families, and Social Development,* by Judith Smetana, PhD, helps parents consider how to do just that. It suggests we move away from the belief that monitoring is as simple as asking your children where they are, who they're with, and when they will be home. Instead, it discusses what adolescents consider "legitimate authority" of parents and reveals that parents really only know what their teens choose to tell them. Armed with this knowledge, we then have to consider what it is that will make teens more likely to share.

In previous chapters, when we discussed connection, we talked about the importance of listening as the best guarantee to keep teens talking—listening without judgment; listening while offering unconditional support; listening while honoring a young person's intelligence and serving as a sounding board while she develops her own solutions. Dr Smetana's work takes it a step further. She reveals what teens find to be acceptable areas for parental guidance and intervention and which areas they expect a hands-off approach. Teens believe that parents have an obligation to be involved with their safety and a responsibility to teach them how to interact with society, while respecting other people's rights and following the law. Teens also believe that parents do not have free reign to transcend on personal territory. If the issue is about their friends or about behavior that doesn't affect safety or their "getting along" with society, it may be out of bounds.

This information informs us how we need to present rules and boundaries. We must make it clear to our children that we have rules because we love them deeply and care for their safety. The rules are not frivolous and certainly don't exist to control them. In fact, we cherish their growing independence and recognize their growing skills and competencies. While some rules are *always* or *never* rules, most are in place only until children gain more experience or demonstrate the responsibility that shows they need less supervision. "*Always* wear a seat belt; *never* drive intoxicated." "You may not drive after dark until you gain more experience driving during the daytime."

Certainly, the toughest area for setting rules and boundaries involves your child's friends. Adolescents especially may not think you have a right to comment on their friendships or even what they do with their own time. I want to underscore this important point: Rules and boundaries should be framed to be about safety whenever possible. If you condemn your teen's friends, you might just make their company more enticing. If you limit them from seeing particular friends, your child might choose to stop talking to you about who they're with and might make up stories that prevent you from knowing where they're going. After all, they think, "This is my personal life and not your business."

Although some believe that peers control teens' behavior more than parents, I disagree. Our strategy has to be to modulate peers' influence in a way teens find acceptable. First, be selective in your comments and rules about friends. Your children really do deserve privacy when issues do not involve safety or negative influence. On the more "controlling" side, you should set general rules that will keep your children safer and won't feel like they were made to counter any specific friendships. Curfew, for example, keeps your child off the streets when things get wild. When you make sure that adults appropriately supervise parties, you protect teens from untold risks and pressure. Next, be subtle about promoting positive relationships. You can make it easier for your child to be with friends you trust by creating opportunities for them to get together. Third, always bear in mind that your child probably wants to do the right thing; he just needs the skills to follow his own internal compass. That's why giving him the tools to navigate the peer world, as discussed in chapters 11 through 13, is so important. The check-in rule and code word allow your child to have face-saving techniques to follow his own values even in the midst of peer pressure.

Finally, remember that there is less to rebel against when teens know their parents care about them. Sometimes it takes an extra effort to help your teen understand that the limits you impose come from your concern for his welfare and safety. The truth is, there are situations in which peers' influence can lead to destructive decisions and others in which they innocently make a situation more dangerous because they create distractions or emotions that make teens lose focus. Driving serves as an example again. We know that peer passengers in a car driven by a new driver substantially increase the risk of crashes. But how do you make a rule about something that, on the surface, seems as innocent as driving friends to the movies? If you say, "I don't want you to have any friends in the car while you are driving," your teen will think, "My friends are my business." *(In other words, "My parents have no legitimate authority.")* "Why do my parents hate my friends? I'll take them anyway and my parents will never know."

Instead, be clear about your motives. "I care about your safety, and because teen passengers distract new drivers, you may not drive with passengers until you have at least 6 months' experience behind the wheel."

Expect push back. It's perfectly normal, even a good thing, for teens to test their boundaries. "My friends are really good; that's probably because other kids act wild."

You respond, "Actually, even great kids get excited talking when they're having a good time. It's too much to expect you to have your eyes on the road, control of the car, and control of your friends. This is nonnegotiable, but it's also temporary. When you have more experience driving and you've shown me you continue to be responsible, you'll be able to drive your friends. In the meantime, I'm happy to get you all where you want to go."

Keeping Kids Talking

Monitoring is less about what you ask and more about what you know. So, how do we get our kids telling us what is going on? First, we listen, rather than react. Second, we make every effort to be responsive to their needs, rather than inflexibly strict. If a reasonable request, accompanied by detailed planning that demonstrates responsible thinking, is denied, your teen will stop talking. She'll take up lying instead. Imagine your daughter comes to you, saying, "I really want to go out to this concert on Saturday night. I'll be home later than usual, but you'll know exactly where I am. I'll stop in and let you meet my date. Don't worry about homework; I'll finish it all before I go out. Also, don't worry about sleep. I'll sleep late Sunday but get up in time to finish my chores." If you respond, "Rules are rules, you know curfew is midnight," don't be surprised when Thursday night comes around and she kisses you on the cheek on the way out the door and says, "Love you. Don't forget, I'm sleeping over at Rachel's Saturday night." Kids lie when they see no yield in talking to us.

Making It Easier on Both of You

Remember, it's a teen's job to explore limits. Teens compare themselves with peers to see what they can handle. They want to keep up because they're always trying to answer one of those fundamental questions of adolescence: "Am I normal?"

When your rules are different than those of other parents, you'll be seen as strict and unreasonable, and your child is set up to rebel. If you work with your community or with the parents of your child's circle of friends to set up common rules and boundaries, everything will go more smoothly. Your child will just expect the rules because everybody else has similar boundaries. He can meet your expectations, stay safe, and be "normal" at the same time.

Building Resilience Videos (www.healthychildren.org/BuildingResilience)

Video 31.1 Balanced Parenting: A Key to Adolescent Success and Healthy Behaviors

Video 31.2 Offering Boundaries and Being Role Models: Adults' Critical Role in the Lives of Adolescents

To learn about the full offering of* Building Resilience *videos, please turn to page 327.

Positive Discipline Strategies

The word *discipline* means to teach or guide. It doesn't mean to punish or control. Parents who discipline successfully see discipline as an ongoing responsibility to teach. The best disciplinarians (or teachers) hold high expectations and give appropriate consequences or allow them to occur naturally, rather than dole out arbitrary punishments when children fall short of those expectations.

Several disciplinary strategies can help children develop control of behaviors and their outcomes. Some of these approaches can be used to spotlight and encourage positive behaviors. Others can be used to steer children away from negative behaviors. Regardless, the most important aspect of discipline is ongoing positive attention.

Paying Positive Attention

When infants cry and a parent's face appears above the crib, babies learn their first lesson about how they control their environment. They can't articulate it, but they know, "If I cry, someone will come and pick me up, feed me, change me, and take care of me." As they get older, children become masters at controlling our attention.

You may have seen this joke (which has been e-mailed around cyberspace) that captures a child's attention-grabbing control. A small boy is sent to bed by his father. Five minutes later—"Da-ad." "What?" "I'm *thirsty.* Can you bring me a drink of water?" "No, you had your chance before lights out." Five minutes later—"Da-aaaad." "WHAT?" "I'm *thirsty.* Can I have a drink of water?" "I told you, no! If you ask again, I'll have to spank you!" Five minutes later—"Daaaa-aaaad." "WHAT?!?" "When you come in to spank me, can you bring a drink of water?"

Children crave parents' attention. When they don't get enough of it, they find ways to make us pay attention by doing something we cannot ignore, like interrupt, whine, talk back, or pick a fight with a sibling. Then our attention is usually paid in negative ways, like scolding, criticizing, lecturing, threatening, or punishing. These negative ways are ineffective and instill powerlessness rather than a sense of control. The cycle continues because kids begin to see that type of attention as what they expect and learn to need from parents.

As we list a litany of reasons why children shouldn't have done something, they don't think about how correct we are. In fact, our efforts tend to backfire because we make them feel inadequate and incompetent. They want to prove our dire predictions or assessment of their behavior wrong.

If we want to diminish negative behaviors, we can short-circuit them by giving kids more frequent doses of positive attention. Unfortunately, we tend to focus primarily on their undesirable behaviors and fall into a pattern of responding only to those. If this has been your experience, here's a simple way to break the pattern. Keep a diary for a week and note all your interactions with your child. When he wants your attention, how does he get it each time? Begin to recognize that many of his annoying or undesirable behaviors may be attention-seeking ploys. How do you respond? Once you become more aware of your pattern, you'll be better able to replace negative attention with positive attention.

I've already mentioned some ways to pay positive attention. Catch kids being good. Show appreciation for the little things they do or say, things we often overlook, such as sharing toys, getting their school gear together on time, or helping with daily chores. Praise them with words that show you have really noticed and appreciated something they have done, rather than generalized phrases like, "You're so terrific." I'm certainly not against telling kids they're terrific, but let them know *why*. "I think you're terrific to help your little brother learn to ride a bike."

Other ways to pay positive attention can occur in simple, daily encounters—play guessing games while waiting in line, tell or read bedtime stories, or ask kids to help you with something pleasant that is not a chore. Children appreciate being invited to participate in grown-up activities, which also helps them feel more competent. "I have to mail a lot of letters. Can you help me put the stamps on the envelopes, please?" "I need to get a present for someone at work. Want to help me pick out something?"

These minor occasions are wonderful opportunities to pay loving attention to our children. The more positive attention we give them, the less they feel a need to capture our attention by behaving in less desirable ways. But let's face it: All the positive attention in the world won't guarantee a child will never misbehave. What do we do then?

Appropriate Consequences

From an early age, children should learn that certain misbehaviors bring unwanted consequences. Hitting younger siblings means a *time-out,* sitting quietly for a certain amount of time away from the center of the action, and losing that positive attention that they crave. Failing to finish homework means loss of television time. Leaving piles of dirty laundry around their rooms means their favorite clothes won't be clean the next time they want to wear them.

These consequences are appropriate because they fit the crime. When parents have to discipline by using a punishment, it should be reasonable and related to the offense so that children understand the direct consequence. When they spill or break something, for example, they have to clean it up or fix it. A consequence that is unrelated to the offense (say, they cannot attend a birthday party because they haven't picked up their socks) takes their focus off the misbehavior and prevents them from thinking about how to correct it. They become defensive or feel like victims. They become angry, focus on your unfairness, and sometimes even want to get even ("I'll show them! I'll never..."). More relevant to our discussion of control, overly harsh or arbitrary punishments send the messages, "You aren't in control. We, your parents, control what happens to you. There's no logical connection between your actions and consequences."

Certain patterns typically emerge when parents try to guide kids toward a safe behavior (such as, "I need to know where you're going and who you'll be with."), get them to adhere to safety rules ("Bike riding requires a helmet."), or contribute to smooth operations of the home ("Fold your clothes; clean the dishes."). The Discipline Cycle diagram on the next page illustrates the flow of communication when it works productively and when it breaks down. As I describe the interactions, try to see what portion of the diagram applies to you. It may be that you have different interactions with different children or that you and your spouse have different patterns.

First we issue an order, like, "Clean up your room!" The child may follow the command, and all is well. If the child ignores us or argues, everyone's stress level increases. We may repeat the order several times. Most kids know their parents' threshold for repeating commands. Some parents repeat them 3 times; others repeat 6 or even 7 times. Children know just how far to push us and how many refusals they can get away with before we give in or get tough.

Why do they do this? Because they are engaging us, holding our attention. The problem is that families caught in this repetitive cycle of commands waste a lot of time nagging and refusing, nagging and refusing.

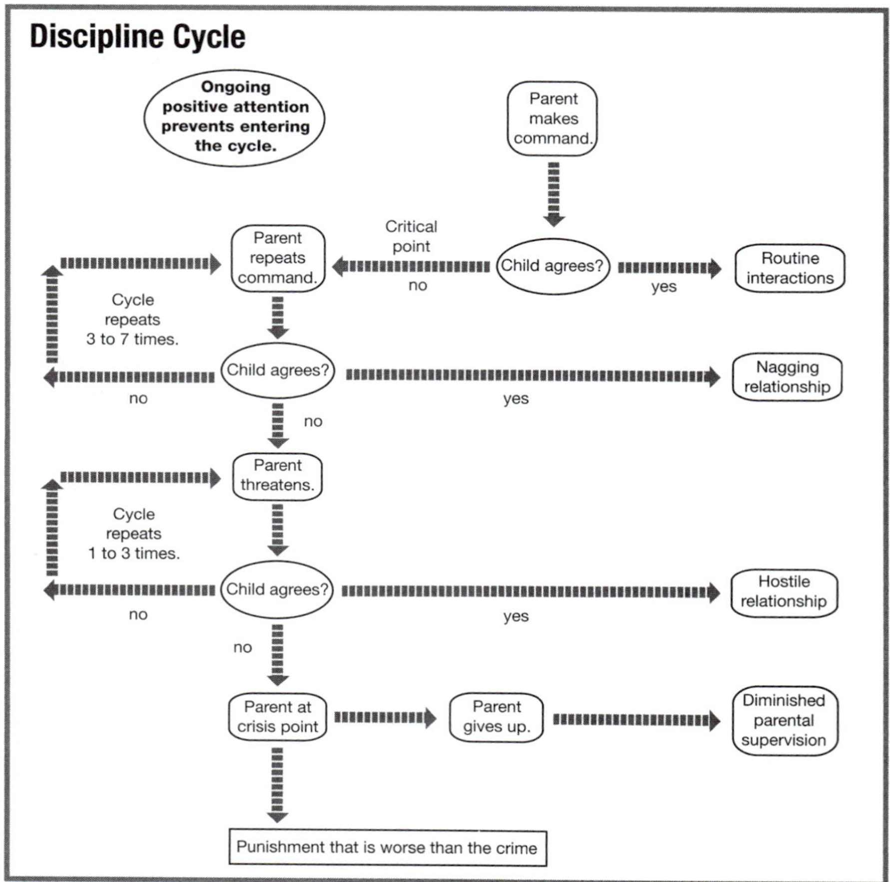

Adapted from Barkley RA. *Hyperactive Children: A Handbook for Diagnosis and Treatment.* New York, NY: Guilford Press; 1981. Copyright Guilford Press. Reprinted with permission of The Guilford Press.

If they don't comply after our first, second, or seventh request, we move up a notch to the threat level. "If you don't clean up your room, you can't go to the birthday party!" Now the child must decide to accept the threat and obey or call our bluff ("I don't want to go to the dumb party anyway!") because if he buys into the threat and complies, our attention will disappear. Either way, the tone in the household moves from nagging to hostile.

If we let confrontations get to this point, we get angry because the child is disobedient and defiant. We are at a lose-lose crossroad. We have 2 options: We can follow through on the threat, or we can cave in. If we follow through with the threat, children don't learn useful lessons. They feel like victims of mean parents; they learn nothing about taking responsibility or solving a problem. They focus instead on how we made them pick up their rooms or kept them from going to a party. The punishment shifts away from the original request or command and now focuses on their rising defiance and disobedience. Missing a party because socks are left on the floor seems unfair to them.

When we get to this point with teenagers, we are sometimes talking about problems and consequences much more serious than cleaning up and going to birthday parties. They may be out after curfew, we may not know where they are, and we're so frantic that our threats become almost hysterical. Most parents are unlikely to say, "You are 25 minutes late. I have been worried sick. I was ready to call the police! I'm going to come up with a consequence so fair and so directly related to your lateness that you will really learn this lesson!" No, hysterical parents instead have adrenaline coursing through their veins and say, "That's it, young lady! You are grounded for 2 weeks!" Parents may consider grounding a gift to themselves because it means they will know where their child is. To adolescents, grounding feels like being sent to prison, and they don't see how 25 minutes even begins to compare to 2 weeks. They learn nothing and become increasingly hostile.

Parents often realize that their initial threats were too harsh, so in a more rational state they take the second option, caving in ("OK, I give up. You can clean your room after the party," or "All right, never mind. You're not grounded. Just be home on time tomorrow, OK?"). When we give in, children learn that they can manipulate us, hold our attention even in a negative way, and still win by not obeying our original request. Children who learn to manipulate parents or simply endure our nagging and anger because they know they'll win in the end are headed for trouble.

To prevent these lose-lose situations, try to avoid getting to that critical point in the first place. The critical turning point is immediately after you make the initial command. Don't let children pull you into these spiraling negative cycles. Instead, make it clear from the beginning that certain behaviors are not negotiable and consequences are immediate. It may seem harsh to have immediate consequences, but it is far better than wasting so much of your valuable relationship time on nagging, hostility, or empty threats.

A word to the wise here: Pick your battles. On those things that really matter to you, have clear and immediate consequences. But remember that part of growing up involves kids' negotiating boundaries and figuring out what they can handle. Parents who make rules about everything or hold a rigid sense of exactly how children should behave in every situation prevent them from benefiting fully from their own experiences of decision-making and boundary-setting.

Advance Planning

You can avoid negative punishment cycles by planning fair, consistent, and predetermined consequences that will occur if your child refuses to comply or behaves irresponsibly. Make these consequences known in a concise, clear way. If you plan ahead, you can set consequences that are reasonable and linked to the problem, and your child will be disciplined instead of punished.

When you are in the middle of a problem or confrontation, give your child options in a calm, straightforward tone. "If you don't pick up your toys, we won't go to the playground." "You can continue to whine or, when you stop, I'll play a game with you." "If you want a ride to the mall, you'll have to finish your chores first." Then stick to your statement. Don't be pulled into the old pattern. By making consequences immediate and linked to his choices or actions, you help him understand that he has some control. You, the parent, set the limits, but he controls his choices and consequences within those limits.

With younger children, trying times may arise when they act out in public or in front of friends, and you'll need to issue a consequence in a way that won't be embarrassing. We want our children to keep their dignity even when they are misbehaving, so we can take them aside and have a brief, firm private discussion. ("How do you think your remark made her feel? Apologize or leave the room.") With very young children, we may need to remove them physically from the scene—take them out of the store when they toss a tantrum.

These challenges take patience and a cool head. We don't want to embarrass kids because that not only instills a sense of shame, but it also puts them in a defensive position ("Why are you picking on me?") so they don't reflect on what they've done wrong. They become hysterical, the adrenaline controls their bodies and actions, and it becomes unlikely they'll behave rationally. Again, we want them to learn that they have control over outcomes, good and bad.

Family Meetings

Sitting down together to solve problems is a great way to allow children to experience more control of their behaviors. Family meetings don't have to be (and certainly *shouldn't* have to be) saved for problem occasions only. They can be used for pleasant purposes, such as discussing family vacations, whether to get a new pet, or what color to paint the house. They can be brainstorming sessions—what to get Grandpa for his birthday or how to convince the local government to plant more trees.

Family meetings can be reactive. "We have a problem, now what can we do to solve it?" They can also be viewed as a preventive strategy. As advance planning sessions, they go a long way in addressing how to respond to situations clearly and directly when they arise. Encourage everyone to brainstorm the potential problem and its possible solutions.

Family meetings give children a safe, relaxed environment to think in advance about their behaviors. This is an opportunity for them to develop more abstract, cause-and-effect thinking as they discuss benefits and disadvantages of possible actions and consequences. Everyone's contribution should be heard and respected in these family discussions. The more input children have, the more likely they will be to comply with decisions. You want your child to propose reasonable, fair solutions and consequences, but don't forget that parents are the final arbiters and ultimately set the limits. You can do this without issuing threats or commands.

The consequences you agree on should be spelled out clearly so that when the time comes to test them, they will be understood and effective. It may be helpful to allow your child to run through some what-if scenarios. "What if I come home too late and I haven't called?" "What if I get in trouble with…?" "What if I am going to be late but call to tell you what the problem is and how I'm handling it?" This process will help your child clarify the purpose of the rules and more importantly, understand the limits of your flexibility.

We Are the Borders Adolescents Need to Stay Safe

To get an idea of the developmental task teens are working on, imagine a table covered with 10,000 pieces of a jigsaw puzzle titled "Who Am I?" They mistakenly think it needs to be completed in time to write their college essays. Think about how you put together a puzzle so complex. You begin with the corners and then move on to the borders. Next, you look at the picture on the cover to remind yourself what you are building. The middle of the puzzle is toughest because you have to rely on trial and error—turning pieces in all directions and occasionally trying to force them to fit.

Parents are critical to the puzzle's completion. Boundaries and monitoring create those borders teens can push against as they work on the harder inner pieces on their own. When we serve as healthy role models, we offer our children a reliable picture on the cover. Adolescents with appropriate boundaries and trustworthy role models can navigate the rest on their own.

***Building Resilience* Videos (www.healthychildren.org/BuildingResilience)**

Video 32.1 Discipline: The Key to Healthy Households and to Young People Learning Responsibility and Self-control

To learn about the full offering of* Building Resilience *videos, please turn to page 327.

Increasing Kids' Control

When discussing problems and solutions with your child, encourage her to negotiate. You are the ultimate limit-setter and certain misbehaviors are non-negotiable, such as hitting another person, verbal abuse, stealing, or whatever you deem unacceptable. But the majority of issues that you will consider with your child will probably be negotiable. When you're discussing individual family members' responsibilities, such as taking care of pets or sharing computer time, it's healthy for children to negotiate schedules, rules, and the consequences for not following them. By actively negotiating, kids reap several benefits. They exert some control of events. They will be more likely to follow through on compromises that they've had a role in reaching. As teenagers and young adults, they will have learned give-and-take skills that will come in handy when they must negotiate with peers, teachers, or bosses.

Whatever consequences you and your child agree on, expect that problems will inevitably arise, so be ready for them with the appropriate consequence. Don't make children feel that they have ever made a mistake in coming to you when they fall into trouble. Let the consequence teach the lesson, but don't let your disappointment in their behavior or your anger take over.

When children mess up, let your essential message be, "Yes, you've done something wrong, but I still love you." Statements like this don't erase or diminish the disciplinary consequence, but they will help ensure that your child feels secure enough to come to you with problems. If we don't send a strong message of unconditional love, even in the face of disappointment over behavior, kids may turn away from us the next time they find themselves in trouble.

A Rein in Each Hand

As children grow, we often feel that we're holding 2 reins. We grip one tightly to keep them safe, while the other is looser as we gradually give them a little more slack to move away from us and explore increasing freedom. We're constantly jiggling these reins, pulling one a bit tighter, letting the other out an inch or two. We don't want to overprotect or control children too strictly, yet we don't dare let them have freedom they can't handle safely. It requires a delicate balance, but the trick is to increase their freedom gradually while at the same time minimize chances that they'll make unwise choices.

We typically think of teenagers as pulling away from parents and asserting autonomy. That's true; it is their job to develop their own identities apart from us. But the process actually begins at a much earlier age. Even the toddler whose favorite word is "No!" is asserting her independence. By age 3 years or so, she may be saying, "No, I do it myself," when you try to get her dressed faster than she's dressing herself. Some children, of course, have innate temperament traits that make them more independent, persistent, or outgoing than other kids. Very few children want their parents to hover over their shoulders, overprotect them, make all their decisions, or otherwise curtail their independence.

Earned Freedoms

We can take advantage of children's natural desire for independence by guiding them along if we put some safety nets in place. *Earned freedoms* are built on the foundation that parents don't hand out privileges and freedoms lightly, and neither do we use them as bribes. Earned freedoms are just that—earned. Here's how to institute this practice in your family.

Sit down with your child and explain the concept that you and she can come up with a plan that serves you both well by ensuring 2 things: her greater freedom and privileges and your need to be sure she's safe and responsible. Together, you draw up lists of what you each want and need. You'll discuss these, negotiate, put them in writing, and come up with a written contract.

Your child may want to stay up later at night, but you need to be sure she gets enough sleep to be healthy and alert for school and play. She may want a new bicycle, but you need to be sure she wears a helmet and rides safely. Your child may plead for a larger allowance, but you want to be sure she knows how to handle money responsibly. She may want to go somewhere with her friends, but you need to know where they'll be, if there will be adults present, and when and how she'll get home. She may be ready to drive, but you need to put into place the restrictions that have been proven to save lives—limiting the number of teenagers in the car, no driving after a certain hour, no cell phone use while driving, exposure to more complex driving situations (like 4-lane highways or bad weather conditions) only after the easier ones have been mastered, and driving on her own only after a significant amount of adult supervision.

From both your lists, you can draft a contract. Her wants should be linked to your expectations of her responsible behavior. If your child requests a later bedtime, for example, she can earn it by meeting your expectation of getting up in the morning, meeting the bus on time, and earning good grades in school. If she wants to go places with friends, she can earn this privilege by calling you at an appointed time to check in and letting you know how she's getting home. If she is ready to drive, you will allow this if she follows your safety plan.

Your contract will work most effectively if you reevaluate it from time to time to see how it's working. You'll probably hit several snags, but try to stick with it and tailor it to be more effective when necessary. Your child will enjoy having more control and will undoubtedly act more responsibly to keep that control and gain greater freedom and privileges. It's a reinforcer of good behavior as well as a deterrent of negative behavior.

The earned freedoms technique works best when you make the privileges and freedoms verifiable. For example, a new privilege can be earned when it is monitored or verified by some measure, such as a certain length of time (say, the number of hours spent watching television or doing homework). If your side of the contract says, "I need to know you're keeping up with your schoolwork," that can be measured by the report card or amount of time spent on homework. If kids aren't keeping up their side of the bargain and their grades are slipping, the consequence is to decrease the amount of time they spend on the television, computer, phone, or other amusements.

In the case of teenagers and safety concerns ("I want to know where you're going, with whom, whether parents will be present, and who's bringing you home and when."), adolescents should be very clear—before they earn freedoms to go out on their own—about how strongly you feel about following the rules. They should know which freedoms and privileges will be unearned (otherwise known as *lost)* if they don't act responsibly to prove they are capable of those freedoms. For example, a parent could say, "I want you to understand that if you are late, I will not allow you to stay out until 11:00 again. You have already proven to me that you're capable of following a 10:00 curfew. You will return to that earlier curfew if you are not able to follow the later one. I think you are ready to handle an 11:00 curfew, so go have a great time."

When you've worked out an earned freedoms contract, go back and consider its effect on the interaction patterns shown in the Discipline Cycle diagram in the previous chapter. Recall the importance of having immediate consequences at the critical point after your first command so you aren't dragged into a fruitless cycle of repeating and threatening, nagging and arguing. Pick your battles and don't overregulate your child's choices. For the big items that involve safety and responsibility, though, parents must have clear guidelines, stick to them, and make the consequences immediate. This stick-to-itiveness and immediate response will be far easier when the consequences are understood in advance—easier still because children (usually beginning at about 10 years, depending on the individual child) have helped formulate that understanding.

Essentially, the contract says, "I will earn this freedom or privilege by being willing to show responsibility and keep this freedom by proving my responsibility. I know that I will lose this freedom when I do not show I can be responsible." Parents have the consequence in advance and at their disposal to use when necessary ("You have not shown responsibility here. You have lost this freedom."). The advantage of revising the contract every few months is that you have a history of past successes—freedoms your child has proven she is capable of handling. When you need to come up with a fair consequence, you could revert to a freedom your child proved able to handle in the past. For example, "You said that if you stayed out until 8:00, you would have time to finish your homework. You didn't finish your homework. You'll have to begin coming in at 7:30 again. You were able to have fun then and still complete your homework."

Improved Communication

The earned freedoms technique can improve communication in your home for several reasons. Most obviously, it will improve because you will be discussing how to help your family function better on a regular basis, but also because you will be hearing your child's self-assessment of what she believes she can handle and you will calmly be able to share concerns.

Perhaps the most important reason is this: When you write down your need to know she's safe and responsible, you are sending your child the message that you're willing to trust her, negotiate, hear her side, and consider her ideas. Most kids expect parents to tell them what to do. They think we want to control them, rather than delegate some measure of control to them. When you first propose the earned freedoms concept, your child may look at you skeptically. As you work through it, she will realize that your motivation is to help her grow safely and that you are willing to listen to her. It is convenient to have a contract to refer to when children misbehave or disappoint you, but realistically, they will make requests for privileges or misbehave in ways you simply didn't anticipate.

Whether you are in a family meeting responding to a child's request or on the spot with a crisis at hand, don't feel that you must make an instant decision. It's fine to say, "Mom/Dad and I need to think about this. We'll let you know after we discuss it." That statement not only buys you some valuable time to reflect without an instant overreaction, but it also models for your child a thoughtful way to deal with challenges.

In 2-parent families, it's ideal when both parents present a unified front in decision-making. But it's not unheard of for parents to disagree! Partners often have differing styles for raising children. After all, we had different sets of parents and different childhoods ourselves. So when we disagree or are unclear about how our partner sees a problem, it's wise to take time out to discuss it. This also heads off the all-too-frequent strategy that children learn early in life—divide and conquer, otherwise known as, "If Mom says no, ask Dad."

***Building Resilience* Videos** (www.healthychildren.org/BuildingResilience)

Video 32.1 Discipline: The Key to Healthy Households and to Young People Learning Responsibility and Self-control

To learn about the full offering of* Building Resilience *videos, please turn to page 327.

Delaying Gratification

Resilient adults can delay gratification. So many things that feel good for a moment can get in the way of success. Especially when we're stressed, we may look for easy answers and feel-good solutions that end up creating more stress in the long run. Those who can maintain self-control while striving toward a larger goal are more likely to move beyond obstacles. Those with grit will view life as a marathon, keeping their eyes on long-term successes (see Chapter 25).

But children? Kids start out being all about instant gratification. "I want it when? *Now!*" They arrive in the world as self-centered pleasure machines, using their charm and cuteness to get adults to meet their every need. Children are quickly socialized to learn that not every desire can be granted immediately. The rice pudding comes after the strained peas. They must learn to wait in line for the carnival ride. They have to do homework before going outside.

Every parent knows it's an ongoing challenge to teach children that they often must wait to get what they want, and sometimes they never get what they want. Parents who are committed to raising resilient children know that it is a critical part of a child's developing self-control. The word "developing" is critical here. This is a developmental process that builds over time. We do an injustice to our younger children if we expect them to have well-developed impulse control.

Control and delaying gratification are not usually considered aspects of discipline, but when we remember that discipline is teaching and not punishing, it becomes clearer that teaching control is a cornerstone of preparing children to have self-discipline for life.

I know you want to make your children smile, hug you, and say, "Thanks, this is exactly what I wanted," as much as I do. I have had to stop myself from showering my daughters with things that made them smile ear to ear. When I learned what they wanted for their birthdays, I had to tie myself to a chair to keep from running out to get it. Even now, when they say they want to go out instead of doing homework, the little boy in me wants to say, "Neat, I want to play too." Fortunately, I am restrained from being so absurdly indulgent because of some adults I know. These adults, who never learned to delay gratification, are quite obnoxious. They push ahead in line, leave work for colleagues to finish while they go off and play, and are unconcerned about others. Not so cute.

So I overcame my impulses and taught my girls that sometimes pleasures are earned, sometimes we have to wait for them, and other times we may never get them. As children, that meant special toys usually had to wait for special occasions, and others were too expensive to buy at all. It meant that finishing homework came first, or that as much as they loved ice cream, it followed a meal. While they always have known they are the priority in my life, they also knew that they sometimes had to wait until I returned patients' phone calls before I could play with them. Now that they are teens, I am careful to make sure they have earned the special electronics or sports equipment they crave. But because I am busier, I try even harder to let them know they remain my top priority and I will be wholeheartedly available to them as soon as I am able.

These small delays of gratification when children are young will prepare them to put in the necessary, sometimes boring effort and time that will reap success later. They learn, for example, that lots of research and homework can create a science project that they can show with pride. The knowledge that an investment of time and effort produces desirable results is also key to choosing positive coping strategies instead of easier, quick-acting, but dangerous ones that perpetuate stress.

The key may be helping children learn that there is value in delaying immediate enjoyment. As long as putting off something pleasurable always feels like giving something up, it is reasonable to expect resistance. What if children and teens could gain an improved sense of self through controlling their impulses? Imagine if they enjoyed the challenge of testing their will or took personal pride in sticking to their values. Do you see how tightly this is linked to overall character and how once again your modeling is more important than what you say? This idea is supported and tested by Eran Magen, PhD, and James Gross, PhD, in their work on how willpower helps people resist temptation.

Children and adolescents who are able to make wise decisions learn to trust their ability to control their own lives. They are less afraid of taking the appropriate risks that resilient people must take to meet and rise above adversity. They don't fear failure. They don't assume they are powerless because they have seen the fruits of good decisions. They learn from mistakes and don't repeat the pattern of decisions that led to those mistakes.

A word of caution here: Young people also have to be forgiving of their human impulses. Nobody wants to delay gratification all of the time. We don't want our kids to grow up feeling guilty for allowing themselves pleasure. As in all things, balance is key. This brings up yet another case in which your love is the linchpin of your child's well-being. Your unconditional love teaches your child to be forgiving of himself or herself even in the face of human frailty.

To learn about the full offering of* Building Resilience *videos, please turn to page 327.

Preparing Our Families for Lifelong *Inter*dependence

If I asked you if you wanted to raise a child who was prepared to be fully independent, I suspect that you would nod yes while fighting a lump building in your throat. We want our children to be capable of navigating the world, but really our goal is for them to ultimately be *inter*dependent with us.

The developmental challenge of childhood that accelerates during adolescence is to gain the confidence to be able to stand on one's own. As hard as it is to watch our children grow up, it is critical to their well-being and to the health of our relationships that we honor their growing independence. When we hold them back, they push us away. When we ensure their safety while guiding them toward independence—sometimes actively and sometimes by just getting out of the way—they appreciate us.

When our grown children know that we honored their need to become independent, they will return to us for that *inter*dependence that defines loving families across generations.

Everyday issues trigger many parent-child struggles but also offer opportunities for fostering independence. Your teenager might think she should be allowed a new privilege just because she's a certain age or her friends are doing it, but she might lack the skills needed to manage the situation. If you focus on preparing your adolescent, you will turn potential sources of conflict and rebellion into opportunities to master new skills and demonstrate responsibility.

Childhood and adolescence is naturally filled with opportunities for trial and error and, ultimately, success. Our challenge is to make sure our children learn from day-to-day mistakes rather than view them as catastrophes. At the same time, we need to be vigilant in helping them avoid those errors that could cause irreparable harm. Just as importantly, we do not want them to miss out on growth opportunities. When we are overprotective, it limits their opportunity to gain valuable positive life experiences and, just as importantly, to make those mistakes that offer them chances to learn how to rebound, recover, and move on. We want young people to make errors under our watchful eyes when we can offer the life lessons that build enduring resilience.

Don't Install Control Buttons

Think about when you had your own children and were considering the level of involvement you wanted your parents to have in their lives. Did you want to keep their visits to a minimum or live in the same community? I'll bet the answer had something to do with whether you felt "controlled" or supported by your parents when you were a teen. Would they respect you as a parent—indeed, as an adult—or try to take over? These control buttons were installed during adolescence. If you want a healthy relationship far into the future, don't install these buttons now. Instead, be authentically excited by and supportive of your child's growing capabilities.

Independence, One Step at a Time

When is your child ready to meet a new challenge? When there are enough pieces in place so the chances for success are enhanced.

A request by your 14-year-old to spend the afternoon at the mall with friends won't hinge on answering on the spot, "Is she old enough?" if you've taught about spending wisely and resisting seductive marketing messages. The day your teen begins to drive won't be so nerve-racking if you've modeled safe driving behaviors and made it clear you will monitor your teen's progress even after he gets his license. Your stomach won't be in knots when she goes on her first date if you have raised her to have self-respect, the skills to recognize and respond to pressure, and the knowledge to protect herself.

Each challenge requires a different strategy. The book I wrote with Susan FitzGerald, *Letting Go with Love and Confidence,* hopes to make parents more comfortable supporting independence in a measured, stepwise manner by helping them think about how to approach a wide variety of issues. It is beyond the scope of this chapter to offer strategies for a multitude of developmental tasks or challenges, but there is a common path you can follow for any one of these tasks.

First, start by observing. Think back to when you childproofed your home. If you just guessed what needed safeguarding, you would have missed opportunities to protect your baby. The first step was to walk around on your knees and see the surroundings at the same level as your toddler. Once you saw the world from his vantage point, you knew to turn that pot handle inward and cover those sockets. That same sort of observing—getting a "kid's-eye view"—will heighten your senses about the challenges your child or teen is likely to encounter. You'll be better prepared to think of how best to phase in new privileges and what kinds of support and monitoring need to be in place.

Next, your ability to individualize guidance rests on considering your child's temperament and unique developmental needs. Although this may sound intimidating, nobody matches the expertise you have on your child. The next step involves listening. Listen respectfully to what your child thinks she can handle and ask what guidance or support she seeks. Invite her to develop a plan with you. Approach the conversation with the attitude that even though she is young, she is still the greatest expert on herself.

Finally, generate a road map of each step that needs to be mastered to gain the skills and confidence that will prepare her to meet the overall challenge. Help her understand that she will gain more independence and privileges as long as she continues to demonstrate responsibility. When she knows that your goal is to help her ultimately get to her goal, she'll be much less likely to complain that you are carefully monitoring the process. Most importantly, she will appreciate your presence in her life, and no control buttons will be installed.

Lest I paint an unrealistic picture, remember that your child will still push you away as part of the uncomfortable journey toward independence. However, when she is confidently standing on her own, she will return to you for the loving *inter*dependence we all desire.

Building Resilience Videos (www.healthychildren.org/BuildingResilience)

Video 35.1 Raising Children Capable of Independence but Who CHOOSE to Be *Inter*dependent

To learn about the full offering of **Building Resilience** ***videos, please turn to page 327.***

One Rung at a Time

Sometimes a decision to take a positive step seems so huge or a goal so difficult to reach that young people feel they can't even think about trying. They feel powerless and scared. They think they have no choices. They sense that they're controlled by outside forces that just push them along.

When young people have no deep-seated belief that they are capable of changing, I use a ladder technique. I've used it with kids who never thought they could succeed in school or never considered that they could become healthier by losing weight or exercising. I've even used it with youth burdened with drug addiction and trapped in gangs. They all have in common the sense of being so overwhelmed, so stuck, that they believe they can't take the first small step, that they have no control at all in their lives.

When your child is at an impasse, use choreographed conversations and active listening on a regular basis and decision trees occasionally. Save this ladder technique for when your child is really stuck and feeling hopeless. Here's how to begin.

Explain that you sometimes get overwhelmed yourself. The first step is to think about where you are in the present moment. Draw out the base of the ladder and write in the dilemma at hand.

Admit that you don't have all the answers, but you do know there are a couple of different possible futures. Write them at the top ends of the ladders as 2 distant but real destinations. One is the positive, hopeful future and the other is what might happen if your child doesn't start to make wise choices. Repeat that you don't know all the answers, but you do know that each ladder has several rungs along the way, leading to the ultimate outcome. Ask your child to suggest what steps will lead to the less desirable end. Because he's feeling overwhelmed and helpless, don't be surprised if he knows exactly what steps lead to the negative outcome. He feels expert at those decisions and actions. Unfortunately, he may see no alternatives for the other, positive ladder.

As you write the steps he suggests, tell him that you find it easier when you divide difficult tasks into many small steps. You keep an eye on the future dream to keep you motivated, but you worry about only one step at a time so you don't become weighed down.

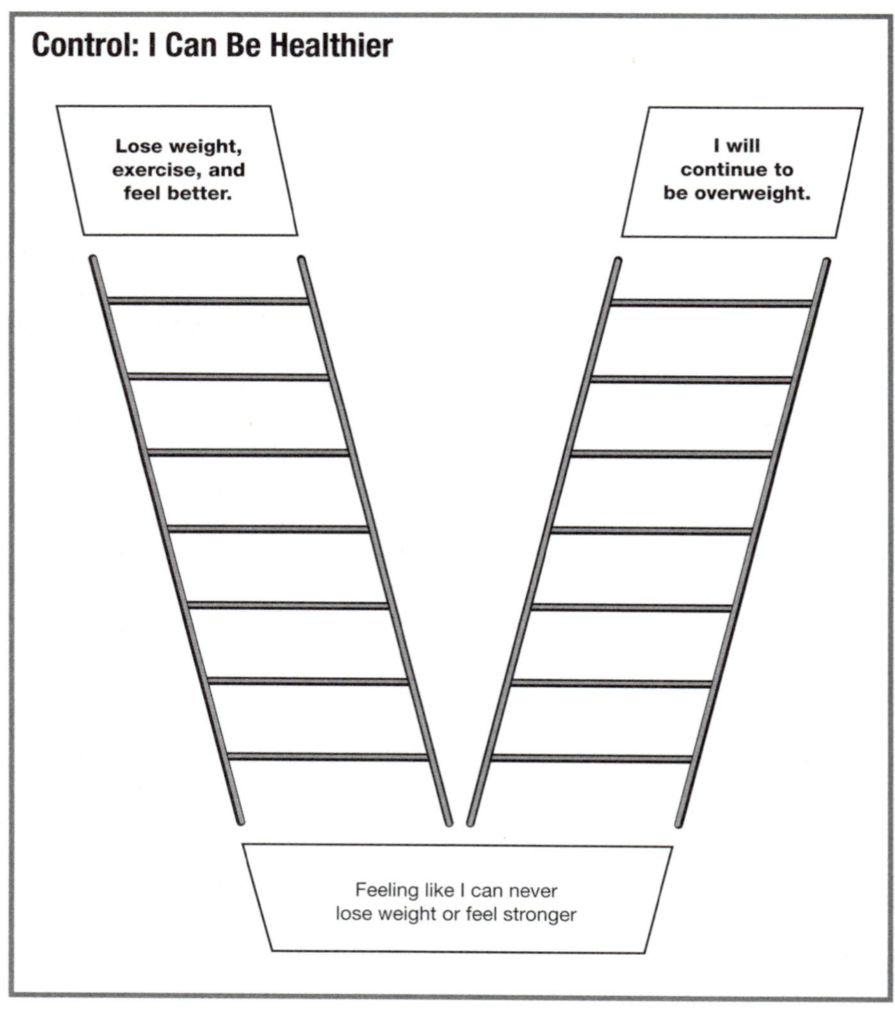

I used this ladder technique with Jung, a 12-year-old boy who was very overweight and unable to participate in the sports he loved. His parents nagged him to lose weight, and some of his peers teased him. Jung desperately wanted to lose weight, but he could only admit that with his gaze on the floor. Until our conversation, he had never talked about how much he wanted to shed the extra pounds. Instead, he'd put on a bravado front: "I don't care. Why do you?" He confided to me that the thought of losing weight frightened him because every time he'd tried in the past, he failed and gained more. He didn't even want to try again; he felt doomed to failure.

I sketched out 2 ladders and asked him what he had to do to keep gaining weight. He knew exactly what to do. He named all the unhealthy habits he had and said he would simply continue them. I noted these habits on different rungs of the ladder. Then I asked him to name one step he could take to get on a healthier path. I assured him that once he was on that ladder, each successive rung would be easier. Jung struggled to come up with a single step, but he eventually decided that he could stop drinking candy water (soda pop). When he returned to my office a month later, he had lost 3 pounds—a huge success! The greater difference was in his attitude. He realized that he had control. He could make a decision and follow it. He had gained the confidence to take further control and began telling me what his next step would be (walking the dog for 20 minutes after dinner each night).

I used another ladder diagram with Leslie, a 14-year-old girl who was trapped in a gang run by her 16-year-old cousin. Leslie was a bright, engaging girl who felt too overwhelmed to escape her dangerous circumstances. She wanted to become an architect when she got older so she could build buildings in her community to keep children off the streets. I tried my best to offer her my "adult wisdom." She appreciated my well-intentioned ideas but told me that I just didn't get how hard it would be to break from her cousin's gang—"That's family!" she explained.

The ladder diagram allowed Leslie to visualize 2 different futures. She knew which steps would continue to propel her toward trouble, but the ladder technique took away the vague nature of "turning your life around" by helping her see that ladders are climbed one rung at a time.

On her first visit, I could not even get Leslie to the first rung of the positive ladder. After a week, she returned and said she was ashamed that she could still not think of one right step. When I told her that just returning to see me was a positive step, she realized that she had some control over events in her life. Her sudden awareness that she had some control melted her belief that she was powerless and trapped by her fellow gang members.

The same girl who spent a week wallowing in her inability to come up with any possibilities immediately began brainstorming ideas she could use to break with the gang. She engaged her mother in a "just blame me" conspiracy (see Chapter 13). When she was facing the most trouble, she would call her mother, who would demand that she come home. Her cousin respected her mother and would allow her to have that special mother-daughter time. Leslie broke from the gang and later attended college.

The key point of these examples is that Jung and Leslie overcame their sense of powerlessness, lack of control, and beliefs that only fate determined their futures when they experienced success in one small first step. The success that gave them an inner sense of control was achieved by using the first part of the coping plan—they broke down a daunting task into manageable steps. Once they felt successful, the expectation of failure that had paralyzed their ability to act disappeared. They could take control. They could succeed.

When people become responsible for their own decisions and actions, they learn to face joyful and disappointing results. They learn that mistakes happen; sometimes they could have prevented them, but the next time they will be more prepared for them. If they are given many chances to exercise control in their lives, they are far less likely to see themselves as passive victims and blame others. This is the core of resilience: When faced with adversity, failure, or stress, kids who have a true sense of control will be able to bounce back. Ultimately, they will be happier, more optimistic, and better equipped to face the next challenge.

To learn about the full offering of* Building Resilience *videos, please turn to page 327.

Not Everything Is Within Our Control

When children know that they can control their environments and influence what happens to them, they hold a powerful key to resilience. It's also important for them (and for adults) to know when they don't have control. Otherwise, we would be banging our heads against walls and wasting vital resources and energy needed to handle those things we can control. People who are unrealistically optimistic will take on unreachable challenges and perhaps miss opportunities to take on those they can conquer. The key is to assess realistically what can and can't be controlled.

My mother-in-law, Regina Schwarcova Pretter, is a case study in resilience. A Czech Jew, she was taken to Auschwitz when she was 17 years old. She survived 3-and-a-half years of hell and went on to raise wonderful, loving children and experience a great deal of joy in her life. When asked the secret of surviving, she says simply, "You fight for the things you can do something about, and you don't waste your energy on the things you can't control."

To overcome any adversity, children must know when they have the power to change something and when they should reserve their energy. Think about anxiety. At some level, it results from the confusion about what we can and can't control. Like all emotions, anxiety can be helpful, but when it's out of control, it can be paralyzing. Isn't it better to know what we can handle, know our confidence is well earned, and have the good sense to recognize what *not* to worry about?

We've discussed the power of discipline to help children gain inner control and understand how much control they have over consequences. When we incorporate clear boundaries into our disciplinary practice, we also teach kids that they sometimes have no control. Any parent would be a fool to watch an 18-month-old who reaches toward the stove and say, "Now, dear, I want you to understand that if you place your precious little fingers on the stove, you will experience a very nasty consequence." Of course you'd shout, "No!" and grab her. Then you would act out big owies as you pretend to touch the stove. That's setting clear, distinct boundaries—no choices, no negotiation.

A 4-year-old has no choice about crossing the street to chase down a wayward ball. A 9-year-old has no choice about bicycling without a helmet. A 16-year-old has no choice to stay out all night. Clear, distinct boundaries. Long-winded explanations or negotiations would be a waste of energy. Children learn not to expend energy on choices over which they have no control.

We can also teach the lesson about conserving energy in no-control situations by modeling. If we do a little self-talk aloud when our children are present, we can model real but selected, well-choreographed conversations. For example

Mother: "Ms Brown is so difficult to work with. She makes me feel awful every day. She keeps nagging me to turn in my reports faster. I'd really like to tell her off."

Father: "I don't blame you one bit. You are already working so hard. What would happen if you let her know what you think?"

Mother: "I'd feel a lot better!"

Father: "For how long?"

Mother: "About a minute, I guess."

Father: "Then what would happen?"

Mother: "I'd lose my job, or she'd keep me on but become nastier."

Father: "Whoa. You're really stuck between a rock and a hard place. Is there anything you could do that would make things better?"

Mother: "I can't fix her bad personality or management style. I'm just going to try to remember that it's her problem. You know, I could try a little harder to grind out a report a bit faster each day and place it on her desk before she has a chance to harass me. But if she does, I'll just smile at her and let it go."

Father: "Sounds like a plan. You'll do what you can do and let go of the stuff you can't change anyway."

Previous chapters introduced strategies that can also be used to help children learn the limits of their control. When we create a zone of safety using empathetic listening skills, children will come to us during their most frustrating and vulnerable moments. We'll naturally want to fix their problems, but we cannot. Even if we could, we shouldn't; instead, we should guide them to come up with their own solutions by using a choreographed conversation or decision tree to help them imagine the end points of various problem-solving strategies. They usually will be able to arrive at solutions that fix or improve the problem.

They may instead reach an impasse—just like real life. That's the moment to give them a hug and remind them that when life gets tough, at least they can always rely on your unwavering presence. Help them understand that some things are simply beyond our control, for grown-ups and kids alike, and the only thing we can really control is how we choose to react. Often, the best thing we can do in these situations is conserve our energy and move ahead without tearing ourselves apart.

To learn about the full offering of* Building Resilience *videos, please turn to page 327.

PART 6

When Resilience Is Challenged Beyond Reasonable Limits

Extreme Circumstances

Parents can do everything in their power to help children develop resilience, but major challenges can test even the most resilient young people. When we know in advance that a crisis is looming, such as a divorce or the terminal illness of a beloved grandparent, we try to prepare children. In times of unforeseen crisis, we'd like to be able to give them a quick booster shot of resilience.

All our good intentions may not be enough because these events put enormous pressure on us and leave us little energy or time to support our children. For that reason, resilience building should be an ongoing, preventive practice of parenting—a routine that builds a child's strength and stores it for unusually critical times. This chapter goes a step further than the 7 Cs model to address circumstances that require a resilience boost. In each situation, parents make a major difference in how children weather the storm. In each case, the key element is that parents model stability and self-care, while reassuring children and adolescents that their safety and well-being is the parents' chief concern.

Please go to www.healthychildren.org/BuildingResilience for discussions on handling divorce, sickness and death, terrorism, war, and natural disasters. We wanted this information available to the public and placed it on our Web site.

To learn about the full offering of **Building Resilience** ***videos, please turn to page 327.***

Turning for Help

The security that derives from a strong connection with parents is the key to resilience. But even if you have the strongest connection and the most competent, confident children equipped with the best possible coping strategies, your children still have limits that can be exceeded when life gets too tough to manage.

We must never believe that resilience means invulnerability. All people, even the most stable and resilient, reach their limits sometimes. It is not a sign of weakness on our children's part, nor is it a sign of poor parenting on our part, when they show their human limitations. When children are not coping well, they may come to their parents silently with telltale signs like tears or a furrowed brow. At other times, they may verbalize their feelings clearly and express exactly why they are troubled and what they need. But usually, parents have to remain alert to subtle indications that children are troubled.

Signs of trouble can include regression. A classic example of regression is a 3-year-old reacting to the birth of a new baby by becoming infantile, sucking her thumb, and demanding much more attention. Other children regress by bed-wetting. Older children and adolescents might have the kind of tantrums they haven't had since they were toddlers—anything to let their parents know they are out of control. Sometimes a child will show signs of regression by being overwhelmingly lovable. Be thrilled when your child wants to snuggle up the way she did as a toddler, but if it is a change of behavior and her need feels intense, allow her to open up about something that may be troubling her. A child who has heightened anxiety when a parent is out of sight may have an increased need to have you near, perhaps to guarantee her safety or security. Or she may be worried about you and only feels comfortable with you in close range.

Children experience stress through their bodies just as we do. They get bellyaches, headaches, muscle strains, fatigue, and even chest pain and dizziness when they're stressed. Don't assume they are faking to avoid school or get out of responsibilities. If you approach children as if they are faking, they will feel ashamed. It is likely that they do not yet understand the connection between their emotions and their bodies' responses. In these situations, it is important to have them examined by a pediatric caregiver to be sure there is not an illness that needs treatment. It is equally important to consider that children with frequent aches and pains that can't be explained by a virus or other illness may be stressed. Pay attention when your child has frequent complaints that prevent her from going to school. Pay particular attention if symptoms are less frequent on weekends or vacations. That will be helpful information for your pediatrician, who will consider the possibility of school being a stressor in your child's life.

Some children who are troubled also show signs of sleep disturbances—sleeping too much or having trouble falling asleep. They may have nightmares or a renewed need to sleep in your bed. Sometimes children don't even know that they're having trouble sleeping. Look for signs of fatigue or difficulty waking up in time for school.

School-aged children often reveal stress through school performance. Remember, school is the job of childhood. Just as adults' performance at work declines with increasing stress, children find it difficult to focus on schoolwork. Anytime grades are slipping significantly, it should be a red flag that alerts caring adults to explore what is going on in the child's life.

In older children and adolescents, always look for changes in behavior. A new circle of friends or radical change in dress style are signs that merit a supportive conversation. Any suspicion that your child may be turning to substance use, including cigarettes, deserves your intensive involvement as well as professional guidance.

Many parents are very attentive to signs of depression, but they make the mistake of believing that childhood and adolescent depression appears the same as adult depression. Adults who are particularly sad or depressed tend to have sleep disturbances, become withdrawn, lack energy, seem to have a lower capacity to experience pleasure, and often express hopelessness. This is true of some children and adolescents, but nearly half of adolescents who are depressed are irritable instead of withdrawn. They may have boundless energy and are likely to act out with rage. I have taken care of many depressed teenagers whose parents are loving and attentive but missed their child's depression because it is sometimes difficult for parents to tell a normal teenager from a depressed one. Normal teenagers have phases where they're irritable at home and have occasional outrageous outbursts. Because parents may have adjusted to this moodiness, they can miss a teen whose rage and irritability are signals of emotional turmoil or depression. This is a critical reason that parents need to feel comfortable turning to a professional for an evaluation.

Finding Help

When a child does reach the limits of her resilience, she has to deal with a sense of inadequacy. It is important that she not also have to deal with the feeling that she is somehow letting her parents down. If you want to make sure that this never happens, let go of the fantasy that your child will be able to handle everything as long as you do everything right. If you view your child's problems as a reflection of you, you won't be able to help her through the toughest times because you'll have to work through your own feelings of failure.

Whenever your child does seem to be troubled, the first step is always to reinforce that you are there to be fully supportive. Listen, be a sounding board, perhaps even offer advice, but certainly give hugs or do whatever you can to ensure that her most important source of security remains constant. If your child seems to need more than you, it is time to turn to professional help.

At this point, most parents have to work through their own disappointment that their child needs something more than they can give. But think of it as an act of love, not of failure. You love your child so much that you will get whatever help she needs to be able to thrive.

Be assured that professionals who evaluate young children have the training to ensure it is a safe, even enjoyable, experience for your child. Ask your child's pediatrician, school counselor, or clergyperson for recommendations, then speak to the professional to find the right match for your child.

It may be tougher to guide a teenager to agree to seek professional guidance. Adolescents may feel ashamed that they can't handle their own problems and worry that going for help confirms that they are weak or "crazy." If you have ambivalent thoughts about seeking professional help, try to resolve them *before* talking to your teen. She will pick up on your mixed emotions easily and become even more resistant. If you genuinely believe that seeking professional help is a positive action, your adolescent is more likely to see it that way.

It is important to help our adolescents to understand a few key points about professional help. First, they need to understand that they deserve to feel good. Seeking help is an act of strength because strong people know they are capable of feeling better, deserve to feel better, and will take the steps to feel better. They also need to know that professionals do not give answers or solve problems but instead try to find the strengths of each person and build on them. Adolescents should understand they will only be guided to become stronger by using skills they already have and new ones that they will be taught to put into place for themselves.

To learn about the full offering of* Building Resilience *videos, please turn to page 327.

When Your Own Resilience Reaches Its Limits

If your goal is to build a happy, resilient child who is prepared to thrive through good times and bad, it's critical that you care for yourself with the same degree of commitment you give your child. This is always true, but it becomes essential when your own resilience reaches its limits.

We parents are role models. By viewing challenges as opportunities for growth, we display a resilient mind-set. We're the models who demonstrate healthy coping strategies. We're the ones who, through our example, make it safe to admit vulnerability and personal limitations. When we acknowledge and address problems, we reject stigma associated with imperfection. When we reach our limits and reach out to others, we model that strong people seek support and guidance.

Parents who instinctually grasp the importance of modeling when the topic is substance use, inappropriate language, or even how to be neighborly are sometimes resistant to demonstrating self-care—why? Perhaps it is because our generation of overstretched parents devotes every last drop of energy to making sure children's material, educational, and emotional needs are met. It seems like a small sacrifice to forgo our "selfish" needs. This is especially true for those who harbor the unspoken but deep fear that because we work so hard, we aren't giving our children the time "good" parents should offer.

As a child and adolescent advocate, I *know* that the well-being of your child rests on your health and personal resilience as well as on the strength of the partnership between you and your spouse. If I thought I could sell you on caring for yourself by telling you that you deserve to be happy, I would. But after years of experience with parents, I know that an approach that centers on you will be appreciated for the moment but forgotten during stressful times. I therefore need to stress that caring for yourself is *not* selfish—it is a selfless and strategic act of good parenting.

Your child wants you to be OK. For you to care for your child properly, you need to be OK. For this reason, it is a selfless act to take care of yourself so you can maintain the strength needed to care effectively for others. Parenting is a long-haul proposition. Maintaining your interests, addressing your needs, and relieving your stress with healthy coping strategies are precisely what give you the energy to give to others.

Let's take this a step further. Do you want your child to grow up and focus all of her energies on caring for her children and lose herself in the process? You are the model. Show that good parents are child-centered but maintain an adult existence. The greatest gifts you can give your child are to live a balanced life and to demonstrate that when life offers us challenges, we take active steps to get back on track.

Falling Back in Love

The best parents reach their limits at times. You might reach that point because parenting sometimes feels like a mystery; no matter what you do, you are not getting the results you want. Maybe you're at your rope's end for other reasons and your patience is wearing thin. Possibly external forces, like peers or media, are influencing your child, her behavior is unacceptable, and you grow frustrated trying to counter those forces. Perhaps something troubles your child so deeply that she takes out her anger on you because only you are safe enough to dump on. It could be that precisely because of how deeply she loves you, she needs to rebel to test her own wings. Remember, our teens rarely hate us; they only hate how deeply connected they feel to us.

No matter what pushes us there, most of us reach our limits and often don't like ourselves when we do. Those flashing moments when we don't like our kids can be even more unsettling. The fact is, one of parents' greatest challenges is being confronted with a situation that leaves them seriously disappointed in their children's behavior or desperately worried about their safety. These moments most directly challenge our resilience and our relationships.

What can we do at these moments? A first step is to reassure yourself that normal development is full of fits and starts. Just because you're in the midst of a crisis doesn't mean you have lost your child. On the other side of the crisis may be a deeper relationship and a son or daughter who has once more learned to turn to you. It may be that your steady presence is all your child needs to right herself, but don't forget that the best of families sometimes need professional guidance. The health of your relationship is worth investing in; assuming that "it will all work out in the end" might be a mistake.

The best resilience-based advice I can offer is to never lower your expectations. Children are fully aware when parents' disappointment and anger overwhelms them. Countless teens have told me they have nothing to lose anymore because their parents have already lost trust in them. I have heard this used as an excuse to use drugs, cut school, even to have a baby. I have seen it lead to depression. Other teens ratchet up their behavior a notch to continue to get the only kind of reaction they can still get from their parents. They notice that their exhausted parents have given up and begun to display that dangerous "Kids will be kids, what can I do?" attitude. As a result, teens learn that the only way to get attention is to provoke a strong-enough reaction to shake their parents' complacency. A very different but ineffective approach is to lower your standards and decide to be your kid's friend. Especially in times of crisis, your child needs a parent with strong, predictable values more than he needs a friend.

These parenting traps can be avoided if we return to 2 of the core messages of resilience. First, children need unconditional love, absolute security, and a deep connection to at least one adult if they are going to be prepared to overcome life's challenges. Second and most importantly, children live up or down to adults' expectations.

Unconditional love gives children the knowledge that all will be OK in the long run. Even when we dislike or disapprove of their behaviors, our children must know we stand beside them. Unconditional love doesn't mean unconditional approval. You can reject a behavior without rejecting your child. Love is never withdrawn or withheld based on a behavior. If you deal with even alarming concerns with this approach, your adolescent will not go down the dangerous path of believing she has nothing to lose. She may send you strong signals of rejection but will eventually want to return to the greatest security she knows, your unwavering presence.

Despite our anger and disappointment, we must never lower our expectations. When parents hold children to high expectations, kids tend to strive for those standards. I am not referring to achievements; rather, we expect consideration, respect, honesty, a sense of fairness, generosity, and responsibility.

This might sound logical intellectually, but it's not easy to turn off the anger when we're confronted with a major crisis or deep disappointment. It's hard to heed the advice to maintain constant love and high expectations when you're worried out of your mind or seething with anger. You need something that will allow you to draw that deep breath to reassess how best to approach the situation. It is time to give yourself the gift of falling back in love.

You fell in love the moment you looked into your child's eyes and were swept away when your baby grasped your finger. Your child might be a teen now, but inside is the baby you held and the child you took to the first day of school. He may be ornery at times, but inside your 14-year-old is the 1-year-old who looked to you for cheers as he took his first steps, the 2-year-old who ran down the sidewalk to greet you as you came home, and the 4-year-old who could only be comforted by you when his bike toppled over. It is not just the memories of childhood that should remind you of how passionately you feel toward your child. Hasn't it been wonderful to watch your teen learn to question rather than always accept?

The knowledge of who your child *really* is can remind you of the highest expectations and greatest dreams you hold for your child. It may give you the fortitude to continue to blanket your child with unconditional love even as you are being pushed away. Not smothering "I can fix this" love, just the reassurance that you are not going anywhere. Reclaiming this love may be just what you need to break the cycle of excuses, threats, and anger that can easily overtake your home in challenging times.

Seeing the little boy inside of the young man causing you grief may be just the ticket that will allow you to change the negative pattern of interactions between you that pushes you to your limits. You need a reset button, but perhaps your self-righteousness and your adolescent's pride and sense of indignation may be getting in the way of starting over. You can't count on him to make the first move. The love that blossomed the day of his birth is precisely what you can draw from to restore your relationship and begin to turn him around. It may allow you to set aside your disappointment and request a vacation from the stress you are experiencing. You need some time together with no friction; the opportunity to enjoy each other again. Go out to dinner, a beach, or a theme park. Promise each other a vacation from arguments. Let him see that he is not rejected. Hopefully he will learn there is something to be gained by restoring your relationship and modifying his behavior. I can't guarantee this will work, but I can assure you it will not make things worse, whereas more fighting and displays of disappointment will.

I am blessed to have 2 wonderful, rather easy daughters. But even guys who write parenting books have their moments. My girls are creative, independent, confident, and occasionally strong-headed (which will serve them well). But let me tell you who they *really* are—they are the children who at the age of 3 made me stop at the side of the road to rescue a soiled, worn, pink teddy bear that was "lost." It was scared and lonely, and they wanted to protect it.

One of them became attached to Eeyore at age 2½ because "Eeyore seems so sad, I want to make him happy." They are the girls who begged me to catch bugs and then free them outside so they could be with their friends. When they were 4, we were traveling and saw a roadside chef preparing dinner. They saw a whole chicken in a pot with its feet poking out. Awareness flashed across their innocent faces. "Daddy, did you know that when some people eat chicken, they eat real chickens!? Why would they do that, don't they like chickens?"

When I took my 10-year-old daughters shopping one day, I considered buying one of those pillows that promises to improve sleep. I wanted it, but the sticker price dissuaded me. The next day, one of my girls spent all her money and gave me the pillow because "I know that if you sleep well it will change your whooooole life."

That is who my girls are. Genuinely good people. Faithful friends. Stewards of the environment. People who have a deep capacity to love and an instinct to protect the vulnerable. Funny, funny girls. Sometimes they drive me crazy, but I can usually sift through their behaviors to uncover the girls I know and love. My knowledge of their essential makeup makes it easier to occasionally absorb their expressed frustrations because I can (rightly or wrongly) reframe it as the flip side of the sensitivity I cherish in them. It's not always easy, but my recollection of who they are restores my senses when my patience wears thin. Most importantly, my understanding of their makeup allows me to always hold them to the very highest expectations—in terms of their sensitivity, warmth, and empathy.

There is no magic formula for good parenting, and no words of wisdom exist to guarantee children won't stray toward some worrisome behaviors. I would never tell you that you don't have the right to be angry and display that anger. Just always remember that the power of your influence lies in the unconditional love you maintain for your child. There is only one place in the world where a child can count on that depth of security. You must remain a stable force so your child can securely navigate a challenging world. Finally, precisely when worrying about your child consumes every drop of energy within you, remember to care for yourself. Your child needs your strength to last; he is learning from you how to recover from adversity.

Building Resilience Videos (www.healthychildren.org/BuildingResilience)

Video 40.2 The Greatest Gift You Can Give Your Child Is to First Care for Yourself

To learn about the full offering of **Building Resilience** *videos, please turn to page 327.*

PART 7

Especially for Communities and Individual Teens

Community-based Resilience-building Strategies

Our goal must be to create a world in which every child has the support and encouragement to develop to his potential. We can visualize that support as concentric circles of guidance, protection, and opportunities. The first and most important protective layer must be parents' high expectations, enduring love, and unwavering support. Other protective layers include extended family, positive peers, school, and community. Whether the community encompasses civic groups, religious organizations, schools, sports leagues, or any and all groups that serve youth, it can promote healthy development by creating conditions in which families can thrive and by offering community-based resources including youth development and enrichment programs.

If you're reading this primarily as a parent, you may find this chapter useful in better understanding how community-based programs can develop extra layers of support for your child. You can also join other parents to create a community of concerned families. Be assured that as your community takes on the challenge of creating an environment where all children will reach their potential, each child, including your own, will be better prepared to succeed.

This chapter focuses on steps that a community as a whole, or a community-based program, can take to shift toward a strength-based, resilience-building philosophy and practice. It also touches on the emotional challenges youth professionals endure as we are exposed to young people who have had difficult or painful lives. Finally, it offers key questions youth-serving agencies can ask themselves as they consider whether they are promoting resilience-building strategies.

The 7 Cs Model: Usefulness and Limitations

This book is designed to give parents tools to build strengths in their children and give communities a common language and philosophy to build on the inherent strengths of youth while lowering risks. If you represent a school, community, or program that's thinking about using a positive youth development or resilience-based strategy to transform the way young people are approached, I congratulate you. I suggest that you consider organizations that will work closely with you to evaluate needs, suggest infrastructure changes, and frame interventions. Although there may be many such programs, I would like to highlight 4 well-respected groups that can rise to meet your needs: the Search Institute (www.search-institute.org); Communities That Care (www.communitiesthatcare.net); Kids at Hope (www.kidsathope.org); and the Penn Resiliency Project (www.ppc.sas.upenn.edu/prpsum.htm).

This book is a translational work intended to take the best of the literature and research and make it easy for parents and communities to act on it. The 7 Cs allow people from many viewpoints and disciplines—from parents to teachers to youth professionals to policy makers to professors—to ask, "What are we doing to promote (fill in any of the Cs), and how can we do more?" Nobody needs to change their framework or approach if it is already strength-based; the goal is to use a common language so we can better hold conversations. This common language can break down the silos that so often prevent different disciplines with a shared purpose from joining together to take effective action.

The 7 Cs are a minor adaptation from the positive youth development movement; they're changed subtly to allow us to address risk while promoting strengths. Rick Little and colleagues at the International Youth Foundation first described the 4 Cs of confidence, competence, connection, and character. This group determined that these were the key ingredients needed to ensure a healthy developmental path. Later, they added contribution because youth with these essential 4 characteristics were poised to contribute to society, and reflexively, youth who contributed further developed the essential 4 Cs.

The resilience movement is tightly linked to and largely overlaps the positive youth development philosophy, but it focuses on the importance of recovery from and overcoming adversity. Although coping is usually included as a part of competence-building in positive youth development programs, it needs to be highlighted as one of the best ways of reducing risks. Positive coping strategies allow youth to manage stress without turning to those quick, easy, but dangerous fixes that we call risk behaviors. Finally, one of the keys to a person's willingness to enter the positive behavioral change process is to hold the belief in one's ability and skills to tackle a problem; this is called *self-efficacy.*

The final C, control, includes self-efficacy in that people with control understand that actions they take can control, or at least alter, their destiny.

For more information on the 7 Cs resilience model and downloadable and printable materials that complement this book (including a teen stress-reduction plan and summary sheets that can be used in school and community forums), visit www.fosteringresilience.com or www.healthychildren.org/BuildingResilience.

Youth Will Live Up or Down to Community Expectations

The first step your community, school, or program can take is to decide how you choose to portray youth. Although we hope that schools and communities are uniformly protective of children and adolescents, the truth is that healthy development can be undermined. Youth can receive subtle and blatant messages that they aren't deserving of resources and high expectations. If we are to build the resilience of this generation, we must enhance the supports surrounding youth while simultaneously making a concerted effort to address toxic undermining messages.

These messages are not intentional. That's why we need to bring awareness to how negative portrayals get inadvertently transmitted. As discussed earlier, unflattering portrayals of youth create self-fulfilling prophecies for 2 key reasons. First, because adolescents focus so much unspoken energy on answering the question, "Am I normal?" teens do what they think is normal. When we focus on problems without paying greater attention to what is going well, teens mistakenly see the behaviors that generate crises as "normal." Second, teens will live up or down to the expectations they believe we hold for them.

A painful example is youth who have incorporated the toxic message into their self-image that academics are not for them. These youth often have resources directed toward them in the form of prevention programs, but they may not have adequate enrichment activities. Despite noble intentions, they may receive a message that kids like them are expected to engage in worrisome behaviors. If prevention programs were better balanced with strength-building and academic enrichment programs, teens would have the positive alternatives clearly defined and a better understanding of the dreams we hold for them.

Remember that all children, even teens, want recognition and attention. What does it mean if limited resources in schools go toward teen mother programs while the academically oriented girls get little additional support, recess is eliminated, and the sports and arts programs are cut to bare bones? Kids might sometimes do what they learn gets attention; our prevention efforts backfire when that happens. Do not misread this as a statement *against* risk-based intervention programs. To the contrary, they are essential. But we err when we don't put as great an effort into promoting and recognizing the positive as we do in correcting the negative.

The reverberations associated with low expectations are not limited to adolescents. For example, schools should be places where every young person can find his area of strength. Some youth will be artistically inclined, others academically. Some will excel on the playing field, others in the computer laboratory. It's important to maintain a wide variety of opportunities in schools so that no young person receives the message that he is incapable or without a special gift. A child whose gifts are not noticed will quickly lose confidence. Think about how tracking may tell even a 7-year-old precisely where he stands. A child learns quickly about expectations when he's placed in the "minnows" or "sharks" reading group. I'm not taking a position on tracking here, only on the care that needs to be taken to ensure each child feels valued and receives the opportunity needed to excel in something.

Youth need to know that most kids are active, contributing, positive community members. But public health messages illuminate the problems of youth, creating a crisis mentality that may be disconnected with reality. Youth absorb the messages that normal teens engage in the kind of behaviors that alarm adults and earn attention on the news. So most of our attention has to focus on noticing and extolling the positive behaviors around us. What can you do as a parent within your community or as a community leader?

- Notice the acts of generosity and compassion shown by youth and spread these good news stories. Don't notice only the heroic acts, but also the everyday acts; recognize kindness and contribution as the norm.
- Advocate for the positive portrayal of youth in the community. Ask for a shift away from media coverage in which only the highest achievers and delinquents get airtime.
- Advocate for public health messages that don't just tell kids what *not* to do but fervently tell kids *what* to do, and recognize that most youth are already doing the right thing.
- Advocate for enrichment programs in communities and schools, especially in those areas most at risk that currently only have prevention programs. This doesn't mean you should suggest that risk-based programs be cut.
- Give youth opportunities to contribute to their communities. When they're out serving others, their value will be noticed and they'll receive those vital reinforcing displays of gratitude.
- Work with the parents in your community so that young people have appropriate role models, rules, and boundaries that ensure safety. If these are seen as normal in your community, adolescents will have less reason to rebel.

Connection to School and Community-based Programs as a Key Protective Factor

Connection to adults within the home, school, and community make a young person feel valued and protected. Youth with multiple connections have somewhere to turn when times are rough. Adults will notice when connected youth are no longer thriving or when they're headed for trouble. Despite this, some young people slip through the cracks. Efforts at ensuring that each young person is noticed by several adults gives each a combined level of protection higher than could ever be offered by just one caring adult. Think of a block of Swiss cheese slices. It is easy to fall through one hole without notice, but if several slices are aligned, it is unlikely to slip through.

Schools and programs can take steps to ensure that no young person passes unnoticed. One program of interest was started under the leadership of principal Richard Simon in a New York school. The school determined that no child should be left without adequate connections. It prepared index cards with a picture of each student, posted them in a private faculty space, and asked teachers to initial if they had formed a positive connection with the student. The cards that had no initials, or only one, were referred to the guidance department and interventions were made, including referral to the Jared Project, a group of volunteer teachers and staff (including custodians and secretaries) who made one-to-one mentor-type connections. In that way, they ensured that all students formed a positive relationship with an adult in the school. This simple exercise is used in schools and programs around the nation to ensure a caring environment and prevent crises. Some schools place rosters on the walls, and teachers place dots next to those young people with whom they feel they have a connection. Students without ample connections are assigned adults to reach out to them. Some kids find it harder to reach out because they may be shy or find passing under the radar beneficial. But no child is anonymous. It is our job to find the special attributes and uncover the unspoken needs of each child in our midst.

Including Youth Wisdom

Young people who contribute to the well-being of their community and are noticed for their efforts will be more likely to stay engaged. We must never forget that youth are the experts on themselves. We increase the quality of programs and the benefits to the participants when we ask youth for advice in designing programs. Young people who help design services may become leaders in those same or future programs.

If you want to guide the youth of a community toward positive behaviors, consider creating peer educators and positive role models. Messages hold a certain resonance when transmitted from someone to whom peers can relate. At the same time, peer educators have more credibility when they're linked with respected adult experts. Understand also who the peer opinion leaders are (not necessarily the best students or class officers) and influence them to model appropriate behaviors.

Every Kid Is Within Reach

The motto of Kids at Hope is "All Children are Capable of Success, No Exceptions!" It is essential that community-based agencies strive to live by that bold imperative. But to really create programming that suggests we believe it, we have to check in with ourselves and view kids a bit differently, especially those who are heavily invested in alienating adults.

Some young people do an excellent job of pushing adults away. This is particularly true of kids who have been hurt or traumatized. They have earned the right not to trust easily. Another group of kids who push adults away are perfectionists who aren't meeting their own standards and therefore invest heavily in the mask of indifference. Sometimes young people join a subculture to show clearly how they fully reject adult culture. Remember that all of these kids grew from the same small children who craved attention. Maybe they didn't get it, or maybe they were bullied or hurt. Maybe their sensitivity hurts so badly that having their consciousness clouded in drugs feels like the perfect answer, or their behavior perpetuates the myth that they really don't care. Sometimes, all it takes is the right adult being there at the right time to help them acknowledge that they actually care so much it hurts.

Not every individual can reach every young person—perhaps because of what you look like, your age, what you say, what you don't say, or who you remind the kid of. That's OK. It is the reason why our programs often use a team approach. It is really a positive thing when you engage a colleague who you think might better connect with a young person. Don't make those connections solely based on gender, age, ethnicity, or race. Rather, link child professionals with kids based on interests, life experience, and temperament. The only thing that really matters is that we don't give up.

Community-based Programs

Every child possesses unique gifts. That is why "one size fits all" programming never works. If each young person is to have the opportunity to thrive, a variety of programs are needed so each child can find his niche. Safe play spaces are necessary so children can exercise while developing their own innate curiosity and creativity. Communities need academic enrichment programs to help some excel and to prevent others from falling behind. Healthy child-centered communities also have spiritual and recreational centers with a wide variety of programs. And finally, any community-based activities that promote family connection or effective parenting magnify the benefit.

How Can Programs Build on the Strengths of Youth?

Some youth programs still exist on the deficit model—they are designed solely to decrease risk and focus on education. Others instinctively understand that young people respond better when their strengths are recognized, but even these programs struggle to shift toward a strength-building approach.

I care deeply about risk and about keeping kids safe, but I've learned from so many youth that the transformative moment in their lives came when a caring adult first really believed in them, when a youth worker or counselor "made me first understand that I wasn't trash, and that changed everything." Our challenge is to pay attention to the positive, the traits that really make us care for a young person, with the same level of intensity that we focus on the behaviors we want to address.

Planting the Seeds

Caring makes professionals vulnerable to pain. If we expose ourselves to others' suffering while feeling a sense of futility, in time, it simply won't feel worth it. Eventually, we may shut ourselves off from compassion, thereby minimizing our potential to facilitate healing. To stem burnout, we have to trust that caring is worth it.

We do this because we are committed to the health and well-being of youth and believe passionately that building strong youth secures our future. We put in long hours, often give more than expected, and sometimes absorb pain to our own detriment because we believe it will matter. If only we could be sure that our investment of time, energy, and passion would pay off.

We all sometimes end our days and wonder if we made a difference. Did I listen well enough to hear what she was trying to say? Was she listening? Did she understand why I was worried? Is he ready to follow through? Does her feeling safe and secure in my office really matter when she returns home to a life of chaos? Does him deciding to make the most of his life while in my presence matter, when he has to do what it takes to survive the streets?

Those of us in practice long enough have had the privilege of seeing the impact of our involvement years later. Perhaps the most gratifying moments—or those that, at least, serve as the greatest reinforcement—come when we later encounter youth who, earlier, we didn't even know were listening. They tell us of a seed we planted. They tell us that we were the ones who helped them understand that they were acceptable just as they were. Or they tell us that they stopped doing drugs, not really because we informed them of their dangers (they had heard all of that before), but because we allowed them to voice that they were using drugs to numb their intense pain. More importantly, we made them feel good about having feelings and competent in finding ways to express rather than hide their emotions. They bring us their own children to show us that they want to create a better life for their offspring than they were given. Then they cry as they say that just as we believed in them, they will believe in their children.

There is no technique that will always be effective, and most don't produce immediate results. But it is worth knowing that a respectful stance rooted in eliciting, reflecting, and building on the existing strengths of youth will at least do no harm. The risk-based approach that focuses on failures or potential dangers can engender shame. Shame reinforces existing negative self-perceptions that can increase stress and lead to a cycle of dangerous choices. A strength-based compassionate approach may not produce immediate change, but it may light a spark. Genuinely trusting that a teen is the expert in her own life may empower her to craft solutions. At the least, it may make her more receptive to the next caring professional who will be there to serve when she is ready to move forward.

Remind yourself that one of the greatest gifts you can give yourself is to restore your spirit with the knowledge that you do matter. The greatest gift you can give the youth you care for is to commit to serving them for a lifetime—to do what it takes proactively to stem your own burnout. A first step is to let go of the need to find immediate, daily gratification in this job and instead to celebrate the integrity of your work, trust the value of your mission, and bask in the knowledge that the seeds you plant sometimes take root. You'll only rarely see the flower that blooms, but it blooms nonetheless.

Reaching Teens: Strength-Based Communication Strategies to Build Resilience and Support Healthy Adolescent Development

The American Academy of Pediatrics (AAP) has a sister publication to *Building Resilience* that offers professionals a comprehensive, strength-based, resilience-building, trauma-informed set of strategies to serve youth. *Reaching Teens* has 69 chapters and more than 400 videos that develop ideas, demonstrate scenarios, and offer youth wisdom (www.aap.org/reachingteens). It offers up to 65 hours of continuing education credits for a variety of youth-serving disciplines. At its core, it is about creating services that build the 7 Cs in youth while also addressing key challenges in their lives.

The 7 Cs as a Common Interdisciplinary Language to Serve Youth

The following pages have questions, grouped by the 7 Cs, that youth professionals can ask themselves as they shift toward a resilience-building, strength-based approach to youth. Feel free to download them from www.fosteringresilience.com.

The Resilience-based Philosophy: Reflections on Our Program

The Essential 2 Questions

Within our walls, do we believe in every young person unconditionally and hold them to high expectations? Do we sincerely believe that every child can succeed?

Competence

- Do we see what young people have done right? Or do we focus on their mistakes?
- Do we help our youth recognize what they have going for themselves?
- Do we help them focus on those strengths and build on them?
- Are we helping to build the authentic skills that make them competent in the real world?
  - Educational skills
  - Work skills
  - Social skills
  - Interview skills
  - Anger management skills
  - Stress-reduction skills
- Do we communicate in a way that empowers them to make their own decisions, or do we undermine their sense of competence by lecturing them, thereby giving them information in a style they cannot grasp? Rather than talking down to them, do we instead deliver information in a manner they understand?
- Do we let them make safe mistakes so they have the opportunity to right themselves, or do we protect them from every bump and bruise?
- Do we praise in a way that notices effort more than it rewards the product?

Confidence

- Do we see the best in our youth so that they can see the best in themselves?
- Do we clearly express that we expect the best in them?
- Do we help them recognize what they have done right? (Confidence comes from knowing that one has competence.)
- Do we help them understand that they have authentic survival skills?
- Do we treat them as incapable children or young adults learning to navigate a difficult world?
- Do we catch them when they are doing the right thing?
- Do we encourage them to strive just a little bit further because we believe they can succeed?
- Do we avoid instilling shame?

Connection

- Do we recognize that adults' unconditional belief in young people—and holding them to high expectations—is the single most important factor determining whether those young people will be able to overcome challenging circumstances?
- Do we enter young people's lives without permission, or do we give them time to understand we are worthy of their trust?
- Do we build a sense of safe community within our walls?
- Do we encourage young people to take pride in the various ethnic, religious, or cultural groups they belong to?
- Do we recognize that for many of our most troubled youth, firm attachment to a stable family might be missing? Further, do we know that our role as stable, caring adults takes on an even greater importance?
- Do we have a television and self-contained entertainment system in every room, or do we create a common space so people share time together? Does everyone exist in their own world, hiding behind earphones and texting distant friends, or is communication happening here?

Character

- Are we helping our youth to recognize themselves as caring people?
- Do we allow them to clarify their own values?
- Do we allow them to consider right versus wrong and look beyond immediate needs?
- Do we help them understand how their behavior affects others?
- Do we help them develop a sense of spirituality that fits into their (not our) belief system?
- Do we value them so clearly that we model for them how important it is

to care for others?

- Do we value each other so clearly that we demonstrate the importance of community?
- Do we value each young person and promote the understanding that when all reach their potential, every child benefits?
- Do we notice the character traits of grit—integrity and tenacity?

Contribution

- Do we make clear that we believe our youth can make the world a better place?
- As we create programs that serve youth, do we include them in the planning process, appreciating that they are the experts on themselves and their own needs?
- Do we create opportunities for each youth to contribute to the community?
- Do we share how important a value it is to serve others?
- Do we help our young people recognize that precisely because they have come through difficult times, they are positioned to guide others in how to improve their lives?
- Do we search in each person's life for another individual for whom they might serve as a role model? Do we use this to encourage them to be the best person they can possibly be?
- Do we help them to understand that if they have messed up in their past, their recovery serves as a model?

Coping

- Do we recognize that so many of the risk behaviors youth engage in are attempts at reducing the stress or pain in their lives?
- Do we condemn young people for their behaviors? Do we increase their sense of shame and therefore drive them toward those behaviors?
- Do we believe that telling youth to "just stop" the negative behaviors will do any good?
- Do we guide youth to develop positive, effective coping strategies?
- Do we help young people understand when their thoughts are magnifying problems? Do we help them to make realistic assessments?
- Do we model positive coping strategies on a daily basis?
- Do we encourage caring for our bodies through exercise, good nutrition, and adequate sleep?
- Can children safely play and exercise outdoors or in recreational centers in our community?

- Do we encourage creative expression? Does our community offer resources and programs in which children and teens are able to learn and practice creative expression?
- Do we encourage written and verbal expression in a way that allows each youth to reveal thoughts in a comfortable manner, whether through talking, journaling, poetry, or rap?
- Do we create an environment in which talking, listening, and sharing are safe and productive?
- Do we model relaxation techniques?
- As we struggle to compose ourselves so we can make the fairest, wisest decisions, do we model how we take control rather than respond impulsively?

Control

- Do we help young people understand that life is not purely random?
- Do we help them to understand that they are not responsible for many of the bad circumstances that may have plagued them?
- Do we help them think about the future, but make it less overwhelming by helping them learn to take one step at a time?
- Do we help them recognize their mini-successes so they can experience the knowledge that they can succeed?
- Do we help youth understand that while no one can control all of his circumstances, each person can shift the odds by choosing positive or protective behaviors?
- Do we understand that youth who have been hurt emotionally or physically may think they have no control and therefore have no reason to take positive action?
- Do we understand that discipline is about teaching, *not* punishing or controlling? Do we use discipline as a means to help someone understand that their actions produce consequences (in other words, life is not random)?
- As we work to build trauma-informed practices, do we understand that traumatized children lost control over portions of their lives, and, therefore, our giving them back a sense of control is key to their healing?

To learn about the full offering of* Building Resilience *videos, please turn to page 327.

Just for Kids: A Personalized Guide for Managing Stress

This chapter is written specifically for young people from 12 to 18 years of age. It explains how stress affects bodies and emotions and suggests ways to manage and reduce stress. I hope you will also give teens an opportunity to read Part 4, Coping, because it will fill in many of the details that can't be included in this brief overview.

Your adolescent will get the most out of the chapter if he or she downloads it from www.healthychildren.org/BuildingResilience. The first part, which explains stress, is included here to model how it is presented to an adolescent. The 10-part plan itself is offered only online.

A Teen's Personal Guide for Managing Stress

What Is Stress?

Stress is the uncomfortable feeling you get when you're worried, scared, angry, frustrated, or overwhelmed. It is caused by emotions, but it also affects your mood and body. Many adults think that teens don't have stress because they don't have to work and support a family. They are missing the point and are wrong!

What Causes Stress?

Stress comes from many different places.

- *From your parents.* "Don't disappoint me, clean up, hurry up, finish this, do your homework, go out for the team, practice your music, try out for the school play, do your best, stay out of trouble, make more friends, don't ever try drugs."
- *From your friends.* "How'd you do on the test, try this, prove you're not a loser, don't hang out with them, don't wear that."

- *Even from yourself.* "I need to lose weight, build my muscles, wear the right clothes, get better grades, score more goals, show my parents I'm not a kid anymore."

And from

- Watching parents argue
- Figuring out how to be independent
- Feeling pressure to get good grades
- Thinking about the future
- Being pressured to do something you know is bad for you, like smoking
- Not being good enough at sports
- Worrying about how your body's changing
- Dealing with sexual feelings
- Worrying about neighborhood or world problems
- Feeling guilty

How Does the Body Handle Stress?

First, here are 2 short definitions.

- *Hormone*: a chemical made by one part of the body that travels through your blood to send messages to the rest of the body.
- *Nervous system*: the brain, spinal cord, and all of the nerves. The nerves send messages between your brain and the rest of your body.

The body is a finely tuned machine that can change quickly to do what we need it to do, like react to stress. The body has 2 nervous systems. The *voluntary* system does what you choose to have it do—walk, talk, move. The *involuntary* system keeps the body running without your even thinking about it—breathe, sweat, digest. The body actually has 2 different nerve pathways in the involuntary system. One works while we're relaxed, and the other works when there's an emergency. These 2 systems can't work together at the same time. It's important to know this because we can shut off the emergency system by flipping a switch and turning on the relaxed system.

Is Stress Always Bad?

Even though stress is uncomfortable, it's not always a bad thing. Sometimes stress helps us deal with tough situations. A lot of stress changes our bodies quickly and helps us react to an emergency. A little stress keeps us alert and helps us work harder.

Ages ago, when people lived in the jungle—where a tiger might leap out at any moment—the emergency nervous system was key to survival. Imagine your great, great, great ancestors, Sam and Zelda, munching on some berries.

Suddenly they saw a tiger and had to *run!* Hormones gave them the burst of energy they needed to escape.

How did their bodies react? First, Sam and Zelda got that sinking feeling in their stomachs as the blood in their bellies quickly went to their legs so they could take off. Then when they jumped to their feet, their hearts beat faster to pump more blood. As they ran from the tiger, they breathed faster to take in more air. Their sweat cooled them as they ran. Their pupils became bigger so they could see in the dark, in case they needed to jump over a log while running away. They didn't think about anything but running because they weren't supposed to stop and figure out a friendly way to work it all out with the tiger.

Our ancestors never would have survived without the stress reaction, but stress helps us do more than run. It keeps us alert and prepared for the next lurking tiger.

Few of us need to outrun tigers today, but we all have problems and worries that turn on some of those exact same stress responses, like that panicky feeling you sometimes get when you're studying for a big test. Your heart beats fast. Your breathing becomes heavier. You sweat and get flashes of heat because your hormones are confused about why you aren't listening to them. Why are you standing still when they are telling you to run?

If Stress Is a Survival Tool, Why Does It Make Us Feel Awful?

Sam and Zelda had few choices when the tiger chased them. Either the tiger ate them or they escaped. As sick as it sounds, if they'd been eaten, they wouldn't have had much to worry about anymore, right? If they lived, you can be sure their burst of energy allowed them to outrun the tiger or at least outrun Zok (their slower friend who was eaten by the tiger). In their run for survival, Sam and Zelda used up every drop of their hormone burst and then took a well-deserved nap.

In the modern world, our biggest worries aren't usually about life or death. We don't really have to run away from our problems. But those same stress hormones stay in our bodies because unlike Sam and Zelda, we don't use them up by running. Instead, those hormones continue to hang around, unused and confused. They seem to be asking, "Why did my body stand still when that 'tiger' attacked?"

It would be better if we had different hormones for different stresses. Hormones to deal with parental pressure would make you love chores. Hormones related to school stress would make you focus longer and shut down your kidneys so you wouldn't need bathroom breaks. But we only have those hormones that prepare us to flee or fight. So it's really important to use your brain to decide what's a real emergency and to use exercise to use up those hormone bursts.

Even when there are no real emergencies, our emotions make our bodies act like there is a huge crisis because the brain controls emotions and stress hormones. If your brain thinks something terrible is happening, your body will react as if it really is! Even a little bit of stress that never seems to go away can confuse the body. It makes the body work harder to prepare for an emergency that may not really be there.

A tiger running at you is a real crisis. If you believe a mild stress (like a math test) is an emergency, you will not be able to study. Your body will be preparing to deal with a real tiger, and you won't be able to concentrate on anything but escaping. The trick is to figure out when something really is an emergency and when your emotions are only treating it like one.

A Review

- Stress is an important survival tool and can keep you alert and focused. But when you're not dealing with a real survival issue, it can make you uncomfortable and interfere with your ability to think through the problem.
- Stress hormones are telling us to run, so exercise uses them up.
- The body reacts to stress when the brain tells the body to prepare for an emergency.
- Emotions play an important role in how our bodies experience stress. How we think about a stressful situation and what we choose to do about it affect how it makes us feel.

How Do People Deal With Stress?

Nobody can avoid all stress, but you can learn ways to deal with it. When you are stressed, it is normal to want to feel better. Anything that makes you feel better is called a *coping strategy*. Negative strategies can be quick fixes, but they're harmful because they can be dangerous and make stress worse in the long run. Think about some of the ways people cope with stress that can really hurt them.

- Drugs
- Cigarettes
- Alcohol
- Bullying

- Fighting
- Sex
- Cutting/self-mutilation
- Skipping school
- Eating disorders
- Running away
- Isolating themselves or withdrawal
- Gangs

Dealing With Stress

These harmful choices may help you feel good for a little while, but some can be really dangerous. They also end up making people worried about you or angry with you. This messes up your life, and you become a lot more stressed. They're especially worrisome if they are a major way you deal with stress because you may turn to these behaviors more often during hard times. This is one of the ways addiction starts. If you are doing some of these things, ask yourself, "Why?" If it is to deal with problems, consider other ways of dealing with the same problems.

There are many healthy ways of coping. Healthy coping strategies are safe and can help you feel better without messing up your life.

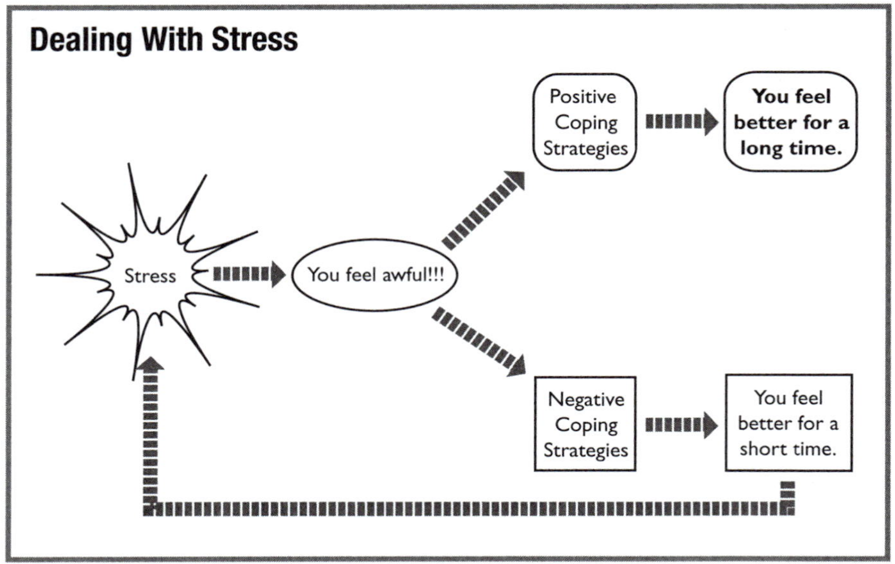

Creating Your Personal Stress-Management Plan

Here is a 10-point plan to help you manage stress. All of these ideas can lower stress without doing any harm. None are quick fixes, but they will lead you toward a healthy and successful life. The plan is divided into 4 parts.

1. Tackling the problem
2. Taking care of my body
3. Dealing with emotions
4. Making the world better

When you read over the plan, you'll notice that you can come up with a bunch of ideas for each point. PLEASE don't think you should try them all. This plan is supposed to help you reduce stress, not give you more. Try out some ideas, then stick to one or two for each point.

You might notice that this plan is almost like building a college or work résumé. This is the sane way to build a résumé; you are doing it to manage your life and remain happy and prepared for success, not to cram in activities to impress someone else. It will ensure you're healthy and balanced, and that's very attractive to colleges and employers.

Please go to www.healthychildren.org/BuildingResilience for the stress-management plan.

To learn about the full offering of Building Resilience *videos, please turn to page 327.*

Parting Thoughts

I remain humbled on a near-daily basis by children, teens, and adults who demonstrate an ability to rise above challenges and maintain their spirit and optimism in the face of adversity. I am certain that those young people who do best, through good and bad times, are those who have parents who are deeply connected and who allow them to stumble and recover.

Resilience is not invulnerability. Even if you could, you would not want to "grow" an invulnerable child or protect him or her from walking through every puddle. Compassion, generosity of spirit, and empathy are often developed from the lessons learned during life's harsher moments. In fact, as your child goes through those times, celebrate his or her sensitivity. We are only as happy as our least happy child, but remind yourself that your momentarily sad or anxious child might be blessed with the depth of feelings that will ultimately lead her to be the caring, kind person you hoped to raise.

I hope that this book has challenged you to come up with the kind of strategies that will fit your individual child. When you revisit this book as your child grows, I hope it will reinforce what you already know about parenting and spur you to come up with approaches that I may have left out but would more perfectly meet your child's needs. Have the confidence in yourself and the courage to trust your own instincts, to know that your knowledge of your child outweighs any opinion that I or any "expert" may offer.

If I had to summarize the essence of resilience-building while standing on one foot, I think I would add a new C: *caring.*

- Care so deeply that your children know that you are crazy in love with them.
- Care so fervently that you hold them to high expectations to be good people—because they will rise to your expectations.
- Care so intensely that you are willing to let them learn that they control their world and that the solutions to most problems lie within their developing wisdom.

- Care by teaching children to care for themselves. Teach them how to relieve stress and move beyond telling them what *not* to do.
- Care enough about your children so that you really know who they are. Rather than hoping they fit into an idealized image you have for them, know their individual temperaments, limitations, and potential.
- Care for yourself. When you model how important self-care is, you give children the gift of learning that it's OK to have feelings, human to reach a limit, and necessary to rejuvenate.
- Care so much about our future that you work to make this world better for all children.

You began caring the day you found out that a baby was coming into your life. You were overcome with caring when that baby grasped your finger, gazed into your face, and seemed to say, "I'm yours; please protect me." As children grow, our greatest challenge is to learn how to say, "You are strong; you can stand on your own." I have tried to give you some ideas to build your children's resilience so that you can prepare them to stand on their own, even to run. But never forget that they draw the security and confidence to be able to thrive from the safety and guidance you offer them. Let them try out their wings and soar toward independence. When they trust that they can navigate the world on their own, they will return to you for the *inter*dependence that has no age boundaries and offers security over a lifetime.

Video Resources

Visit www.healthychildren.org/BuildingResilience to view 15 videos on a variety of topics including stress management and coping, discipline, using praise appropriately, and other resilience-building approaches.

Additionally, more videos are available for purchase to reinforce and solidify the strategies offered in this book. These are from the resource *Reaching Teens: Strength-Based Communication Strategies to Build Resilience and Support Healthy Adolescent Development.* The index that follows gives you the opportunity to view some of the same materials professionals will use to learn how to better support resilience in young people. For more information, please visit www.aap.org/reachingteens.

Chapter Title Video Number	Title of Video	Presenter	Run Time (approximate)
Chapter 1: Why Resilience?			
No related films			
Chapter 2: Stress and Its Effects			
2.1	Recognizing and Managing Stress in Children of Different Ages	Ginsburg	8 min
2.2	Stress Management and Coping/Introduction	Ginsburg	1 h 28 min
2.3	Stress Management and Coping/Section 1/Tackling the Problem	Ginsburg	8 min
2.3.a[a]	Stress Management and Coping/Section 1/Tackling the Problem/Point 1: Identify and Then Address the Problem	Ginsburg	4 min
2.3.b	Stress Management and Coping/Section 1/Tackling the Problem/Point 2: Avoid Stress When Possible	Ginsburg	2 min
2.3.c	Stress Management and Coping/Section 1/Tackling the Problem/Point 3: Let Some Things Go	Ginsburg	2 min
Chapter 3: Ingredients of Resilience: 7 Crucial Cs			
3.1	Applied Resilience: The 7 Cs Model of Resilience	Ginsburg	31 min
3.2	Building Resilience in Your Child: The 7 Cs Model of Resilience	Ginsburg	25 min
3.3[a]	A Brief Presentation of the 7 Cs Model of Resilience	Ginsburg	4 min
3.4	The Power of Unconditional Parental Love to Help Teens Get Through Even the Hardest of Times	Vo	4 min
3.5[a]	Is It Possible to Give Our Children Unconditional Love While Also Holding Them to High Expectations? Absolutely.	Ginsburg	5 min
37.1	Modeling Resilience for Your Children: Defining and Defending Your Priorities	Sugerman	2 min

[a]This video is freely available for viewing at www.healthychildren.org/BuildingResilience.

Chapter Title Video Number	Title of Video	Presenter	Run Time (approximate)
Chapter 4: Not Letting Others Undermine Your Child's Resilience (or Psych You Out!)			
4.1	The Teen Brain: A Balancing Act Between Thoughts and Emotions	Catallozzi	4 min
4.2[a]	Ignore the Negative Hype About Teenagers: Expecting the Best From Adolescence Will Pay Off	Ginsburg	5 min
Chapter 5: Getting Out of the Way			
5.1	The Benefit of Allowing Our Children to Deal With Challenges	Sugerman	2 min
5.2[a]	The Toughest of Balancing Acts: How Do We Protect Our Children AND Let Them Learn Life's Lessons?	Ginsburg	6 min
5.3	Because We Need to Learn How to Recover From Failure, Adolescence Needs to Be a Safe Time to Make Mistakes	Ginsburg	3 min
Chapter 6: The Value of Play			
6.1[a]	The Importance of Play in Promoting Healthy Child Development	Ginsburg	13 min
Chapter 7: Noticing, Praising, and Criticizing			
7.1[a]	Using Praise Appropriately: The Key to Raising Children With a Growth Mind-set	Ginsburg	7 min
Chapter 8: Authentic Success			
5.3	Because We Need to Learn How to Recover From Failure, Adolescence Needs to Be a Safe Time to Make Mistakes	Ginsburg	3 min
7.1[a]	Using Praise Appropriately: The Key to Raising Children With a Growth Mind-set	Ginsburg	7 min

[a]This video is freely available for viewing at www.healthychildren.org/BuildingResilience.

Chapter Title Video Number	Title of Video	Presenter	Run Time (approximate)
Chapter 8: Authentic Success, continued			
8.1	Raising Children Prepared for Authentic Success	Ginsburg	7 min
8.2	Perfectionism: A Barrier to Authentic Success	Ginsburg	34 min
Chapter 9: Thinking Clearly			
9.1[a]	The First Step of Managing Stress: 3 Critical Questions	Ginsburg	3 min
Chapter 10: No More Lectures			
4.1	The Teen Brain: A Balancing Act Between Thoughts and Emotions	Catallozzi	4 min
10.1	Facilitating Adolescents to Own Their Solution: Replacing the Lecture With Youth-Driven Strategies	Ginsburg	15 min
10.2	Teens Told What They "Should" Do Will Lose the Ability to Learn What They Can Do	Rich	3 min
Chapter 11: "I Get It!"			
No related films			
Chapter 12: Changing Behavior Step-by-step			
12.1	Peers and Friendships: Insights Into the Complex Positive and Negative Impact Youth Have on Each Other	Kinsman	20 min
12.2	Peer Negotiation Strategies: Empowering Teens AND Parents	Ginsburg	18 min
12.3	Peers and Friendships: The Voice of Youth	Youth	45 min

[a]This video is freely available for viewing at www.healthychildren.org/BuildingResilience.

Chapter Title Video Number	Title of Video	Presenter	Run Time (approximate)
Chapter 12: Changing Behavior Step-by-step, continued			
12.4	Helping a Young Person Own Her Solution: A Case of Using a Decision Tree to Prevent Violent Retaliation	Ginsburg	12 min
Chapter 13: Shifting the Blame to Save Face			
12.1	Peers and Friendships: Insights Into the Complex Positive and Negative Impact Youth Have on Each Other	Kinsman	20 min
12.2	Peer Negotiation Strategies: Empowering Teens AND Parents	Ginsburg	18 min
12.3	Peers and Friendships: The Voice of Youth	Youth	45 min
Chapter 14: Media Literacy			
14.1	Parents' Role in Helping Youth Manage Media	Rich	7 min
14.2	How Does Media Figure Into the Lives of Kids?	Rich	35 min
14.3	Media's Effect on Our Youth	Strasburger	18 min
14.4	Replacing the "Big Talk": Media's Potential to Foster Parent-Child Communication	Strasburger	2 min
14.5	Why Vulnerability to the Influence of Media Varies by Developmental Stage	Strasburger	2 min
14.6	Our Discomfort With Technology Must Not Prevent Us From Discussing Media Use With Our Children	Rich	2 min
14.7	Cyberbullying	Rich	3 min
14.8	Media as a Super-peer	Rich	3 min

[a]This video is freely available for viewing at www.healthychildren.org/BuildingResilience.

Chapter Title Video Number	Title of Video	Presenter	Run Time (approximate)
Chapter 15: Not Being Broken			
15.1	ADHD: From "Disorder" to Manageable Difference	Ginsburg	10 min
15.2	A Focus on Parenting Teens With Chronic Diseases: Balancing Protection With the Need for Youth to Make and Recover From Mistakes	Pletcher	5 min
15.3	Helping Youth and Parents Understand That Alongside the Challenges of Having a Chronic Disease Often Comes Long-standing Strengths	Pletcher, Peter	3 min
15.4	Guidance for Parents: It Is Your Role to Be Protective, But Seeing Your Child With Chronic Disease as "Fragile" Can Unconsciously Undermine Your Child's Progress	Pletcher	6 min
15.5	Learning Differences in Adolescents	Catallozzi	26 min
Chapter 16: Building Confidence			
16.1	Addressing Demoralization: Eliciting and Reflecting Strengths	Ginsburg	34 min
16.2	The Depth of Our Caring Positions Us to Enter the Lives of Youth and to Be Change Agents	Singh, Vo	6 min
16.3	Sometimes Youth Who Have Survived Adversities Have the Biggest Hearts and Largest Dreams	Diaz	3 min
16.4	Young People Speak of the Power of Being Viewed Through a Strength-Based Lens and the Harm of Low Expectation	Youth	18 min
Chapter 17: Connection			
3.4	The Power of Unconditional Parental Love to Help Teens Get Through Even the Hardest of Times	Vo	4 min
3.5[a]	Is It Possible to Give Our Children Unconditional Love While Also Holding Them to High Expectations? Absolutely.	Ginsburg	5 min

[a]This video is freely available for viewing at www.healthychildren.org/BuildingResilience.

Chapter Title Video Number	Title of Video	Presenter	Run Time (approximate)
Chapter 17: Connection, continued			
17.1	If We Are to Build Strong Men Destined to Be Good Husbands and Fathers, We Need to Raise Our Sons With Love and Affection	Bell	2 min
Chapter 18: The Art and Importance of Listening			
18.1	Listening: The Key to Guiding Your Child	Ginsburg	5 min
Chapter 19: Strengthening Family Ties			
12.2	Peer Negotiation Strategies: Empowering Teens AND Parents	Ginsburg	18 min
Chapter 20: Widening the Circle			
No related films			
Chapter 21: Some Cautions About Connection			
21.1[a]	Preparing to Cross the Chasm: Our Teens Hate Us Because of How Deeply They Love Us	Ginsburg	7 min
21.2	Even During Your Toughest Parent-Teen Moments, Remember That Your Teen Loves You so Much, It Hurts	Sugerman	1 min
21.3	Why Teens Push Us Away: "I May Not Know Who I Am, But I Sure Know I'm Not You!"	Sugerman	3 min
21.4	The Critical Role of Continued Parental Involvement During the Teen Years	Campbell	8 min

[a]This video is freely available for viewing at www.healthychildren.org/BuildingResilience.

Chapter Title Video Number	Title of Video	Presenter	Run Time (approximate)
Chapter 22: Supporting Resilience in Military Families			
22.1	Supporting Military-Affiliated Youth	Lemmon	34 min
22.2	Military Families: The Importance of Staying Connected	Lemmon	2 min
22.3	Maintaining Family Connections During Deployment	Ginsburg	3 min
22.4	Addressing Perfectionism in Military Youth	Youth, Lemmon, Ginsburg	4 min
22.5	Military Youth: Service, Resilience, and Leadership	Lemmon	4 min
22.6	A Plea to Military Parents: Caring for Yourself Is the Best Way to Help Your Children Thrive	Lemmon	1 min
22.7	Seeking Help Can Be an Act of Strength	Lemmon	13 min
22.8	What Can I Do to Help Military Youth Navigate Through Adolescence?	Lemmon	32 min
Chapter 23: Nurturant Connections Offer Meaningful Protection Against the Effects of Childhood Trauma			
23.1	Parents' Vital Protective Role in Helping Children Thrive Despite a Trauma	Ginsburg	3 min
23.2	An Overview of Trauma-Informed Care	Ginsburg	23 min
23.3	Trauma-Informed Practice Part 1: What Happens to Youth From Traumatizing Environments?	El Centro staff, Covenant House staff	49 min
23.4	Trauma-Informed Practice Part 2: The Positive Force That Traumatized Youth Bring to the World	El Centro staff, Covenant House staff	8 min

[a]This video is freely available for viewing at www.healthychildren.org/BuildingResilience.

Chapter Title Video Number	Title of Video	Presenter	Run Time (approximate)
Chapter 23: Nurturant Connections Offer Meaningful Protection Against the Effects of Childhood Trauma, continued			
23.5	Trauma-Informed Practice Part 3: Essential Elements of a Healing Environment	El Centro staff, Covenant House staff	47 min
Chapter 24: Character			
24.1	Every Human Interaction Is a Cross-cultural Experience	Singh	1 min
24.2	The Easiest Way to Be Culturally Humble: Saying, "Teach Me About You"	Singh, Diaz, Bell	2 min
24.3	Unconditional Love and High Expectations Protect Your Child From Society's Lower Expectations	Campbell	4 min
24.4	A Gift to Our Children: Preparing Them to Question, Rather Than Accept, Racist or Discriminatory Messages	Vo	2 min
24.5	Personal Challenge: Raising African American Males in a Society That too Often Portrays Them Negatively	Lewis, Campbell	11 min
24.6	"Rules of Thumb" Can Be Helpful, But Generalizations Often Produce Harmful Unconscious Biases	Vo	1 min
Chapter 25: Grit: The Character Trait That Drives Performance			
5.1	The Benefit of Allowing Our Children to Deal With Challenges	Sugerman	2 min
5.2[a]	The Toughest of Balancing Acts: How Do We Protect Our Children AND Let Them Learn Life's Lessons?	Ginsburg	6 min

[a]This video is freely available for viewing at www.healthychildren.org/BuildingResilience.

Chapter Title Video Number	Title of Video	Presenter	Run Time (approximate)
Chapter 25: Grit: The Character Trait That Drives Performance, continued			
5.3	Because We Need to Learn How to Recover From Failure, Adolescence Needs to Be a Safe Time to Make Mistakes	Ginsburg	3 min
7.1[a]	Using Praise Appropriately: The Key to Raising Children With a Growth Mind-set	Ginsburg	7 min
25.1[a]	Grit: A Character Trait Linked to Success	Ginsburg	8 min
34.1	Delayed Gratification	Ginsburg	9 min
Chapter 26: Contribution			
26.1	Stress Management and Coping/Section 4/Making the World Better/Point 10: Contribute	Ginsburg	4 min
Chapter 27: Getting a Grip on Stress			
2.1	Recognizing and Managing Stress in Children of Different Ages	Ginsburg	8 min
2.2	Stress Management and Coping/Introduction	Ginsburg	1 h 28 min
27.1	A Simple Explanation of How Stress Affects the Teen Brain	Vo	5 min
27.2	The Forces in Teens' Lives That Produce Stress	Vo	6 min
27.3	Youth Speak of the Forces That Create Stress in Their Lives	Youth	14 min
27.4	Youth Speak of How Stress Drives Behavior	Youth	10 min
27.5	Achieving a State of Optimal Health: Stress and the Health Realization Model	Singh	1 h 28 min
27.6	The Adolescent World: Who Said Anything About the Teen Years Being Care Free?	Youth	18 min

[a]This video is freely available for viewing at www.healthychildren.org/BuildingResilience.

Chapter Title Video Number	Title of Video	Presenter	Run Time (approximate)
Chapter 27: Getting a Grip on Stress, continued			
27.7	The Adolescent World: Navigating School Pressures	Youth	14 min
27.8	The Adolescent World: Navigating Relationships at Home	Youth	13 min
27.9	The Adolescent World: Navigating a Stressful Environment	Youth	14 min
27.10	The Adolescent World: Being Held to Low Expectations	Youth	4 min
Chapter 28: Taking Action			
2.2	Stress Management and Coping/Introduction	Ginsburg	1 h 28 min
2.3	Stress Management and Coping/Section 1/Tackling the Problem	Ginsburg	8 min
2.3.a[a]	Stress Management and Coping/Section 1/Tackling the Problem/Point 1: Identify and Then Address the Problem	Ginsburg	4 min
2.3.b	Stress Management and Coping/Section 1/Tackling the Problem/ Point 2: Avoid Stress When Possible	Ginsburg	2 min
2.3.c	Stress Management and Coping/Section 1/Tackling the Problem/Point 3: Let Some Things Go	Ginsburg	2 min
9.1[a]	The First Step of Managing Stress: 3 Critical Questions	Ginsburg	3 min
26.1	Stress Management and Coping/Section 4/Making the World Better/Point 10: Contribute	Ginsburg	4 min
Chapter 29: Taking Care of Your Body			
27.5	Achieving a State of Optimal Health: Stress and the Health Realization Model	Singh	1 h 28 min
29.1	Stress Management and Coping/Section 2/Taking Care of My Body	Ginsburg	32 min

[a]This video is freely available for viewing at www.healthychildren.org/BuildingResilience.

Chapter Title Video Number	Title of Video	Presenter	Run Time (approximate)
Chapter 29: Taking Care of Your Body, continued			
29.1.a	Stress Management and Coping/Section 2/Taking Care of My Body/Point 4: The Power of Exercise	Ginsburg	8 min
29.1.b	Stress Management and Coping/Section 2/Taking Care of My Body/Point 5: Active Relaxation	Ginsburg	6 min
29.1.c	Stress Management and Coping/Section 2/Taking Care of My Body/Point 6: Eat Well	Ginsburg.	2 min
29.1.d	Stress Management and Coping/Section 2/Taking Care of My Body/Point 7: Sleep Well	Ginsburg	16 min
29.2	Brain Hygiene: The Very Basics of Stress Management	Vo	1 min
29.3	Limiting Empty Calories From Drinks: A Small Step Toward Better Nutrition	Ginsburg	5 min
29.4	Mindfulness in Practice	Vo	33 min
29.5	The Body Scan	Vo	16 min
29.6	Awareness of Breathing	Vo	8 min
29.7	Mindful Walking	Vo	4 min
29.8	Getting Practical: Bringing Mindfulness Into Your Life	Vo	13 min
29.9	Mindfulness as a Means to Increase Self-acceptance, Diminish Shame, and Defeat Self-hatred	Vo	3 min
29.10	Mindfulness as a Tool to Increase Your Clinical Effectiveness	Vo	5 min
29.11	Managing School-Related Anxiety	Ginsburg	11 min

[a]This video is freely available for viewing at www.healthychildren.org/BuildingResilience.

Chapter Title Video Number	Title of Video	Presenter	Run Time (approximate)
Chapter 30: Taking Care of Your Emotions			
30.1	Stress Management and Coping/Section 3/Dealing With Emotions	Ginsburg	23 min
30.1.a	Stress Management and Coping/Section 3/Dealing With Emotions/ Point 8: Take Instant Vacations	Ginsburg	4 min
30.1.b	Stress Management and Coping/Section 3/Dealing With Emotions/ Point 9: Release Emotional Tension	Ginsburg	19 min
30.2	The Tupperware Box: A Case Example	Ginsburg	13 min
Chapter 31: Styles of Discipline			
31.1[a]	Balanced Parenting: A Key to Adolescent Success and Healthy Behaviors	Ginsburg	15 min
31.2[a]	Offering Boundaries and Being Role Models: Adults' Critical Role in the Lives of Adolescents	Ginsburg	2 min
31.3	Parental Involvement: Balancing Consistency and Flexibility	Campbell	4 min
31.4	Guiding Parents and Teens to Understand the Shifting Balance Between Parental Control and Teen Decision-Making	Sugerman	13 min
31.5	Balanced Parenting: We Should Be Like Lighthouses for Our Children	Ginsburg	3 min
31.6	Teen Driving	Ginsburg	27 min
Chapter 32: Positive Discipline Strategies			
32.1[a]	Discipline: The Key to Healthy Households and to Young People Learning Responsibility and Self-control	Ginsburg	11 min
32.2	Helping Our Children Solve the Puzzle of Adolescence: "Who Am I?"	Ginsburg	2 min

[a]This video is freely available for viewing at www.healthychildren.org/BuildingResilience.

Chapter Title Video Number	Title of Video	Presenter	Run Time (approximate)
Chapter 33: Increasing Kids' Control			
32.1[a]	Discipline: The Key to Healthy Households and to Young People Learning Responsibility and Self-control	Ginsburg	11 min
Chapter 34: Delaying Gratification			
34.1	Delayed Gratification	Ginsburg	9 min
Chapter 35: Preparing Our Families for Lifelong *Inter*dependence			
35.1[a]	Raising Children Capable of Independence but Who CHOOSE to Be *Inter*dependent	Ginsburg	11 min
35.2	Adolescent Development 101	Clark	41 min
Chapter 36: One Rung at a Time			
36.1	Gaining a Sense of Control: One Step at a Time	Ginsburg	14 min
Chapter 37: Not Everything Is Within Our Control			
2.3.c	Stress Management and Coping/Section 1/Tackling the Problem/Point 3: Let Some Things Go	Ginsburg	2 min
37.1	Modeling Resilience for Your Children: Defining and Defending Your Priorities	Sugerman	2 min

[a]This video is freely available for viewing at www.healthychildren.org/BuildingResilience.

Chapter Title Video Number	Title of Video	Presenter	Run Time (approximate)
Chapter 38: Extreme Circumstances			
3.4	The Power of Unconditional Parental Love to Help Teens Get Through Even the Hardest of Times	Vo	4 min
38.1	Supporting Youth Through the Grieving Process	Kinsman	13 min
38.2	Dealing With Grief by Living Life More Purposefully	Ginsburg	7 min
38.3	Children of Divorce Can Become Perfectionists to Spare Their Parents	Sonis, Ginsburg	6 min
Chapter 39: Turning for Help			
3.4	The Power of Unconditional Parental Love to Help Teens Get Through Even the Hardest of Times	Vo	4 min
22.7	Seeking Help Can Be an Act of Strength	Lemmon	13 min
39.1	Helping Your Child Whose Physical Symptoms Might Be Related to Stress	Kinsman	3 min
39.2	Knowing When You Should Worry About Your Child: Seeing Problems in Context	Sugerman	3 min
39.3	Helping Youth Overcome Shame and Stigma (and Doing Our Best to Not Be a Part of the Problem)	Ginsburg, Feit	37 min
39.4	Asking for Help Is a Sign of Strength	Sugerman	1 min
39.5	Helping Youth Understand That Talking Literally Makes Them Feel Better	Kinsman	2 min
39.6	Supporting Youth Through Depression	Kinsman, Feit, Chaffee	41 min
39.7	Anxiety	Kinsman	19 min
39.8	Bullying Must Not Be Viewed as a Routine Part of Growing Up	Ginsburg	9 min

[a]This video is freely available for viewing at www.healthychildren.org/BuildingResilience.

Chapter Title Video Number	Title of Video	Presenter	Run Time (approximate)
Chapter 40: When Your Own Resilience Reaches Its Limits			
37.1	Modeling Resilience for Your Children: Defining and Defending Your Priorities	Sugerman	2 min
40.1	When Your Own Resilience Reaches Its Limits	Ginsburg	8 min
40.2[a]	The Greatest Gift You Can Give Your Child Is to First Care for Yourself	Ginsburg	4 min
40.3	Our Feelings Are Contagious: We Help Our Children When We Care for Ourselves	Vo	3 min
40.4	Adolescents With Chronic Disease Need Parents Who Care for Themselves	Pletcher	6 min
40.5	Parents Model Healthy Versus Unhealthy Coping	Ginsburg	3 min
Chapter 41: Community-based Resilience-building Strategies			
41.1	"It's About the People Who Are Here"—The Central Element of an Adolescent-Friendly Space	Sidhu	3 min
41.2	Love and Respect Are Key Ingredients to Creating an Adolescent-Friendly Space	Diaz	4 min
41.3	Checking in on Yourself: What About Your Own Adolescence Might Flavor Your Interactions With Youth?	Ginsburg	9 min
41.4	Making Inroads With Youth Who Put Up Barriers	Arrington-Sanders	6 min
41.5	The Tupperware Box: A Model for Releasing Trapped Emotions	Ginsburg	18 min
41.6	We Do Not Serve Others Well When We Are Not Centered	Singh	2 min
41.7	Deep Boundaried Connections Restore Our Own Energy	Singh	2 min

[a]This video is freely available for viewing at www.healthychildren.org/BuildingResilience.

Chapter Title Video Number	Title of Video	Presenter	Run Time (approximate)
Chapter 41: Community-based Resilience-building Strategies, continued			
41.8	Mindfulness Allows Us to Remain Fully Present Even Amidst Our Exposure to Suffering	Vo	8 min
41.9	How "Choreographed Conversations" Can Prevent Burnout While We Still Give Youth What They Need	Ginsburg	8 min
41.10	Have I Really Made a Difference? Trusting That Our Presence Matters	YouthBuild Covenant House Youth, Ginsburg, Diaz, with other faculty	44 min
Chapter 42: Just for Kids: A Personalized Guide for Managing Stress			
No related films			

[a]This video is freely available for viewing at www.healthychildren.org/BuildingResilience.

Video Presenters

Professionals and youth from several organizations shared their wisdom in the videos. Their contributions are greatly appreciated.

Renata Arrington-Sanders, MD, MPH, ScM, FAAP
Assistant Professor
Division of General Pediatrics and Adolescent Medicine
Johns Hopkins School of Medicine
Baltimore, MD

David L. Bell, MD, MPH
Assistant Professor of Pediatrics and Population and Family Health
Department of Pediatrics/Heilbrunn Department of Population and Family Health
Columbia University Medical Center
Medical Director, The Young Men's Clinic
New York, NY

Kenisha Campbell, MD, MPH
Assistant Professor of Pediatrics
Perelman School of Medicine at the University of Pennsylvania
Medical Director, Adolescent Primary Care & Family Planning
Nicholas and Athena Karabots Pediatric Care Center
Craig-Dalsimer Division of Adolescent Medicine
The Children's Hospital of Philadelphia
Philadelphia, PA

Marina Catallozzi, MD, MSCE
Assistant Professor of Clinical Pediatrics
Columbia University College of Physicians and Surgeons
Morgan Stanley Children's Hospital of New York
Assistant Professor of Clinical Population and Family Health
Columbia University Mailman School of Public Health
New York, NY

Tonya A. Chaffee, MD, MPH, FAAP
Associate Clinical Professor of Pediatrics
University of California, San Francisco
Director, Teen and Young Adult Health Center
Medical Director, Child and Adolescent Support Advocacy and Resource Center
San Francisco General Hospital
San Francisco, CA

Liana R. Clark, MD, MSCE, FAAP
Adolescent Medicine Specialist
Philadelphia, PA
Medical Director, Global Vaccines and Policy
Merck & Co, Inc.
West Point, PA

Covenant House Philadelphia
Philadelphia, PA

Angela Diaz, MD, MPH
Jean C. and James W. Crystal Professor
Departments of Pediatrics and Preventive Medicine
Icahn School of Medicine at Mount Sinai
Director, Mount Sinai Adolescent Health Center
Mount Sinai Hospital
New York, NY

El Centro de Estudiantes
Philadelphia, PA

Karyn E. Feit, LCSW
Adolescent Social Worker
Nicholas and Athena Karabots Pediatric Care Center
Family Services, Children's Seashore House
The Children's Hospital of Philadelphia
Philadelphia, PA

Kenneth R. Ginsburg, MD, MS Ed, FAAP, FSAHM
Professor of Pediatrics
Perelman School of Medicine at the University of Pennsylvania
Craig-Dalsimer Division of Adolescent Medicine
The Children's Hospital of Philadelphia
Director of Health Services, Covenant House of Pennsylvania
Philadelphia, PA

Sara B. Kinsman, MD, PhD
Associate Professor of Clinical Pediatrics
Perelman School of Medicine at the University of Pennsylvania
Craig-Dalsimer Division of Adolescent Medicine
The Children's Hospital of Philadelphia
Philadelphia, PA

Larkin Street Youth Services
San Francisco, CA

LTC Keith M. Lemmon, MD, FAAP
Chief, Division of Adolescent Medicine
Department of Pediatrics
Madigan Healthcare System
Joint Base Lewis-McChord, WA
Assistant Professor of Pediatrics
Uniformed Services University of the Health Sciences
Bethesda, MD
Clinical Associate Professor of Pediatrics
University of Washington School of Medicine
Seattle, WA

Valerie J. Lewis, MD, MPH, FAAP, FSAHM
Adolescent Medicine Specialist, Department of Pediatrics
Clinical Scientist, Division of Community Health and Health Studies
Lehigh Valley Health Network
Allentown, PA
Assistant Professor of Pediatrics
University of South Florida Morsani College of Medicine
Tampa, FL

Nadja G. Peter, MD
Assistant Professor of Clinical Pediatrics
Perelman School of Medicine at the University of Pennsylvania
Craig-Dalsimer Division of Adolescent Medicine
The Children's Hospital of Philadelphia
Philadelphia, PA

Jonathan R. Pletcher, MD, FAAP
Assistant Professor, Pediatrics
The University of Pittsburgh School of Medicine
Clinical Director, Division of Adolescent Medicine
Children's Hospital of Pittsburgh of UPMC
Pittsburgh, PA

Michael O. Rich, MD, MPH, FAAP, FSAHM
Associate Professor of Pediatrics
Harvard Medical School
Associate Professor of Social and Behavioral Sciences
Harvard School of Public Health
Director, Center on Media and Child Health
Division of Adolescent Medicine
Boston Children's Hospital
Boston, MA

Simran Sidhu, MJ
Executive Director
YouthBuild Philadelphia Charter School
Philadelphia, PA

Nimi Singh, MD, MPH, MA
Assistant Professor, Department of Pediatrics
Division Head, Adolescent Health and Medicine
University of Minnesota Amplatz Children's Hospital
Minneapolis, MN

Jo Ann Sonis, LCSW, DCSW
Licensed Clinical Social Worker
Craig-Dalsimer Division of Adolescent Medicine
Division of Gastroenterology, Hepatology and Nutrition
The Children's Hospital of Philadelphia
Philadelphia, PA

Victor C. Strasburger, MD, FAAP, FSAHM
Distinguished Professor of Pediatrics
Founding Chief, Division of Adolescent Medicine
University of New Mexico School of Medicine
Albuquerque, NM

Susan T. Sugerman, MD, MPH, FAAP
Adolescent Medicine Physician
President and Cofounder
Girls to Women Health and Wellness
Dallas, TX

Dzung X. Vo, MD, FAAP
Assistant Clinical Professor
Division of Adolescent Health and Medicine
Department of Pediatrics
British Columbia Children's Hospital
University of British Columbia
Vancouver, British Columbia
Canada

YouthBuild Philadelphia Charter School
Philadelphia, PA

Index

A

B

C

D

Q

R

S

T

U

V

W

Y